It's a Long Lane That Has No Turning

It's a Long Lane That Has No Turning

Bill McCaffrey

Dedications

I dedicate this book to Mae and Francis (Mike) McCaffrey, my parents, and to all the other saints who may never be canonized, but who will always be an inspiration to people who need to be inspired to keep on keeping on with their lives of love, faith, integrity, caring, and all the other positive characteristics that saints have.

I also dedicate this book to all its wonderful characters, who made growing up in North Philly in an Irish Catholic family in the '50s the most wonderful life ever. My brothers, Fran and Vince, my sisters, Maureen and Theresa are major characters and they are truly wonderful.

Special dedication must be given to Anne Morrissey McCaffrey, my wife, for being patient (at least on the outside) with me.

Foreword

I always knew I was lucky but it took writing *It's a Long Lane That Has No Turning* to show me just how lucky. *It's* gives me the opportunity to tell my kids, and grandkids and nephews and nieces, grandnephews and grandnieces all about life for Irish Catholics in the heart of Philadelphia in the '40s and '50s. Things in life were and still are backward.

An old jalopy convertible is more fun than a new Corvette, for example. Having Charlie's pizza is a ball but getting dressed to impress others at an expensive steakhouse is ok, I guess, as long as you don't splash gravy on your Brooks Brother's shirt or your imported Italian silk tie. High Mass is far more spiritual, hence, enjoyable, than fifteen minute, hard-to- keep-up-with low Masses said on a side altar. Wimpy guys start fights; big guys fight their fights. Bottle caps are better than marbles. Wireball requires more of a touch than a slider. Spraying people with fireplug water either by hand or by bottom beats ducking kids at some exclusive country club pool with all kinds of restrictions, even after you paid a month's rent for one day in the pool. Street tackle with no equipment proves a man's manhood more than a hockey fight. Sister Prophetess' prophecies were on the money, not like the "Chosen Prophets;" you see on TV, who are way off base and uncommonly rich at the trusting, loving, believers' expense.

Eccentric people like Otto the Outrageous, Bif with one F, and Slash with a head too big for a hat, make better friends than schemers who are quote "perfectly normal" unquote. Roof racing across roofs with forty-five degree angles would be a more challenging Olympic event than sweeping a stone down an alley. Saints are happier than sinners. Having parents who give up everything for you is better that a new Jag and a cold shoulder. Sitting in a rundown, leaking boat with your Pop and brothers hoping but not really caring to catch crabs has it all over speeding across the bay in an expensive boat creating wakes to give fishermen a little jolt and wasting precious gas. The local talent found in Irish pubs or gin mills brings more tears to your eyes than the multimillionaire singers' CDs. Having wonderful sisters brings more pride to a boy than having his own bedroom, TV, computer, car, and iPad combined. We drove the nuns crazy, not the other way around. The neatest people are on paper routes, not Wall Street or Madison Avenue. You never complained about the nuns to your parents and your parents would not think about lawsuits against them. The working poor help the poor using *their own money* and they do not go about bragging about it. Well-to-do, phony politicians use other people's money and never stop bragging about their *concern* for the *little guy.* The poor little guy might never get the thrill of working with Zeke the Mad Barber or the bartenders at Paddy's Pub; the people "concerned" about them recommend that they don't work. Batting with a broken bat with a nail driven right through it makes a real bat a real treat.

Feeling secure with two honest, hard working, patriotic, and loyal parents gives a boy and girl a better life than parents, who are too busy to be loyal and unconvinced that honesty or traditional family lives pays. Eating eggs, oysters, fish, and oatmeal on Fridays is a sign of pride and is no big sacrifice. The darker the ashes on Ash Wednesday, the better you make a statement about being a Catholic. Latin masses were more spiritual and intriguing than masses in the vernacular languages. Baseballs with cowhide covers are great to hit but not as much fun as throwing a baseball covered with electricians' black tape, which sticks to your hand when you try to throw somebody out. On the other hand, if you don't have tape, the thrill of watching a ground ball as the string unwinds to the outfield until all that is left is an orange core is hard to beat.

I hope that the stories which make up *It's a Long Lane That Has No Turning* will bring laughs, sorrows, and good old fashioned tears to everyone who takes the time to read it. I can't wait until you meet and get to know people like Renaldo the Purloiner, Deafy with perfect hearing until deafness was needed to get out of trouble, and Billy Pegleg, who won three sprint races at the Penn relays. The Horse Head Lady and crazy Joan of Arc of Edith Piaf are cool and insane, but not on a par with the Crazy Lady though, who killed her husbands when they became uninteresting or ceased to be attentive to her. The beautiful Violet made collecting on my paper route a pleasure, especially since she was near the end of the route and worth working toward. Switch, who taught people how to drive, never met a corner bar that he could pass by and let the student "learn how to let a car idle" while he stopped in. I pray that I did justice to these people and the rest of our more interesting and eccentric friends and neighbors.

If nothing else, I hope that anyone who reads *It's a Long Lane That Has No Turning* feels the same appreciation and love I have for the people who I loved in the '40s and '50s and still do.

My thought at the time as I remember them are in **bold** letters.

Introduction

"You must be perfect, like your heavenly Father is perfect: you should live your life like a Saint; Saints were people like you and me. They were your age once. You can be a Saint if you start now. Besides, the options to Sainthood are not very great. Why wait until you are an adult to try to be like a Saint? Start today, right now. William, you look so pale and serious. What is wrong?"

From that moment on, I had these words memorized. Sister St. Raphael, Sister of Saint Joseph (S.S.J.), my sixth grade teacher, started the day teaching sixty inner city kids, boys and girls, a great life lesson. She went on to teach six or seven other lessons until 3:30p.m. She and the other Sisters did this every school day for many, many years; about thirty plus years for some. There were no grading days off, no teacher's meetings days, no substitute teachers and no spring or even Easter break. In eight years, we had one visiting Sister but just for the morning session.

I'm sure that I didn't answer Sister's question. However, I do remember feeling concerned and overwhelmed by her words. I knew for sure that I would never be a Saint; I knew myself too well. I didn't always treat people with respect. I didn't always do my homework to the best of my ability. I wondered about the options to being perfect. Maybe Sister was right. Maybe the options stunk. I knew that I couldn't be perfect, even for ten minutes. Sister once said that only God was perfect, yet she asked us to be perfect. Sister said that we may start then; there was no need to wait to be an adult.

What can I do? What did she mean? I'm already not perfect. I can't start now; I'm too used to being imperfect. I always knew that Jesus was perfect, but He had to be perfect; He is God. It probably was easy for Him; yeah, that's it: He had to be perfect; it was easy for Jesus. Even the perfect Jesus thought about imperfection when He asked His Father to let Him out of the Crucifixion.

Pop always kneels at the Consecration even when he's standing in the aisle. Pop was the only one who knelt during the Consecration at the Communion Breakfast Mass in the gym. I will always kneel at the Consecration. Pop seems perfect to me; so does Mom. My parents are saints. I'm not.

How can anyone be perfect? Heck, even my parents *aren't perfect* and they are always honest, helpful, kind, and generous. Does perfection mean that I always have to do my homework? Can't I lie a little bit now and then again to myself to save myself from feeling guilty? By the way, were the Saints happy people? She didn't say they were. Why did Sister think I was pale? What if I did Saintly things and was never canonized; would that count? Sister looked very serious and I better start feeling serious from now on. I'll change right now. There will be no more criminal activities for me.

I bet that Jesus is angry because I helped put Anthony down the sewer to get pimple balls. God, I'm sorry that I sawed off a perfectly good broom handle to make a bat for Halfball. I really couldn't tell if Mrs. Kelly had the broom out for the trash or if she placed it near the trash cans. Yes I could, it wasn't trash. Next time I play on Johnson's lot, I'll ask for permission. I'll ask the dental students at Temple if it's ok to play rough tackle on their property. I'll replace the grass we dug up even if it wasn't me who dug it up. I'll repay my parents for the broom handle. Do I have to repay everybody for everything I used without his or her permission? I really wish that I didn't take the pretzels off Sister's desk at her birthday party. She said, "God knows who took the pretzels and there is no need to apologize to her, apologize only to God who saw you". Are these things mortal or venial sins? Maybe I can get to confession this afternoon. The penances from Father Akers' are easier than those from Father Reagan. I certainly don't want to be turned into a pillar of salt. I'm twelve, is it too late for me? Have I gone overboard? I didn't need two hands full of bottle caps; why didn't I leave some for somebody else? Has God already given me seventy times seventy breaks as it says in the bible according to what the bishop said at mass? I hope He never stops forgiving people.

As I continued to age, I played and replayed this scene in my life repeatedly, especially in the past few years, and with a higher level of intensity during the last couple of years. I listen to all the commotion about Irish Catholic guilt and I read about and listen to stories of lifelong psychological problems brought on by the Sisters in Catholic schools who beat people up and laid guilt trips on them. I hear and observe all the mocking of the Catholic hierarchy when it comes to Catholic issues like Mary, birth control, same sex marriages, the sacraments, premarital sex, abortion, embryonic stem cells, cloning, pedophilia and celibacy. I wonder why so many Catholics, including some of our priests, have joined in on the bash-Catholicism bandwagon. What's with Catholic Universities? Do they think that making heroes of people who teach and practice anti-Catholic beliefs while putting Catholic beliefs in the background makes them a big time, fully accredited academic university? Why do so many Catholics act very non-Catholic-like? Catholics believe in divorce at the same level as Protestants. Some Catholics think that abortion is a valid solution to an unwanted pregnancy. Some bishops, priests and sisters are in that group, I am sorry to say. Maybe this Catholic thing is too tough. Maybe it is not a fun life style.

The Catholic thing is supposed to be a lot easier now that the Mass is in the local language because the Latin Mass meant little because you couldn't understand a word that was said. Young Catholics will never know what it felt like to stand behind the priest looking at the altar and the ever present Crucifix as the congregation, priests, and altar boys praised God, using the same language all over the world. This common language was part of what Catholicism was all about being "one church". There was quiet time during Mass, especially during and after Communion, when silence was truly golden. High Masses were much longer, optional and simply magnificent if the choir was good. St. Stephen's had a great choir and a bishop as its pastor, Bishop J. Carroll McCormack and priests Frs. Martin, Fitzpatrick, Melley, Curran, McDevitt, and many visiting priests. We were blessed with the Sisters of St. Joseph, Chestnut Hill, the SSJs.

The magnificence of the high Masses captured you and held the congregation spellbound and emotionally captive for the entire Mass. Some other churches had choirs, which sang in the background of what was happening at the altar. During high Mass and on special holy days – the only times hymns were sung in Mass - a choir sang the hymns in Latin and the mystery of the Mass and the Eucharist became *more* mysterious but faith started to shine through with the beautiful praises to God. People needed God. They were poor and they had lousy jobs. They wanted more for their children, even if they had to put their lives on the line in Europe or Asia to preserve our freedoms as well as persevere in their difficult situations. These people expected nothing and asked for nothing. They got what they expected and *did* get what they *didn't* ask for.

Altars had to have relics of saints inside them. It'd be a fine day in hell before Mass would be said on an unconsecrated table in Father McNamara's church. Altars were sacred and chalices were gold or gold plated inside the cup. Priests and only priests could touch the chalice and most of the time visiting priests had a black box with their personal chalices. The chalices were beautiful if they were ornate or not. Most were ornate. Many times, I asked the priest where he got his chalice. Some had their chalices handed down from deceased priests; some were custom- made. One priest's father made his chalice with silver from Montana and gold from Utah and Nevada; it was just beautiful and it was the first time his father did anything with precious metals. His father was a subway conductor for the Philadelphia Transit Company (PTC).

Why does just about every Catholic I know remember not to eat or drink anything, except water, from midnight right up to the time they receive Holy Communion? Today, only an hour must pass before the reception of the Holy Eucharist while Catholics do not eat or drink anything, except water. Some Catholics think that is too tough and it's ok to eat or drink right up to their entrance to the church. There is little pride in the Catholic things any more, none. For whatever it's worth, Catholics took pride in not being able to eat or drink anything after midnight on the night before we received Holy Communion until we actually received the Body and Blood. I know of no one who complained or who would dare go to Communion if they ate or drank after midnight. Ask any non-Catholic fifty-five and over, "What's the first thing that comes to mind as you think about your Catholic buddies back in the 40s and 50s?" The answer ninety percent of the time will be either they didn't eat meat on Fridays or they ate fish and macaroni all during Lent. Maybe the response will be, "They went to Mass every Sunday or they told the priest their sins. They went to Catholic school where the boys wore white shirts and ties and the girls wore uniforms". The uniforms were usually blue dresses, passed down from an older sister, a close relative or a friend of the Sisters. Some might answer that they had to go to confession at least every other week. Some observant friends will tell you that they got ashes on their foreheads. All of these remembrances will remind the Catholic how proud he or she was to be a Catholic.

Ask many Catholics what comes to their minds and you'll get: The Sisters that beat me for no reason. Mortal sin and what it did to me. All boys or all girls high schools; having to go to Mass on Sundays, First Fridays and Holy Days; May processions and the embarrassment of wearing a white suit while walking around the church grounds with the boys/girls.

You will get these responses, but hang on a minute. On second thought, there will be a follow up to these responses. Their responses will probably be something like this, "Actually, I learned a lot from the nuns and they put up with me. I felt good going to Mass. I never really stayed with my Lenten pledge even though I complained about having to give something up; I was more prepared for high school than my friends; I was more prepared for college than most of my friends; fear of mortal sin kept me out of trouble. I wanted the darkest ashes I could get."

The Sisters taught the basics to fifty or sixty students (We had 62 in the 4th grade). They taught all the subjects and they maintained order in the classroom. They updated their grade books for all those students by hand and their entries were perfect. They used ink with no margin for error. We never had substitute teachers for a day; I remember one for less than a *half day* in eight years. I probably was proud of the things we as Catholics had to do. Every Philadelphian: Catholic, Protestant, Jewish, Moslem, or, yes, some atheists, answered with the name of the nearest Catholic parish to the question "Where do you live?"

Sister St. Raphael shakes me up. Her words struck home.

Even now, I have the same feelings about Sister's words about perfection as I did in third grade. Only now, I have seen saintly people, not perfect people. I have seen people pursuing perfection, consciously or unconsciously, mostly unconsciously. I have also seen people pursue some of those options to Sainthood that Sister mentioned. Sainthood can't be easy, but it is a good life from what I've observed. Fighting against the need to be Saint-like is not such a good deal from what I have felt and observed. It's tiring and uncomfortable. In third grade, I had a very short personal history to reflect on. At sixty-eight, my personal history is longer and at times seems like an eternity. I can reflect for hours now.

I am writing this book to tell you about the people I remember as I grew up in Philadelphia in the forties and fifties. I am writing about the *people* I knew based on my recollections and glorifications of these wonderful people. The events and the places that will provide you the background drop to put everything in perspective will be the theme of the next book.

If you're a country, small town or suburban kid, you will love these people like I do even though you don't know them. If you are an inner city kid at heart, this book will bring back memories.

It all began when I was four years old and the period is from 1946 to 1956. Enjoy the Philadelphians that you meet in this book. There are so many wonderful and mysterious people for you to get to know like Otto the Outrageous, Renaldo the Purloiner, Zeke the Mad Barber, Horse Head Lady, Bif with one F, Maria, Violet, Deafy, Sr. Prophetess, Uncle Matt, Slick, Slash, The Iceman, The Pretzel Man, the Moving Man, Rodney St. Clare, Dr. Ida, and many more.

I had to restrict the stories in this book to descriptions of the most interesting people. My next book will have stories about these people. My third book will be about my high school and my years with IBM.

My thoughts at the time, as I recall them, are in **bold** letters. Enjoy!

Table of Contents

1

Reese Street – the Beginning – 1946

It had to be a hot, muggy day because it was Philadelphia and it was August. I was throwing a pimple ball against the marble-like front steps of 2243 North Reese Street, I wasn't being called to come into the house, and I was outside for hours. This meant it wasn't raining. My younger brother, Vince, was coming home from the hospital today. I imagined that my mother would be in the shotgun seat of Uncle Arthur's black car, a Packard. Packards had neat hood ornaments. Uncle Arthur had the neatest. It was a silver lion just waiting for someone to touch the car. The car shined like no other car. The insides were gray and silver. The president could feel like a big shot riding in the Packard. The car was old and beat up pretty well when Uncle Arthur bought it but new car owners probably envied my Uncle. Uncle Arthur won't have a problem parking right in front of 2243 because no one on Reese Street owns a car and all the Reese Street kids play on the brick pavement. The kids I knew were too young to play in the street though the street was safe, except when the Iceman or the Milkman was delivering. Pop would have been in the car, anxious to introduce my brother Fran, my sisters Maureen, Theresa, and me to Vince, but he had to work; he always seemed to anyway.

Pop was a "piece worker" in a bearing factory. He polished bearings every night for many years. Piece workers were paid for what they did - how many bearings they polished. A father of five kids ranging in age from five years to five days could not afford to miss work. Pop worked the second shift to get the bonus shift afforded to second and third shift workers. I was about three weeks away from being four when Vince came home. Fran was five, Maureen, three, and Theresa, one. It would be great to see Mom again and to meet my little brother. It would also be great to see Uncle Arthur's car, especially the hood ornament on his Packard.

I didn't count the days Mom was gone but it seemed like weeks. I miss having her home although Pop was fun, playing the mad Scotsman or saying good morning to the walls and the chairs and to all of us. He let us play outside all day and we took him up on that. I'll miss him when he goes back to work at nights. Pop told me that Mom stayed home when I was born. I often thought about a stork making home deliveries. I was impressed that they really did make these deliveries.

It's cool to be born at home. No wonder I love my bedroom and neighborhood. I will miss Pop's famous lunches - the kind that he made when Mom was not around - when Mom goes to have Vince.

Pop was famous for putting everything in the icebox into a pan and frying the pickings with eggs and milk. Lenten omelets really kept us wondering what was in them because oysters, cheese, tuna fish and other non-meat ingredients often made the cut. I remember tomatoes, potatoes, relish, and maybe a chicken gizzard or two. I looked forward to Mom's fried chicken once she got back into the kitchen. Everything happened as expected and on cue when Mom came home.

Baby Vince is home; Mom is home too, looking very happy and healthy. Uncle Arthur's Packard car looks great, especially the hood ornament. I enjoyed the ride Uncle Arthur took us around the block two times. The fried chicken is on the table; it was as expected. Life is good and I have a birthday coming up soon.

A couple weeks after Vince's arrival, his Baptism took place in St. Edward's Catholic Church. We had a house party to celebrate the Baptism. Aunt Rose, Mom's sister, whispered to Vince. She was telling him how lucky he was to be a Catholic, with Scotch and Irish blood and quite good health. Aunt Grace, Pop's sister, agreed with Aunt Rose's comments and added that the McCaffreys were very prominent in St. Edwards's parish.

"My Granddad, your great Granddad, donated a lot of money to the church and a stained glass window with the McCaffrey name is in the church," is the way Aunt Grace put it to Vince, who kept asleep during these exchanges.

I heard it all and I was impressed. I didn't know what a stained glass window was, but I knew what it meant to donate a lot of money to the church. It didn't occur to me at this time that my father shouldn't be worrying about how many bearings he could polish in an hour if his father and Granddad were donating money to the church. They must have been rich.

Reese Street was a wonderful place, especially 2243. Billy was born in that house at 1:00am on September 15, 1942. I was Billy. All the houses on Reese Street were row homes, houses connected to other houses. Philadelphia is famous for row homes. The sidewalks were made of bricks and the front steps of all Reese Street homes look like white, imported marble. Trust me, they were not white, imported marble; they weren't even domestic marble. They were cement. The women of Reese Street scrubbed their steps with Old Dutch cleanser, a sturdy brush and some good old-fashioned elbow grease to create this effect and to provide an insight into the care and love they had for their families and their neighbors. Reese Street was spotless and the first things you noticed were the front steps. Everyone seemed to want Reese Street to look good. All the neighbors wanted Reese Street to be a great place to live. It was! The residents had no money to speak of but they owned a feeling of pride that made them somehow quite well off.

2243 had the neatest attic. It was a place where you could go and experience the thrill of being in a strange place, especially when it was raining. When I was in the attic and it was raining, I felt safe, secure, and cozy. It was as if I saw my cabin in the woods after a long day of hiking. It was cold and I could see smoke coming from the cabin's chimney. There is much more to tell you about Reese Street and I will.

2

Paddy's Taproom

Grandmom and Granddad Maguire lived a few blocks from our Reese Street house. Mom took us to their house at least once a week. Their house was located on Darby Street, "strategically" located next door to Paddy's Taproom. My Granddad was a great strategist. Part of his strategy, I'm quite sure, was to have a house based on the old adage, "location, location, location". His idea of location was as it related to a taproom, not as it related to a good financial investment. Granddad's name was Dan Maguire and he looked just like you'd picture Dan Maguire. Granddad was the quintessential Irishman and a frequent patron of Paddy's. He was born in Ireland, but left at an early age because of a lie and a dispute with his father. My great Granddad, who owned a profitable business, detected the odor of cigarettes. One of his employees was smoking and when confronted about this forbidden act, blamed my Granddad, who was about 12 years old at the time. My Granddad didn't argue or defend himself and a dispute began. My great Granddad simply couldn't put with lying and my Granddad knew that his father would side with the employee. The employee got Granddad drunk a few times, which would have enraged my great Grandfather. This fact was on my Granddad's mind, I'll bet.

Granddad left home and fortunately for me headed for Scotland then to America to land from time to time in Paddy's. Granddad never saw his family after he left home.

Paddy's patrons were working people, who enjoyed a drink (or two) and a good conversation. Some enjoyed the drink (or two) more than the conversation. Some, just a few that is, didn't realize that conversation was available. None of these people drove a car, which was a luxury they hadn't even considered. Most of the men were veterans of the World War II. Mr. Quinn was a veteran who got shot in the leg. He looked tall to me. He wore glasses and, of course, walked with a limp. Buggy, that is, Mr. Quinn, didn't talk about his injury but I know that he was helping his buddies out of terrible situation when it happened. Uncle Dan knew the whole story but told me very little. Mr. Quinn pulled some soldiers out from a tough situation; that's all I know. Mr. Quinn never talked about his injury or the recognition he never got. He limped and that was that. He was a wartime hero in my eyes for his service and humility. Mr. Quinn enjoyed Paddy's, thank God. I want him to enjoy everything.

Paddy's was a great corner taproom with truly wonderful clientele. I went there on a few occasions when Mom's brother, uncle Dan, came home on leave from the Navy. Uncle Dan took me into Paddy's to help me "learn good manners" and to introduce me to the world of "Irish culture". On numerous occasions, I saw Uncle Dan hand somebody a dollar or two. He knew who needed the money and he seemed to suggest to the person receiving the money to go home and be with his family. Uncle Dan always brought the second round. One of his cronies, usually Buggy, would buy the first round. I was never to call Buggy, "Buggy". His name to me was Mr. Quinn.

The bartenders at Paddy's were a brawny lot. They were the right men for the job because they exemplified all the traits of a patron of Paddy's. They enjoyed a good conversation, especially when they were the listeners. They could mix a mean whisky drink; they could tap a keg and pour a beer with a perfect head at the same time, and they could keep things under control. I often thought that the producers of Hollywood movies should have gone to Paddy's to screen test the bartenders. They could have played G-men, cowboys, ranchers, athletes, and any other macho-type role. I can think of two or three bartenders who would be perfect for the role of Sean Thornton in "The Quiet Man". John Wayne is a natural for a role as the bartender at Paddy's or is the bartender a natural for the role of Thornton. I'd like the Duke to play a bartender at Paddy's; maybe the Duke and I could team up.

The bartenders could have been contestants on Jeopardy too, because they could talk about many topics, especially politics, Notre Dame Football, boxing, and Catholic beliefs. During one of the conversations about boxing, Uncle Dan said that he was taking me to a fight at the Cambria, where he fought under his older brother's name, Mike Maguire, because he, Uncle Dan, was too young to fight professionally. We would have gone, too, if Paddy's closed at 5pm, when I left, not 2am, when Uncle Dan left.

Occasional bar room brawls changed the friendly nature of Paddy's. It never was a big deal really, because these bartenders could break up a fight before it got too out of hand. They could literally throw someone out of Paddy's and on to the street without breaking a glass or missing an order for a drink from a non-fighting patron. The sober patrons could empathize with the brawlers. Most of them were in fights sometime in their "careers" at Paddy's.

One morning Grandmom and I were walking to her house when a patron tumbled out of Paddy's front door. The man looked just like Andy Capp. He had too much to drink and was the obvious loser in a hopefully short-lived fight. The fight was probably over who was better, Dempsey or Louis or Sugar Ray or maybe Leahy or Rochne. It was a given that these two Notre Dame coaches were rated one and two in the world; the order was the question. Grandmom went over to help the man and to encourage him to get up and go home. The man hardly moved for several minutes, but he finally got up and started to walk towards Paddy's. Grandmom knew the man and turned him around pointing him to his house. Grandmom helped him brush off the dirt on his tweed sports coat so that no one would suspect he was in a fight. She handed him his well-worn, plaid cap, which followed him on to the street where he landed with a bounce. The Irish always wore caps like the paper boys did in the thirties and sports coats that cost little money but that looked good because the Irish could wear clothes. The Irish I knew were clotheshorses. They still wear the caps and sports coats.

The man started for home. I noticed him throwing his arms in the air as if he was arguing with himself or trying to make a point to himself as he walked down the street in a strange way: as if his upper torso was a spoon stirring a pot of Irish stew. His cap somehow ended up on his head, pointed in the right direction. The sports coat fit well; the cap fit perfectly. He looked great, from a distance, except maybe that his coat pockets were hanging out. I thought that his bad day was just beginning and the unpleasant part was yet to come. Maybe his wife and kids will be kind to him; maybe it was the first time he was in this condition; I hoped so. I also hoped that people would be kind to this man because he was probably a veteran of the war, with many personal battles and bar room brawls under his belt. Maybe he could stop at the end of the corner and have a Philadelphia soft pretzel from the underground pretzel shop. That might wake him up and cover up his breath. I hoped that he would buy a few extra pretzels as peace offerings to his family.

Thanks for my family God. They are saintly like Sr. St. Raphael talked about. I wonder if I will ever pick up people who had too much to drink when I get older. I know Mom and Pop would pick the man up. They are always doing something for somebody. Pop is courageous; he saved a young man's life by risking his when Pop pulled the man away from a fast moving train. Why does the man still hate Pop? Mom said that the man lost both his legs and he couldn't live with himself. I'll be in fights at Paddy's when I get bigger and famous at Notre Dame and Yankee Stadium. I wonder if the patrons are all immigrants from Scotland and Ireland. I know that some of the heavier drinkers are war veterans because I heard one of them talking about his tour of duty when an unknown customer wanted to start up a conversation. I'm certain that Paddy's bar tenders collected money for the man with the cap and gave it to him before they tossed him out. Oliver told the man where he was and not what he did.

War veterans are real heroes. They risked their lives for us. Man do I appreciate them. Will I ever be a war veteran? These heroes never brag. I think that their beers should be free because they fought for our country and the whole world. When I finish my rookie season with the Yankees, I'm going to give Paddy thousands of dollars so that war vets can get all the free beer they want. Does Buggy believe in God? I'll bet that God loves Buggy for what he did for our country, especially because he hurt his leg. Do soldiers really kill people and get killed? Soldiers and sailors must really love our country; look what they do to keep it safe and beautiful. The bar tenders and customers at Paddy's really earn their education by working hard all the time and protecting our country.

God, please don't let Pop drink too much. We need him. This place stinks with the odor of beer and filth. Is it easy for Grandmom to pick up drunks? Is she a good person who does good deeds for people? Maybe that's why Mom is so good. Pop,

how did you survive Japan and all those battles? I guess you don't want to talk about the war because we are all too young. Why don't you go to Paddy's? Everybody hangs around the radio when the Notre Dame game is on. Mom, thanks for keeping us together and happy during the war. Pop, you didn't have to go to war, why did you? You must really want to protect us kids.

I can't stand the sight of the stray cats and vicious dogs around here. But I give them credit; they are surviving and I'm sure that they are fighting other dogs and cats every day. The filthy dog dirt all over this street makes me sick. People have to get to work; they don't have time to clean dog dirt from their shoes. I wonder if Portobello was this dirty when Granddad and Grandmom lived there. I wonder if there are times when they wished they stayed in Scotland. Nobody will fight Granddad because he is strong. He carries water meters every day to people's houses. Uncle Dan might have a problem though. Even though he fought at the Cambria, he doesn't appear ready to fight after two or three hours at Paddy's. I hope I'm wrong because Uncle Dan is a man of conscience, like Pop and he will not back down if his beliefs are challenged.

Actually, Grandmom and Granddad's house is nice. It is always clean and the ship clock and the statues of Our Blessed Mother and the Sacred Heart of Jesus are beautiful. Grandmom has Saints' medals pinned all over her apron. That's her jewelry, I guess. The jewelry was sacred, not expensive. Grandmom's custard pies are the best. I think she gets them at the German Bakery on Germantown Avenue, near Dawn Donuts. I'm so lucky to be part of this family. I hope that I will never hurt the feelings of my parents and grandparents. I hope that the people in Paddy's are happy and proud of themselves. They should be proud and happy. I hope the men feel appreciated. No one who fought in any war should pay taxes or for their beers. I'd like to ask the women if they were in the war. I'm sure that some were. I'm sure that they are too humble to talk about it, like the men are 99% of the time. The veterans at Paddy's never initiated conversations about the war and they gave short answers to anyone who wanted to know what it was like.

Pop, I'll probably play football for Notre Dame some day. It might be tough to make All-American, but I think I can make it. I

know that you also want me to be the first American Pope, but I got pale and worried when Sister talked about perfection and being a saint. I want to play center field when Mantle leaves. I can't play third base because I hate ground balls; they go crazy when they hit rocks on our field, near the railroad spur.

Why do they call Paddy's a gin mill? Pop, I bet that you can sell some of your paintings for good money at Paddy's. Some of the women do wash for sailors and soldiers who are on leave. Buggy must be angry about things. If he's not he's a real hero.

Mr. Quinn was always the one to start the singing at Paddy's. He got the songfest going with a brief solo. Some of the others, men and women, chimed in. Not everybody sang solos and those that did only tried to sing. Pop would be great here but he didn't go to Paddy's very often. Pop had a great voice and he knew many songs. Conversations continued during the singing, but stopped instantly when Seamus Muldoon, a bartender and frequent customer, started to sing. He could sing beautifully like John McCormick, the famous Irish tenor. Seamus brought many a tear to yer' eyes when you heard:

"Oh Danny Boy, the pipes, the pipes are callin' from glen to glen and down the mountain side". "Goodbye God bless you mother dear; I hope your heart won't pain; but pray to God your soldier boy you'll see again; and when im (sic) out on the firing line it will be a source of joy to know that your (sic) the mother of an Irish soldier boy". "Oh my Kathleen you're going to leave me all alone by myself in this place but I'm sure that you'll never deceive me ..." "When Irish eyes are smiling..." Me mother 'Ma Cree'..." The Rose of Tralee..." Seamus was the best.

Seamus was short and slim, maybe five nine and one hundred and thirty pounds. He worked in the Clover Cleaner's during the week and at the bakery on 5th Street on Sundays. He lived on Fairhill Street. His clothes looked like a Marine's probably because he was a Marine. He came from "the closest place to heaven on earth; Eden before the snake" in the south of Ireland. He wore dress clothes to Paddy's. He carried his paperboy cap when he was singing and when he wasn't. The cap was his trademark, like Groucho's mustache. He didn't smoke or drink the hard stuff. He brought his two sisters over from Eden. They lived with him and he bragged about them all the time. "Ave Maria, my older sister, and Elizabeth Mary Gabriel, the younger one, are starting college in the fall. Ave has credits from home, but they won't take all of them. They'll work at Breyer's Ice Cream until they start school. Liz is going to Penn and Ave is trying to get to Princeton; we'll have to see what happens. Me Mom is proud of 'em and me. Dad is pointing them out to all the other saints in heaven".

The Irish people are such sentimentalists and emotional when it comes to family, religion, and country. My favorite song that Seamus sings is the "Irish Soldier Boy". Grandmom sings this ditty while she folds her arms in front of her and sways from left to right. Mom finds it too hard to sing; Granddad was not too kind to his family when he had a few too many. He laughed at his kids when they tried to sing or recite poems or just about anything. Everybody sang "Danny Boy" and "Mother Ma Cree".

This neighborhood makes me feel so proud and yet so sorry for the Irish and the Scots/Irish because they work hard, remember their past, and want their kids to be better off than they have been. Why doesn't Leahy recruit from neighborhoods; not everybody gets to finish high school. He could recruit them to finish high school and play football there. They play Rugby and Soccer and Football will come naturally. Many of the Fighting Irish fought in the war; so did Leahy. He knows what the guys can do and how they'd never let a chance to go to Notre Dame get by without an all out effort.

The Fighting Irish are here and in every big city – and Taproom – and there is no need to go to high schools to get players. High school players can't be tougher than someone who fought the Germans and Japanese. Danny O'Dea, the first shift bartender, carries two big barrels of beer from the basement and smiles the whole time. He'd destroy Michigan or Army single handedly.

There were a few women at Paddy's, but I didn't get to know them very well. They called me Sweetie and told me that I was adorable with my jet-black hair. The women didn't ask if I knew their daughters or if our class was the furthest along; far ahead of the other classes. I didn't pay attention to beauty in those days, but Maureen O'Hara came to mind when I talked to one or two. Sarah (don't know her name) was from Ireland, County Clare, and was hot headed as well red headed. I saw her threaten a visitor to Paddy's that she would "shoot darts into your eyes if you ever intentionally bump into me again". Uncle Dan admired the women and he told me so. Pop also admired the women who worked so hard, especially Mom, had difficult lives during the war worrying about their husbands at war and trying to raise kids – Mom had four at the time – and paying the bills. The jobs that these women had weren't cushy office jobs; they were "men's work" like factory work as riveters, piece workers on an assembly line, mechanics, and truck drivers. They probably drove cabs and engineered trains and subways. They cleaned streets and sewers. They did office work if they were lucky. They took PTC public transportation to get to and from work. They sure did sacrifice for their families and their country.

They rushed home from work; they had to, to get dinner for their kids, who needed more attention than the rivets or the component parts on the assembly line. They monitored homework, led the family prayers, controlled access to the bathroom, cleaned up after everybody, and made sure that all the kids were ready for bed and for school the next day. It's a wonder how these women at Paddy's had time for a beer or two; though I'm glad they did. Maybe their kids were grown or they had no kids. I didn't pay attention to that level of detail. All I know is they were special, like the male patrons and the bartenders.

I'm going to steal Zeke, the Mad Barber's poster of Rosy the Riveter and hang it up in here. I hope the mustache and beard somebody drew on Rosy comes off with water.

I loved these people and I admired them. They paid me with Coca Colas, which I took to our table to enjoy with a few potato chips. Someone should have told them of my chemical reactions to a Dawn donut. I can sit perfectly still for an hour at least if I knew a Dawn donut would be my pay. Doesn't matter; these people were the heart and soul of our country. They worked hard for everything they had. Most of them were God fearing, if not necessarily church going, people. They put up with the "Irish like to drink and fight" image, despite their kind and delightful temperaments.

They were not connected so they couldn't expect favors from corrupt politicians. Since they were people of an integrity that was ok for them; they wouldn't know how to get special favors anyway. They wouldn't do anything that would bring shame to their parents and their beloved homeland. They paid top dollar for everything because they didn't bargain or negotiate prices. They trusted that they weren't being overcharged, which they were. They paid their taxes as required by law and on time. They loved their new country, despite the fact that most were from Ireland and Scotland, who were working hard at crummy jobs and dealing with all kinds of biases to raise their families. Their parents put up with "Irish need not apply" and "Shanty Irish" signs. They were true philosophers, educated by life's experiences, not necessarily by textbooks. They weren't like the intellectuals who ponder themselves out of truth and reality.

Paddy's customers talk about everything from their jobs to their jobs in Ireland to politics and sports and family life and, finally, the Church here and in Ireland.

I never saw my parents in Paddy's, but they possessed the wonderful characteristics of Paddy's customers. Mom was an immigrant from Portobello, Scotland, a suburb of Edinburgh. My father, Pop, was from Philadelphia. He was a veteran of the World War II. Mom raised four kids while Pop was fighting on a destroyer escort, the USS Jacquard, in the Pacific. I wish that Pop was with Uncle Dan and me at Paddy's because I know that he would enjoy the discussions, especially the discussions about Notre Dame and the Fighting Irish football team, which Pop loved. I loved Notre Dame too. I sang the Victory March all the time and I saw myself in the Notre Dame backfield and on the defense, showing Southern Methodist that Irish Catholics could play some football. Some of the bartenders at Paddy's could have played for Frank Leahy at Notre Dame now that I think about it.

The women who stayed home are like Mom, but not as saintly, I think. They had a lot of work to do and they must have been lonely and tired. Now that I think about it, they were just as saintly as Mom is; there is no degree of saintlessness; you are a saint or you're not a saint. I don't think canonization makes the saint, a real saint. That would be unfair to all our neighbors, all war veterans, Mom, Pop, and all the people I see saying their rosary during mass. Everybody at Paddy's and on Carlisle Street is a Saint.

Most of the women were veterans of working at home and in factories during the war to keep their families and our economy going. All of these people were fun to be with, especially for a ten or eleven year old, who got Cokes and pretzels simply for being in the right place at the right time and with the best of breed people. It wasn't all play, however, and I did have some serious work to do. I enjoyed my job at Paddy's and the pay was good.

My primary responsibility was to tell each man that I knew his daughter and that she was the prettiest girl in the school. About ten different girls were the prettiest at any given time. I also had the responsibility of letting these same men know that their child was the best student in our class, especially in arithmetic and spelling and that our class was way ahead of the other classes. I forgot that some of their children might not go to St. Ed's. Nobody asked what school I went to, thank God.

My job with the women was to do nothing most of the time and to get a fresh supply of potato chips when they ran out. One woman, named Geraldine. (I could never call her Geraldine though she asked me to. I didn't know her last name. I had to call her Mrs. Whatever her last name was) introduced me to her daughter, who was ten or eleven, like me. ""Fiona, meet Billy Maguire. I think he's in your school", say hello. "Hello." "Hello", was my reply. I don't like to mince words. That was it and I was glad; not a big to-do, just two polite hellos. "He's Danny's nephew and he's the one I told you about with the black hair", was how Geraldine unintentionally embarrassed me.

It's McCaffrey, not Maguire, and Mom calls me Billy, everybody else calls me Bill, except Pop who calls me Billy the Bull even though he saw me dodge a grounder and under throw a throw from third to first. It really didn't matter what I was called. Fiona didn't care what I was called or even know the difference between Billy and Bill. I'm glad that Fiona's mother didn't get into what chapter are you on? What spelling words do you have this week? Did you get gold or silver cards or none at all? Fiona isn't in my class. I think she goes to another Catholic school.

Pop, I'll probably play football for Notre Dame some day. It might be tough to make All-American, but I think I can make it. I know that you also want me to be the first American Pope, but I got pale and worried when Sister talked about perfection and Saint I want to play center field when Mantle leaves. I can't play third base because I hate ground balls; they go crazy when they hit rocks on our field, near the railroad spur.

3

Buggy

My grandfather, Mom's father and Uncle Dan's father, told me this about Buggy. My uncle Dan lost half his hearing diving for sponges off Sicily. He was in the Navy during the war. He said sponges; Buggy said German mines. His medic recommended that Dan go home. Dan refused to leave. He would've stayed if he lost both legs. He hated the way the Germans bullied all Europe and some of Russia. Buggy refused to go home also like Dan. Buggy, Uncle Dan's best friend was in the Army. They enlisted at the same time.

In France, Buggy saw a couple soldiers limping, one was helping the other along into enemy fire. He ran out and helped them both get out of danger. Some shrapnel hit his leg. Everybody was safe and the injured soldiers thanked Buggy many times. Buggy was on the receiving end of help himself at another time. The incident also happened in France.

Buggy was hurt when he tripped on an enemy mine. He was unconscious for several hours as he laid in the fields, close to the enemy. An ally's tank patrol finally spotted him. They brought him to safety but the medic said he was dead. The French planned to bury Buggy in France, near the place they found him. The Allies had no other choice. A Dutch soldier noticed Buggy's miraculous medal and rosary. He removed the medal and put it aside planning to get it back to Buggy's family with his dog tags and rosaries. The soldier, named Cal, tried to take Buggy's rosaries out of his pocket when Buggy instinctively pushed the soldier's hand away. The soldier was aghast and he wept and ran to tell the others.

"The guy's alive, believe me," exclaimed a wide-eyed, half-believing Cal.

"He can't be; you must be mistaken Cal. He was dead when I declared him dead," replied the medic with a level of confidence that someone who was sure that two and two equaled four.

"Come with me, I'll prove it," sputtered Cal as he grabbed the medic's arm and pulled him toward Buggy.

"This isn't funny Cal, you know that," the medic warned Cal.

The two of them went to see Buggy and, to their amazement, he was sitting up asking where he was. "Where are my dog tags?"

"Where's my miraculous medal? I want that medal," Buggy continued in a rare mood of panic.

"Mr. Quinn here are your medal and tags. I declared you dead, sir. You were dead sir; I'm sure of that."

"I'm not dead anymore so get me back to my platoon," insisted Buggy.

"I'm afraid that you'll be with us for sometime Mr. Quinn," added Cal as he tried to pull himself together. "We will help you find your squadron".

"Call me Joe or Buggy; my father's Mr. Quinn," Buggy said using his Irish pride tone.

"When I tried to take your rosary away, you pushed my hand away. Dead soldiers, even American soldiers, don't do that. You are right Joe; you are not dead anymore. We are glad you are alive. What happened? Do you know Joe?" asked Cal who had a million questions that he needed to answer when he talked to people about this incident.

"I was the point man out on patrol with my platoon. I heard shots and looked around to see the others going back. I ran to catch up with them and that's all I remember," said Buggy as he kissed his medal and rosaries. He put both the medal and the rosaries around his neck.

"We're a tank operation with English and Dutch soldiers. We're headed to HQ and HQ knows about you; we sent them a message. You will be safe. Does all this seem unreal to you Joe?" inquired one of the officers.

"Yeah and I prefer Buggy from people who save my life," said Buggy to honor his heroes.

"People? People didn't do this. Were you ever declared dead before Buggy?" asked the shortest soldier with the unheard of ponytail, who pushed his way toward Buggy.

"Once before and that's enough times for now," said Buggy as he prepared to tell the stories.

"Once in a prize fight in the states when a real pro punched me right under the chin. It was a direct hit like if you turned around and sucker-punched me - just a cold, unexpected very hard punch right to the jaw. The ring doctor, who wasn't a doctor, said I died. He said that he was good in the sciences, the so-called doctor, I mean, in high school so we agreed he could be the ring doctor. Barry, that's his name, had terrible handwriting, a true sign of a doctor, and played the role of doctor well. He tried to take my temperature with a weather thermometer after the big hit. There was no movement of "that red line", as Barry called the mercury. He called for help; a doctor he knew from cleaning his office part time. Doctor what's his name with a Polish name like Klaus or Clause determined over the phone that I died. The boxer who hit me went into a hysterical mood. The red car took me to St. Christopher's Children's hospital. The cops used red cars. It was around the block and two more blocks," summarized Buggy in a serious way although it sounded unreal.

"I saw a beautiful girl about a teenager in years. She had a blue dress-like dress, like my second grade Sister wore, only light blue like the faded blue sign near Paddy's Taproom, my favorite restaurant. She told me to get up and praise Jesus and don't feel ashamed. She gave me these rosaries and told me to say them all the time and to remember her at tough moments, like this. My chaplain reblessed, blessed a second time (sic) them for me when I got here. The doctors and nurses knelt down and said a Hail Mary and a Glory Be. The doctors didn't believe my story when they interviewed me for their records. I told Fr. Kelly, the famous Jesuit from our neighborhood, and he told me to pray for healing, not physical healing, mind you, but mind-like healing. He thought I lost my mind. He blessed my rosaries and told me they were nice but nothing special. I never counted his blessing as a "real blessing".

Buggy's eyes opened wider than what seemed normal for a man his size. His face turned red as if he blushed after a cute little girl kissed him.

"Next month after that incident, I was going with Dan to get into the Army. He was Navy. I saw on channel six and in the Bulletin a man's picture who thought he saw Mary, the Mother of God. He described the girl I saw to a T. The TV announcer tried to hold back his laughter, but he couldn't. The man, who didn't look cooky, said that Mary knew he'd be laughed at but to move on until someone listened and believed him. The man sold all his things and gave the money to people laid off, which was what Mary told him to do. He walked around all day long like he was nuts. He greeted everyone and told the homeless to be not afraid and to love God. He had no money but he met up with a couple robbers who told him to empty his pockets. He obliged the robbers and showed them he was broke. One of the punks wanted to take the rosaries away and as he moved toward him, the punk froze in place. He couldn't move. His friend took off and ran as fast as he could towards the subway," remembered Buggy, who could never forget what he heard on TV.

"The robber pleaded with Mary to intercess (he meant intercede) for him so he could run away too. The robber didn't run to the subway like his friend. He walked down a street saying the Seven Sacraments and the Fruits of the Holy Ghost aloud over and over".

"Mary, tell your Son that that kid doesn't know what he's doing; he has no money and this looked like a sure thing. He won't rob again and he might become a priest or a bishop or even a saint. I heard he said these words when the cops came. I knew I had to meet the man who saw Mary. He was special and he was serious, not a fool or a fraud. He communicated with Mary, I'm sure of that. He was worth listening to," continued Buggy to an awestruck, non-Catholic, half-believing audience. Buggy prayed that he could meet the man who communicated with Mary.

"A similar incident happened to me shortly after I heard about this situation," Buggy related. "Some punk walked up behind me and put a gun to my back. He wanted all my money or he would shoot me. He told me to put my wallet on the ground, which I did. Then he told me to put all my loose change next to the wallet. I took out my rosaries and I turned around to face my assailant. I asked if he wanted the rosaries as well and he froze. He told me not to tell anyone what happened and he walked away, leaving the wallet".

Buggy was a couple days away from going to basic training when he went to Paddy's Taproom for the traditional beers that the bartenders gave to all the people going to the war. He turned the corner and was about to open the door. In fact, he was so close that he could hear the conversations about him and that he was about to become a real man. He expected some harassment; it was part of the ritual. He was wearing his favorite A's hat and his favorite shirt. The shirt was a gray Dickey work shirt. Buggy said it meant the humility and pride, both at their proper level that our neighborhood stood for. Of course, he carried the rosaries he got from the nuns when he helped them move some furniture. He wore his medal outside his shirt.

Buggy closed his eyes for a minute and saw Breyer's lot and the fights that he and Dan started. He saw Emily O'Neill, his one and only crush. He saw Cagney, Bogart, Grant, Tracy, Gable and his favorite, Duke Wayne. He saw several leading ladies, all-smiling at him as if they were waiting for him. Buggy wanted to be an actor. He practiced acting by saying his favorite lines in the mirror repeatedly. He was good; he knew it and he trusted Jesus to get him a small part in a cowboy movie. He'd move up; he knew that too. He was tall, maybe six-two, and lean just like the Duke or Cary. He was better looking than Bogart, Cagney, Tracy and the Duke. He felt good about that but he wanted to be in westerns until he became famous. Then he would use his looks to be a leading man.

He used his older brother's Old Spice. He was certain to get some jokes from the ladies about his aroma. He didn't care. "I might meet Emily or Maureen O'Hara, you never know," he said to himself. He hated beer and he didn't drink it.

He never had beer to keep cold in Vera's refrigerated Coke box as the other thirteen-year olds did a few years before. He saved Ovalteen in the box instead. He was his own person; he knew it and he liked it more than his looks or muscles. He combed his thick, jet-black hair into his well-known DA. His Flagg flyers were polished and he knew he'd be the center of attention. He used Simonize to polish his shoes. His shoes didn't look polished but he thought they did and that was enough for him.

"Young man, where is the nearest subway station? What stop is Sts. Peter and Paul's?" asked two nuns, who were lost and who interrupted Buggy's entrance into Paddy's Taproom.

"You need Broad Street and that's far away. You can't walk it sisters. Do you have cab fare?" asked Buggy as he looked at his watch and wallet realizing that he had no money to give them.

"No, we don't, but we like to walk," said the smiling nuns.

"No, it's too far. Wait 'til I see if anybody at the bar can help. Do you want to come in?" asked the courteous young Army recruit.

"Well, if you don't mind sharing your big night with us," said the taller of the two sisters.

"'For he's a jolly good fella. For he's,...'" the patrons were singing the traditional entrance song for their honoree. They stopped when they saw the sisters. The men took off their hats and the women greeted the sisters at the door and walked them into the lounge area where there was no smoke at the time. Megan McCarty knelt down in front of the sisters and held their hands. O'Malley, the retired Navy Commander, who came to Paddy's Taproom from the Main Line for all going-away-to-war-parties, knelt down too but he kissed their hands.

"What'll you have Joe? How 'bout the nuns; wadda (sic) they want do you think?" asked Muldoon, an older bartender with a mustache.

"Give me three Canada Dry's," requested Buggy who had no money because the drinks were supposed to be on the house.

"What are their names? What's their order? Maybe they know my sister; she's a sister somewhere in Mayo," peppered Muldoon on to Buggy.

The good sisters heard the good bartender.

"I'm Sr. Prisca and this is Sr. Blandina. We are both Sisters of Our Lady of Peace and Love," volunteered the younger nun.

"Your blue dresses are very beautiful and cute. I never saw such huge rosaries. Are they real wood?" asked Rose O'Grady, the best woman dart shooter at Paddy's Taproom, whose real name is Kathleen McNamara.

"Where is your convent? Do you have brothers and sisters? You're not ugly. Why did you become a nun?" asked Skimmer the cab driver with a lisp and hunched back, who never leaves a tip for the bartenders.

"Thanks for the compliment about our habits. The light blue reminds us of Mary, our Patroness and our Mother. We make our own rosaries from the Garden's trees. Our convent is in our rooms. There are plenty of rooms in our garden. There will be a room for all of you. We believe that all people are our brothers and sisters. I agree that Sister Blandina is beautiful. I almost didn't become a nun. Any more questions?" responded Sr. Prisca.

"Where do you teach?" asked Mrs. McCarty.

"We teach everywhere we go. We don't use books or words unless we really have to. Our friend suggested this place and we respect Him so we follow His directions," said the beautiful nun.

"No more questions, but here is $50.00 for you sisters. You can take a cab both ways," volunteered Liam, another bartender, who passed a hat around and took money out of his tip box to round off to $50.00. Liam's three sisters are nuns somewhere in Ireland.

"Thank you. Sr. Prisca and I will add this to all of your storehouses of riches near our rooms," said Sr. Blandina.

"Can we go to your convent?" inquired Joe.

"There are many rooms and nothing would make us happier than to have you with us. Joe, we honor you and all the military for your service to our country. I know that half of you are veterans of the wars. You saved the lives of millions of people and you showed what freedom feels like to many others. Your Father and Mother love you for what you did so far with your life and for whom you are now," said a serious Sr. Blandina.

"Sisters, wait for me while I clean up and I'll go with you," stuttered Peter, a faithful patron.

"Thank you Peter, but we'll go alone," said both sisters in perfect unison.

"How did you know my name Sisters?" asked Peter, who knows nobody outside Paddy's Taproom and his church.

"Peter, how can we not know your name? All the souls think the world of where you live. Your parents tell every soul all about you and your sacrifices on their behalf. In fact, all of you are heroes in our eyes, women and men. Joe and Dan are also talked about in a favorable light. We must go now. When Joe gets off the phone, tell him we love him and we will pray for him when he is in France and Italy. We want you to have these miraculous medals. They are plain medals but they were blessed by the Father," explained Sr. Blandina to Peter, a baffled ordinary person with an extraordinary heart.

"Give Joe this little token of appreciation for letting us interrupt his party," Sr. Prisca asked Peter.

Buggy ran down Darien Street for a half block trying to find the sisters but they couldn't be seen. He opened the red velvet bag that tied on the top to see what the sisters gave him. "Don't lose this medal, Joe and pray the rosary each day for the souls in Purgatory and for Russia's conversion" read the unsigned note. Somehow, Buggy just knew what the sisters wanted him to know when he opened the bag, their names. He found something out about these names. Prisca and Blandina, are unusual; they are saints' names. These saints were young virgins who, died for their faith. Prisca was a young girl who openly professed her faith when she was tortured and thrown in with lions. Blandina was brutally tortured and killed because she would not deny her Catholic faith.

Buggy pledged to God that he would do His Will even if it meant death or serious injury. He gave the red velvet bag to his mother and father on the day he left for Ft. Hood. He promised to say the rosary at least once a day. He became a Crusader in his own mind. His quest will be "Freedom and Justice for All Forever". He dropped the names Buggy and Joseph and decided that he was Joe. He reserved the name Buggy for very special people in his life. Nothing could stop him from pursuing his quest. He had faith; that is all he needed.

He wouldn't be an officer but he would be an effective leader because he would lead without titles or service medals. He would lead by his actions. If he needed words to lead, he would use them. He has always led by example. Did he ever meet the man who gave up everything after he saw Mary? Uncle Dan promised to tell me sometime.

Somewhere along the way, Buggy learned that actions speak louder than words. His friends knew him for what he did, not for what he said.

4

The Ragman

On Lawrence Street, near Reese, was a rag shop, which was owned and operated by the Ragman we called Cee-Gar. The rag shop was an old warehouse, which had stacks of discarded newspapers and many types of old rags. Cee-Gar was a short, stout, man with a ruddy appearance, a stogie in his mouth – Cee-Gar – at all times, a five o'clock shadow, which was visible at one am, and a t-shirt, which was spotless at 8 o' clock in the morning. After a short time stacking newspapers, say, until 8:30, the combination of sweat, stogie extract, and ink made the t-shirt look like it went through a two-day dirt fight and lost. He chewed on the stogie, which was probably better for him than smoking it, but it made a real mess. When Cee-Gar was ruffled, he would pull the stogie from his mouth as if pulling the pin off a hand grenade and spit out the most disgusting brown mess you've ever seen. He dared not smoke in the warehouse full of papers and rags. The Ragman always rolled his pants up from the bottom. He always wore dark pants, which he tucked in his white socks, which took on the look of his t-shirt. Stogie stains got to his socks. I do not know how they did, but they did. His belt was partially unbuckled, leaving the end without the buckle dangling. His pants always threatened to drop down and his shoes were the soft kind with no laces. His closely cropped hair had a hint of gray. His hair was so course that you wondered if he had to wear gloves when he washed it. If Zeke, the mad barber of North Philadelphia, would meet this challenge and make Cee-Gar's hair look good, a new world would be opened to him: styling. If Zeke could style Cee-Gar's hair, he could style a Brillo pad.

Cee-Gar held a hook in his hand. He used this hook, which was similar to the hooks that longshore men used on the wharfs, to grab a stack of papers or rags and throw them onto a pile. Our Ragman, Cee-Gar, could throw a 20-inch stack of newspapers on top of a one-foot pile easily. He could throw a 25 pound bundle of rags 30 feet, to the opposite end of the warehouse. He also knew everything about rags. He knew the different types of fabrics and their uses. He literally sat on a chair and sorted the rags by fabric type and condition. It was quite an art. Cee-Gar would pay by the pound for old newspapers and rags. There was a scale built in the cement floor of the rag shop. The scale hardly moved for two hundred pounds, so I assume it went to a ton marker at least. There was a blue line painted on the floor, which was the closest point a person, other than Cee-Gar, could get to the scale. The weight marker was easy to see. Little kids with two old Sunday Bulletins to weigh would call him Mr. Ragman Cee-Gar. Cee-Gar gave Mary Jane candies to the little kids for anything less than seventy-five pounds and a penny a pound for every pound over seventy-five pounds. Old rags were hard to find. Newspapers were everywhere. Cee-Gar paid the same amount for each so most people brought in newspapers.

Nobody seemed to like our Ragman. He had no friends or enemies. He wasn't married. I never saw him in church or going to church. He was unfriendly and all business. No one would dare put bricks inside a bundle of newspapers at Cee-Gar's but it was a common practice at other rag shops.

The Ragman was a workaholic; he started early in the morning, like 5:30am and finished long after most people finished working. Pop said that Cee-Gar learned his work habits from his parents, who escaped from Germany during the war to find opportunities for the Ragman and his siblings. Ragman's parents weren't Jewish but they saw terrible things happening in their beloved country and they felt they had to get away. Pop knew this because he knew the Ragman when they both played football on Beyer's lot.

Pop told me the whole story about Cee-Gar: "Bill, your favorite Cee-Gar man has a name and I want you to use it at all times. His name is Mr. Horst Von Stolcz. You can call him Mr. Stolcz and remember to be respectful. Mr. Stolcz dropped out of school in the fifth grade and started to work for the same broom factory I worked for when I dropped out in third grade. He was an usher at the Strand and nobody dared sneak in when he was on duty. I ushered at the Uptown during this time but I heard all about Horst and how he held would-be 'sneaksers-in,' as we called them. Horst and I lived a couple blocks from each other and we played many choose-up football games against each other. He was tough and I had a tough time blocking him and tackling him when he ran with the ball. Horst's brother, Ed, was in France during the war. Ed was a finesse football player, who could run and make all kinds of fancy moves and never let a defender touch him. Ed played in the defense backfield and he caught many speedy backs from behind. If he made an interception, which he frequently did, he was gone to the end zone. He was just too fast for anybody to catch him once he got a step on you. Ed and Horst would have been great high school players if they stayed in school. Horst had to quit like me because his family needed the money and he didn't seem to be too interested in school. Ed quit school to make money for the family too. He was an excellent student who didn't get the chance to go to North or wherever he would have gone".

"Both Ed and Horst played semi-pro football for the Frankford Yellow Jackets on Sundays. Ed was older and played semi-pro ball when he was seventeen, but Horst lied about his age and played when he was fifteen or sixteen. He told the commissioner of the league that he was nineteen. In those days college players played semi-pro on weekends. Everybody needed money and was willing to work for it. Ed was a very good semi-pro player. He received letters from colleges all over the place. He did not finish high school or elementary school so it couldn't work out. It was such a shame for Ed. With the right breaks, he would have been an All American.

"The Stolcz brothers joined the Army on the same day. Ed went to train for secret missions in Europe. When he left for the Army, he promised that he would return to finish high school and get a good job so he could marry his girl friend, Molly Malone, who lived two houses from his house. He did come home one time, after his special training. He took Molly to the Uptown when I was ushering and we let them in free because they were doing so much for our country. Molly couldn't wait to get another name; Molly Malone heard the song with her name sung by different people she met all the time".

"Ed stopped in Paddy's Taproom Tavern during this leave and all the patrons went crazy singing George M. Cohen songs and buying each other beers. Horst was leaving for the Army at just about this time. He too went in Paddy's Taproom and he too heard songs and joined in on the merriment. All the male patrons and some of the women were in the military at one time or another and you could hear *Anchors Aweigh, Army Blue* and *From the Halls of Montezuma* and songs about girlfriends and families on Susquehanna and Darien Streets for hours. Like a well-rehearsed choir, the Irish and Scottish men and women sang their favorite Irish rebel songs. Buggy sang "There Ain't Nothing like a Dame" and some women sang "I'm Gonna Wash That Man Right Outta my Hair". Horst left the day after all this. Ed left a couple days later and never made it back. He died in France when he was the point man of a large patrol. Ed's parents were finished; it was too much for them to take".

This is too much for Pop to remember. I feel honored that Pop wants to tell me this story.

"Ed's parents lived in relative seclusion. Molly vowed to never marry or even date other men. I don't believe she ever did get married. Horst came home and essentially stopped talking to people. He went back to the Army and transferred from Italy to Philadelphia as a recruiter. He had a difficult time recruiting young men and women because his heart wasn't in it and he got out of the Army after two years. His discharge was Honorable and he wore Ed's dog tags with his own for a long time. He could not find decent work so he started his own business. He was a Ragman from that point on. He never went in Paddy's Taproom. He was alone all the time. He was severely damaged emotionally by Ed's premature death".

When someone came into the rag shop with a cart filled with papers or rags, Mr. Van Stolcz would stop what he was doing; throw the papers and rags on to the scale; show his nasty, intimidating face and proceed to weigh and assess the value of the "merchandise". He would level the slide at the top of the scale, moving the little weights on the slide until the bar was perfectly level. He normally didn't even think before he said, "seventy- five cents, take it or leave. If you don't take it, get those papers outta' here". Cee-Gar was tough and he had the hook. We never made much money doing this, but Mom must have thought it was worthwhile. One time we borrowed a broken up old wooden cart from Cee-Gar and filled it with papers and rags. Try to picture Tevyah, the father in the "Fiddler on the Roof" when he was pulling his cart; that was Fran all the way. On the way back to the rag shop, a wheel fell off the cart. Papers and rags went everywhere. We had to run to catch the papers by stepping on them so they wouldn't blow away. Mom was so embarrassed. Fran and I scampered all over to retrieve the papers and try to put the cart back together. I couldn't keep my eyes off Mom. She was in tears, which was unheard of for her. I was in tears too. I froze for a few seconds before I got back to chasing after papers. I was so upset at seeing Mom so upset. I couldn't take it.

Mom, it'll be ok. Don't feel embarrassed. You are such a good person. Nobody is laughing at you. Why did we have to get THIS cart anyway? Why doesn't the Ragman take better care of his carts? The Ragman won't intimidate Fran and me when we return this cart; he better not. Charlie the Crook said he puts rocks inside the papers to get more money. Sister jokingly, I hope, suggested that we put wet papers in the middle of the bundles when we were collecting papers for the foreign missions. Mom, please go home. Fran and I can take care of this. Mom, I'm going to build you the best home in the world some day. We can start looking at houses as soon as I get out of grammar school. Nobody will laugh then. God, I wish that Pop were here. He would fix everything. Fran is a hard worker. He could take Pop's place I guess if he had to. He will make a great president. He'd be a better pope than me, but he can't be both.

At Fran's suggestion about two months later, we borrowed another cart from Cee-gar. We gathered papers and rags and accumulated enough money to buy Mom a surprise gift. Mrs. Swosta, a non-Irish or Scottish Catholic, took us to a store on Germantown Avenue to pick out the gift. For a dollar, we could buy this very nice Plaster-of-Paris pink lamb, with a bow. We had fifty-five cents.

"Do you have a dollar?" whispered the woman at the counter hoping that we didn't, I think.

"No, we have fifty-five cents, but we can come back tomorrow with forty five cents more if you'll hold the lamb for us," I said thinking about either shining shoes, or getting the cart out and going to Lehigh Avenue where there were plenty papers and some rags.

"That's alright. If it's for your mother, I can take fifty cents. You keep the extra nickel to start saving for next year's Christmas," whispered our favorite businessperson as she smiled and wrapped the lamb in old newspaper.

Mrs. Swosta told us that we got a great bargain and that Mom will cherish the gift. The woman whispered because her store was crowded and she did not want to embarrass us. I've never forgotten that moment.

Mom loved the gift. She said that we shouldn't have done it, but she would always cherish the lamb. Everything was right again. Cee-Gar was Mr. Stolcz and he was a good person again. The neighborhood was the best. Fran proved why Pop thought that he would be the first Catholic president.

Mrs. Swosta was right about the cherishing the gift. Things are ok now, but why did my Mom, a Saint in every sense of the word, have to endure such humiliation? Sometimes this neighborhood stinks to the high heavens, like now. Why is there so much filth around here? Why is all this dog dirt around here? Why can't people keep their dogs under control? Darn it, sometimes you get dog dirt on your shoes and you can't get it off. Some people have to go to work with smelly shoes.

At least Mom smiled when she saw the lamb. It was nice of the woman to sell us the lamb at a great bargain. The woman said that she wished that she gave her mother a lamb like ours' because her mother died and she misses her. The woman was crying and I knew that she wanted to give us a great bargain. Mrs. Zwosta was German, Russian, or something else other than Irish or Scottish, yet she took Fran and me to get the lamb. She was Catholic and her side of the street had higher steps, which were as shiny as the Irish families' steps. Mrs. Zwosta knew that Mom would cherish the lamb. How'd she know that?

Fifth Street is getting so busy and traffic is getting tough. The Rose Hill Street kids think they are so much better than we are. Mom, I'll be a good student. Pop, I'll play for Notre Dame and I'll be the first American Pope, just like you want me to be. I'll need to play for the Yankees for a little while after college. Mom, I think it's good that you were born in Scotland. I always tell my friends that you were born in Scotland. Mom, you're small but smart.

When we returned the broken cart and had our papers weighed by the Ragman, it was forty-seven pounds. He didn't say a word as usual. He gave us *three dollars.*

5

Pop, the Artist

Pop was a terrific artist. He couldn't be an artist by trade because he was raising five kids and his income had to be based on an agreed to salary, not on the whims of some art dealers and buyers. As I mentioned, Pop was a bearing polisher. He polished bearings for a steel manufacturer, using sand paper and his experience to hone the bearings to the size and quality required by the customers. I'll bet that his work was perfect; he was a perfectionist and a true artist. He worked the second shift as long as I remember. He and Mom needed the additional ten percent pay differential that came with the second shift. Pop went to art school on the GI bill. Pop would take me to art school with him. I was the model. I was never sure why Pop wanted a model that had one ear larger than the other, an odd shaped head, and no experience sitting still for any length of time. I do remember how the other students and the teacher would comment on Pop's talents with watercolor, oils, charcoal, and pencil. He had a great touch and a wonderfully creative eye for color. Purple mountains, bluish hills, and purplish pink deserts were Pop's trademarks. You really have to see his work to believe his unique coloring could be effective. He did still life, portraits, landscapes, and many paintings of Indians and cowboys.

Pop, I was proud when the other art students came over to your canvas to see what the master was doing. The other guys thought that you had the best talent, even though you painted with strange colors.

Pop, did I embarrass you at the art studio; you know, with the ear thing and the crazy shaped head? Your artwork makes so many people happy. The colors on your pallet look sharp. I'm going to have tons of your paintings in my house when I get

married. We'll put your paintings and drawings in the house that I plan to buy for you and Mom.

For two hours every week, I would pose for Pop and the other students, who were probably on the GI bill too, while they stared at me, pondered a bit, then painted. When we took a break at the end of each hour, we ate donuts. I was getting the best of the deal – a donut would have been worth at least two hours straight of posing. When we took a break, the art students put their pallets aside. I still remember how the paint tubes lined up in rows on the table next to the easels. The pallets had the multicolored dabs of paint filling it up except for the part where the artist put his thumb. It looked like multicolored mud splattered on a wall. It looked like a multicolored Rorschach's chart. Pop amazed me with the way he mixed paints to create the blues, purples, pinks, and the pale faces of a six grader with jet-black hair and an odd shaped head.

The sessions went fast and Pop and I had a long walk home. When we walked home, Pop and I would race. Pop, who was a slim and trim athletic type man, who could run like a gazelle, always lost these races with me.

"Mae," Pop would say, "Billy is really fast; he'll be a good athlete someday! Frank Leahy is always looking for fast players". I heard this comment and never forgot it. Pop didn't save all his artistic talents for his art class, believe me.

Mom and her friends met each week to have tea and conversation, probably a custom brought over by their Scotch and Irish parents. Pop would draw cartoons of the women, who couldn't wait to see themselves in Pop's latest edition. The cartoons were funny, as I remember, but never insulting, but definitely funny. The women would look at the cartoons and picked themselves out from among the others. They roared and wanted a photo of the cartoon. Pop had artistic talents other than sketching and painting. Somebody took a picture of one of Pop's cartoons. It was the talk of the Reese Street people and the families of its subjects.

When Pop came home from work, usually at 1am or so, on the eve of one of our birthdays, he would hard boil an egg and use whatever he could find around the house to make it look like the birthday boy or girl. He would pencil in the eyes and mouth and put something on the egg that looked like hair or ears, usually grass for the hair and carefully trimmed paper for the ears. My egg, of course, usually had one ear bigger than the other one, which went well with my odd shaped head. The egg was the perfect shape of my head. One time Pop made me a holster for my birthday. He cut out some oilcloth and sewed it together to get me ready in case Bob Steele or Hopalong Cassidy or Roy Rogers was putting together a posse to pursue the bad guys. No commercial holster could have made me happier. No other gift could make me happier.

Pop, I know how much you love Notre Dame because it's a Catholic college, named for the Blessed Mother, which has a great football tradition. I'm beginning to know the "Cheer, cheer for old Notre Dame" song. Do you really think I'm fast? Do you sometimes wonder if I will ever go to Notre Dame and play for Leahy? I heard you say something like that. You can really kick a football, Pop, you can do anything. I wish that you were rich so you can be an artist like you want to be. Why doesn't the GI bill find you a good job as an artist? I wish that I could be just like you. I'll never lose the holster, Pop, and no gift that you will ever give me could mean more to me. This is my favorite birthday.

Maybe I won't get married because I have to be the Pope some day. Putting in four years in a Catholic college like Notre Dame is a good step toward the Vatican. I guess that I'll have to figure out how to get my playing time with the Yankees. I hope that I can make it through grammar school without any trouble. I'm not sure I can do all these things and be a saint at the same time.

We moved further north to Carlisle Street in the middle of my second grade. Traffic on 5th Street was becoming dangerous. Pop and Mom rented 2243 N. Reese Street and they wanted to own a home. All good reasons to move, no doubt about it, but the extra benefits of living on Carlisle Street were icing on the cake. There was the long walk to school, the same length coming home for lunch, again, back to school and finally come home from school, a total of four miles.

6

Doc the Clock and Gatemouth

I mentioned that the walk from 3044 North Carlisle Street was long, exactly a mile. Normally it would take about fifteen to twenty minutes to walk it. On cold days, it would take no more than fifteen to run it. From our house on Carlisle Street to Broad Street took thirty seconds if we were not quite awake or ten seconds coming home after school. We ran into some interesting people along the way. Some were more interesting than others, much more interesting than plain 'ole sane people. I will tell you about a few in the more interesting category.

I don't know where the grill was but I saw the bar many times at the Clearfield Bar and Grill. I saw the bar as I walked to school in the mornings, at 5:00am and at 7:30am. Maybe the grill was in the back or next to a wall; maybe the grill was the cast iron cover on the pavement. I don't know why or how but steam came out of that cover all year long. I never saw a woman in The Clearfield Bar and I was happy for that. The bartenders didn't look like they could bounce out any unruly characters. It just wouldn't be right to see a woman being harassed and no one capable of stopping the harasser. I couldn't go in the bar alone to act as if I was looking for someone because there was no one to talk to about school and what we were covering or that I knew their daughter and she was the prettiest and smartest girl in class. I did all these things at Paddy's Taproom. It wouldn't work because the patrons here were mostly Protestant or from another neighborhood. I don't know how I knew this. I just guessed, I guess. Their kids went to public school, probably Mueller. All the kids that I walked to school with got to know one patron very well.

Doc was the neighborhood Akoki Akakievich, the poor soul in Nikolai Gogal's *The Overcoat*, who couldn't get anyone to repair his overcoat. Doc wouldn't find anyone either even if he had an overcoat. He walked the streets wearing a well-worn, cozy looking jacket bearing the name Frankford Yellow Jackets. The Yellow Jackets were a football team that played semi-pro games around the Philly area. Doc didn't play; he couldn't. He was about five foot one or two and he was frail. Moreover, he wore glasses and had a slight limp. Sometimes the limp wasn't so slight, like when he was asking an adult to either buy him a drink or give him money for a drink.

Doc came up to me once or twice and resolutely disclosed a hidden fact about himself, "I'm Doc the Clock and I'm always on time and you're 'gonna be late for school if you don't run. And don't blame the Clock man if you are."

The clientele at the "Field" or "Clear" – either one of these nicknames would work – worked the swing shift from about 9pm to 6am the next day. They liked Doc; they understood him. Doc liked the guys at the Clear and as a sign of appreciation for the beers they bought for him, he would sing a few songs.

If I had a hunch that Doc would be singing some morning, I would leave a little bit earlier than usual to hear him. My hunch paid off one time out of about fifty tries but it might have been Doc's best performance. I heard Doc singing some Eddie Fisher tunes. Let's just say that Doc wasn't Eddie Fisher by any means. It didn't matter; the guys enjoyed the singing and Doc went through all Eddie's motions. The Clock pressed his left chest area and he sang "Downhearted" and smiled as if on camera while singing "O Mein Papa." Even the guys shooting darts stopped to listen to the crooner, who was also a clock. Doc sang Bing Crosby tunes sometimes. He always finished his Crosby tunes with a poorly done imitation of Barry FitzGerald as a Catholic priest in the "Quiet Man". I enjoyed Doc's singing and imitations. He did John Wayne, Eartha Kitt, and Jimmy Stewart too, all poorly.

I wish I knew these Clearfield Bar guys better. They'd be interesting to listen to and learn from. I guarantee that I will stop after work when I have an adult job and some extra money. Paddy's Taproom opens up at least by 9am. I know that because I was there at 9 with Uncle Dan once. The guys at the Field must need the extra money you get for working the swing shift or they would work the first shift. I'll work the swing shift if I stay in the area. Pop always works the swing shift for the extra money.

I think that most of the Clear patrons were in the war. They are at that age and they look healthy. Doc the Clock must have struck it rich today because his breath clearly revealed that he was able to sucker many people into contributing to his health fund, which was needed to pay for the surgery he needs to keep his leg. He must have limped around all day. I will ask Doc the Clock if he was in the war but I suspect that he wasn't since he's so small and has a limp - sometimes. If he was in the Army or Navy, I will show him more respect than I do. I don't listen to or say hello to Doc the Clock when I see him walking around. He always looks angry and unwilling to talk. Doc the Clock puts beer bottle caps for me next to the steps of the corner house made from big brown stones and the forty- five degree angle lawn, which I think he mows for money. He watches us play Dead Man's Box and knows we need bottle caps. I don't know where Doc the Clock lives. Doc the Clock probably doesn't always know where he lives either. It all depends on what he can find.

Doc the Clock seems to head for the subway station at night. He might use the subway to go home or he might sleep on the platform. Everybody knows where the broken turnstile is. Doc the Clock could easily fit through it. He wouldn't have to pay. Doc the Clock's Ertha Kitt imitation is his best. I think Doc would like to see the Yankees play but the A's moved out. I could show him how to stand in front of the bleachers' entrance and look anxious to get into the game but have no money. No, he could show me a thing or two about begging by guilt.

I won't forget to invite Doc to see me play for Notre Dame against Penn at Franklin Field. I hope Doc the Clock and all the other Akoki-like poor souls are warm and comfortable when they sleep. Holy Mary, Mother of God, take care of Doc. Nobody loves him and he knows it and feels it.

Going north on Broad Street I could see several beautiful row houses. These were not like the row houses on Reese Street and Carlisle Street. These houses were three or four stories high and brown stones provided the foundation to them. Inside their first floors were offices and a large parlor. I think some dentists and lawyers had their offices in these houses. At the end of the street, the thirty- one hundred block, Allegheny Avenue, was a drug store. I went there once or twice if Entine's was closed or didn't have what Mom or Pop wanted. Bobby Gillespie's father liked rock candy so he brought some for his dad when we went to Hunting Park or Confession. I always felt sorry for the druggist because he could do better on the other side of Broad Street, where the subway station was. People could come out of the station and go right into the store. There were no unusual people in the drug store, but one of the most unusual was nearby. One other thing, Entine's had great malts and hot dogs. Renaldo the Purloiner drank many "ah" malt and "purchased" many boxes of Whitman's chocolates at Entine's. The Allegheny Avenue drug store had nothing to eat or drink. Gatemouth worked at a small restaurant, called Gulliver's Alley, near Allegheny Avenue after you cross Allegheny Avenue going north. He took orders, especially "to go" orders. He had the nickname Gatemouth because, in the opinion of the big guys, his mouth looked like a gate with openings at every other tooth. He had to smile because the boss told him to be friendly to the customers. When he smiled, the gate was open for view. Gatemouth had a strange body or Gatemouth had a problem with posture; either way, Gatemouth appeared to bend to the left and the right at the same time, like an S. If he looked in a carnival mirror, he'd look normal. He was very tall. He wore black Ked's high top sneakers. He was skinny and he wore tee shirts all the time, even at church.

Gatemouth wore a long white apron and always had a pencil on his right ear. His hair was jet black and parted in the middle, like Alfalfa's of Our Gang. Come to think about it, Doc the Clock sounded and reminded me of Alfalfa. Gatemouth wore sneaks that he never fully tied. His short-sleeved shirt gave one the chance to see the world's skinniest arms.

"What can I get for you, sir?" uttered Gatemouth, the insecure Gatemouth.

"Two vanilla malts with extra malt and a ham and cheese sandwich," the big shot big guy from the east side of Broad Street way past 5th Street replied, looking like he was the affluent businessman he will never be.

The phony buyer knew very well that he wasn't going to pay for the malts and sandwich. His plan was to make Gatemouth go to the back to make the malts and sandwiches while he filled his coat. He filled his coat with TastyKake pies, cakes, candy, and other goodies that he could fit in the coat in five minutes. Some of the other hot shots who did this wore someone else's long overcoat to double a short coat's take. After running to Johnson's Wax field, they dump out their "winnings" and split the take. Gatemouth stood there with two malts and a sandwich. This happened many times, mainly on the afternoon of a Phillies or A's game. Those big shot losers had to have something to eat on the way to the game.

The big guys on our side of the street wouldn't do that to Gatemouth and they'd call him by his real name. I noticed that Perry walked away. He's a big guy, a good person and he plays football for North, which means he's tough. I think you have to go through a Marine obstacle course to make North's team. That's what Tommy Pitts told me when I told him I'm going to Notre Dame on a football grant in aid. Gatemouth told Mr. Sheehan that he had a black belt in Judo when he was hired. If Gatemouth could act, he could play Icabob Crane in "The Legend of Sleepy Hallow" or the Scare Crow in the "Wizard of Oz". If the big guys messed with Gatemouth after work, he'd massacre them with Judo chops. Someday the red car will pull up and the big shots will have to get in and go for a ride.

I hope the medical students or the dental students from Temple are in Gulliver's Alley when the guys con Gatemouth. They'll do something. They have to do something because they're taught to help others in distress. Plus, they carry around needles with poison for protection.

At Erie Avenue, there was a fancy restaurant called, Horn and Hardarts, H&H or Hornie's for short. It was fancy because it had many tables and chairs and a long row of food. You put a tray on the chrome bars in front of the food and slide it stopping when you see something you want and can afford. I can't forget how many different kinds of breakfast foods H&H had. Someone behind the food would ask what you wanted and dish it out for you. The kids I walked to school with and I ate pancakes at H&H after first Friday masses. The cost was reasonable, ten cents, and the pancakes were delicious. On the wall behind the cashier, who sat on a high wooden chair at the end of the food line, were about a hundred small boxes lined up like the slots in a hotel that hold keys or mail. The slots had glass doors, which opened when someone put in the correct amount of change to buy the food inside. It was called an Automat and it was popular with people who were in a rush and unable to walk through the line. I once blew my fudge money to buy a small chocolate cake in the Automat. The people, mostly women, who worked for H&H were friendly and kind. They were also Irish, real Irish directly from the docks of Ireland to Ellis Island to Philadelphia. They wore women's handkerchiefs on their right shoulders. Maggie Mae, a waitress who looked for us each first Friday, wanted to know who was an altar boy. When she found out, she'd ask for prayers every time we served. In exchange, she promised to pray that we would become Cardinals, like Cardinal Dougherty or Cardinal Cushing. Maggie Mae meant it. Her face would change when she mentioned Cardinals. Her smooth skin wrinkled a little when she smiled and gave us a wink and a nod as if to say, "trust me, you're going to make it". Other than Maggie, there were no regulars to talk to or about at Hornies; though I felt at home with all the waitresses with their Irish brogues.

Erie Avenue was the final milestone on the way from Broad Street to St. Stephen's Catholic elementary school at Butler Street. Erie Avenue was a busy avenue and cars came for many directions. Trolleys, cars, buses and people converged on the complicated crossings. Germantown Avenue crossed Broad and Erie. It took fast feet to cross this intersection. Despite what Pop said, I had slow feet.

7

The Joke's on Terrence Fitz Martin

Terrence Fitz Martin, who came to America less than a year before, reminded Sister about the County they both came from and he told her what it looked like today. I thought Terrence was putting Sister on. "Your old school is now a Pub, Sister," the black headed Irishman self-righteously told the good, very old, very proud, very trusting, very homesick Sister.

"What a pity, Terrence; and the church, is it still on the corner?"

"No Sister, the church was taken down to build a new one near the bookmaker's cottage; I think it's called Our Lady of Sorrows, now. The parishioners who stayed with the new church wanted that name so they could ask Mary to add the county to her list of sorrows. Most Catholics now go to St. Mary's and they still complain to Vicar O'Malley about St. Theresa's. The Catholics send their kids to Sorrows. The bricks from St. Theresa's are being used to build a new convent for St. Mary's. The new convent will overlook the Mary of the Lake. There's talk of a second pub, called O'Malley's and it will be next door on the east side to the new convent. You know Sister, that Mac Day's Pub is next door on the west side.

Come on Terrence, enough is enough. You piled on more than Sister can handle. The bookmaker's cottage and eight sorrows for Our Lady; what's that all about? Sister won't verify what you're saying. She trusts a fellow Irishman. Her old school is probably still a school.

Sister nodded and shook her head right to left and left to right in dismay. Terrence's countenance displayed the look of someone who had to tell a friend bad news from the home front. His mind, however, was a different story.

Terrence is cruel and he seems to enjoy it. I bet he was never in Sister's hometown or was from the same County. He can't wait, I bet, to write a letter to his friends exaggerating what just happened. They shouldn't sell Bonomo's Turkish Taffies in the winter. That stuff is messy to eat and hurts when you're hit with it on cold mornings. Pete the Cop should stop kids from whacking kids on the back of their heads with Bonomo's.

I wonder if Terrence plays tackle football at Hunting Park. It'd be worth the walk to play just one game and rack him up. Really, Terrence is a good guy. He's smart and he's funny. His father died and his mother came to this country to start a new life for herself and her four kids. Sister told us all this when she introduced him to our class. He looked scared that day. All the Irish Sisters ask him questions to get information and, most of all, to hear his brogue. Mom had to talk to her neighbors when she came over from Scotland. They made her talk and they loved to hear her. She felt they were insulting her.

8

School in the Morning

Sixth, seventh, and eighth grades were the best, no doubt about it. We learned a lot about a lot. We had Arithmetic, Mathematics Problems, History, Geography, Religion, Reading, Grammar, Poetry once a week, Picture Study once a month, and Palmer Method Writing, which no one ever did when the practice was over. Palmer Method made no sense to me. Sister knew it and gave credit if you were close or maybe even if you weren't close. We had to hold the pencil between our thumb and forefinger. That's ok; however, the other three fingers had to ride across the paper with all three fingers touching the paper. We did pages of zeroes and pages of forward slashes. It was like asking me to hold my broom handle bat with the left hand on top of the right when I was at bat in Stickball. I got my certificates of successful completion of Palmer Methods I, II and III. II and III were the same as I, but you were supposed to be an expert by then. I got worse; so did everyone else I saw. The girls probably did it well. Sisters stopped pushing the method on us and we ended the last few sessions of part III discussing comic books or praying for the conversion of Russia; we could choose. I was the only one praying for Russia and I was the only one who got a holy card with a picture of the Guardian Angel smiling over two boys in a wheat field. I prayed for Russia because I knew the boys would be messing around, I'd be a leader of the group, and word would flow down to Carlisle Street. I couldn't afford to get in trouble with Sister. My parents would get angry that I was making life miserable for the Sisters. The girls discussed Archie and Nancy comics. They discussed who they'd rather be, Veronica or Betsy from the Archie comics.

Sister thinks I am praying because I was in deep thought. Actually, I am thinking about boxing at Gallagher's cellar and which autographs I still need to get to complete the A's, Phillies

or maybe the Yankees. I should have gotten the decision over Joey Ryan last week. He didn't land a punch and Gallagher's brother gave him two of the three rounds. I hit him all over the place.

Our Sisters taught all the subjects for about six or seven hours a day. The girls wore uniforms and the boys wore white shirts and plain blue ties. A couple boys wore Davy Crockett ties, but Sister didn't have their sense of humor. The colorful ties came off rather easily and the boys had a chance to redeem themselves when they returned from lunch. They redeemed themselves with plain blue ties. Renaldo the Purloiner stole a gross of Davy Crockett ties from the American store on 5th Street. He also stole cigarettes that day and introduced some of the guys to them and the 30th district police station. Robert Thompson and all the girls were always good. The boys needed reminding to be good from time to time. Overall, there was silence in the classroom and none of the boys ever talked down or loudly to the Sisters. Their fathers would kill them after Sister whacked them with a yardstick or a pointer. I preferred the yardstick, but there was no negotiating.

Some boys just don't understand that it's costly to mess around. Jimmy Thompkins is messing around and he is looking at me. I have to ask a question to avoid getting wacked along with Jimmy. He always brings others into his world of messing around. He tells everybody that Erin Flynn is his girl friend. Erin is always crying about that. I think she likes all the boys with Mc in their name but me the most.

The girls did all their homework before it was due. The boys did some of the homework when it rained and turned it in exactly when it was due.. The girl's homework was clean and readable. The boys' homework tended toward unclean, unreadable and incorrect most of the time. The Sisters in grades one through six were six or seven feet tall. Our seventh and eighth grade Sisters dropped down to five feet five. Once Sister stopped me at the door before class was to begin.

"William, did you study your poem?" Sister asked everybody as they walked in the door and we didn't know it. If Sister was grilling someone, the others had to go to the end of the hall.

"Yes Sister, I did."

"Good then. Now recite the first five lines," Sister said wondering, I think, if I really did.

Man did I luck out. I happen to like "If". Thanks God. I will always study my assignments from now on; I'm a changed person Blessed Mother. Don't squeal on me to your Son. This is a miracle. I'm sweating. I can't wait to get started saying the poem.

I recited Kipling's "If". "If you can keep your head when all about you…" "That's fine William; you're the first boy to complete the assignment," Sister said.

"Sister, I'd like to complete the poem; it's my favorite," I said wanting extra credit so I could lock in a gold card.

"No, I have more students waiting outside for something but don't know what that something is," Sister replied sensing my obsequious nature.

She waved her right hand, the one with the oversized ring finger, to signal me off the stage.

"You'll be a Man my son," I whispered to myself and to the girls.

The girls knew that I was trying to polish apples for the teacher and the teacher knew it too. What the girls didn't know was that I wanted to show the new kid who was smart and appealing to the girls.

Robert Thompson must not have been able to recite his homework: Good, maybe the girls will view me as the smartest boy in class. I think I should show Marie and Judy how to play Halfball. That way I can impress on them my athletic abilities. Nah, nothing will make up for the odd shaped head of mine. I'm going to Paddy's Taproom this weekend; I can't wait. Sister's grade book is filled with numbers written with a pen. There are no errors. Her white bib is always pure white. She must not like pizza. She must be perfect in what she does.

Poem, not poems or poetry, and Picture Study were the two subjects that the Sisters taught that were artistic. We had Poem about once every two weeks and Picture Study maybe once every three weeks or once a month. We memorized poems but never discussed their meanings. We memorized the paintings in our Picture Study book, which was an odd size, about the size of a postcard and a half or an unfolded wallet. It had a shopping bag brown cover and there were less than fifteen paintings in the book, maybe eight to ten. We discussed the colors and the characters in the painting.

What was between the man and the woman in Millet's "The Angelus?" What was the color of the horse in Sir Edwin Landseer's "Shoeing the Bay Mare?" were typical test questions.

We didn't discuss the things Pop and the other students discussed at the Art school, like balance, tone, color, movement and style. At the end of the final English exam, there were two Poem questions and three Picture Study questions. We had to fill in the blanks for the Poem exam and answer questions about the colors or the number of characters in the painting or the painter's name. Pop said that he liked the paintings in the book. I could tell that he didn't like the type of questions we got. Mom liked the paintings too, but really liked the poems when I read them to her so I could go out and play Wallball or Halfball. Wallball looked like Handball but a player had to bounce the ball on the pavement so it bounced off the wall. I didn't have to read the poems really but I enjoyed doing it.

After the fill-in-the-blanks questions, the last two questions, on the final English exam were always: Name a biography you read this year and name a fiction you read this year. Give the author's name for each book.

I don't know how the girls answered, but thirty boys out of thirty boys answered the biography question by either "The Mickey Mantle Story," by Yogi Berra and Casey Stengel or "Cardinal Dougherty's Life Story," by Cardinal Spellman. These answers didn't change for three years. The story about Cardinal Dougherty was popular the year he died. Neither of these books existed. Sister knew that but she also knew that the Poem and Picture Study classes were a joke.

I can't put "Treasure Island," by Robert Lewis Stephenson as my fiction on the test because Sister wouldn't believe me. She'd think I was making it up. Bishop McCormack is Cardinal Dougherty's nephew, the Man from Uncle, they call him, and he'd better not see the examination answers. I almost put the Cardinal Spellman Story by Cardinal Dougherty, but the other way around works every year.

The rest of the English final exam was grammar and sentence structure. We had to diagram at least three sentences: active voice, no prepositions or superlative adjectives; passive voice, no dangling participles or pronouns, and quotes from the church's hierarchy. I don't remember the details but we had to diagram sentences.

Sister has to guess at our grades. She couldn't possibly grade the final exams for all twelve subjects for sixty kids before next week. Sisters must work all night to grade exams and put down

our grades on the report cards. Using quotation marks bothers me. I hate the Mathematics Problems' exam. High school has tons of them according to the Tioga T's. I get sick after I read a problem. Sister gave about five of us pieces of fudge because we got at least five out of the ten problems correct. That's embarrassing. Richie Neuber got fudge and a strawberry candy-icing cup with the small spoon. At least five girls got fudge.

Twice a year, we moved to another desk in our classroom. We made a big deal of it and Sister knew what we were doing. Everyone had to take their books out of their desks and stand against the wall. Sister, who had a chart all filled out, called out the names and pointed to your new seat. Naturally, every boy wanted the back rows. The girls probably didn't care but would be happy up front.

"The first four rows will be for the boys," Sister could read sinister minds, "The girls, of course, will be in the last four rows. Martha, Miss Connelly, you will be sitting with the boys if you continue to chatter with Miss King. Miss King, do you want to sit with the boys?"

"Yes Sister, I mean no Sister".

"You mean; 'yes Sister', but it won't work Miss King".

Sister knew which boys messed around and she seated them (me) next to the boys that didn't mess around (not me). The girls could choose wherever they wanted to sit; they weren't confined to the assigned seats on Sister's chart. When I say messed around I mean only occasionally. Sister had almost total control of her class. We sat still and didn't say a word. Teacher's pets folded their hands and rested them on the desk. Wise guys who had the nerve to tempt Sister's patience would have their knuckles reddened with a ruler, which was always in Sister's hand. Nobody walked around the room and nobody ate or chewed gum. Drinking soda or any beverage was impossible. We all stood up if the Bishop or another Sister entered the room.

"Good morning, Bishop". "Good morning, Sister".

Some of the boys called Sister "Stir". "Stir, Stir, I know, I know the answer, Stir" This was intentional. I never could believe those boys. I'd never say Stir unless I was making a cake and I needed the batter. Do you think I'd do such a thing? You're right, I guess, I did.

There were very few mortal sins in the classroom, but defacing the desks or tables came awfully close.

"Sister, this table I got has names carved in it," complained Michael Cavanaugh as he stood up and pointed his left shoulder and right index finger to the artwork. It says "Bill & Gina" and "Jim & Kim".

"William and James are you the Bill and Jim I see here? Did you carve your names into the table?," Sister wanted to know. "You were sitting in those seats," Sister reminded us though she didn't have to.

"Yes, and we used this pen knife that I got for the scouts. We both used the same knife," Jim and I answered together. How could we deny our misdeeds? It would be too risky to try to convince Sister that the carvings were there when we got the desks.

"Sister, I did Bill & Gina," I came clean. "I did Jim & Kim" offered Jim McDevitt following up on my courageous admission.

"Who is Gina, William, I mean Bill?," asked Sister as if she didn't know.

"Gina Lollobrigida from the movies," I confirmed what I believe Sister was thinking.

"Kim Novak, she's a movie star too," Jim didn't wait to be asked.

"You two stay at this current table and tell me how you'll repair it".

Sister's in charge of the altar boys and the safeties. Now what? I thought Sister Helen was going to hit us with her famous Cat o'O Nine tails. I can easily fix this with sand paper. I can't blame Michael for telling on us. He wouldn't get in trouble anyway, though, but he didn't know that. His name is not carved into the table. Mom and Pop will go nuts if I'm taken off the altar. Someone should tell Gina and Kim about the sacrifices we are making on their behalf. Maybe they'd give us a poster or an autograph or something else.

9

Tough Assignment but Somebody's Got to Do It

A Catholic girls' high school was in St. Stephen's parish. The most sought after assignment, even more than Midnight Mass on Christmas, was to serve at the Little Flower High School. I got the assignment twice and it was something else. The school was right across the street to Hunting Park. I could see the baseball diamond where I got knocked over playing third base for the 10th Street Corinthians. The nuns at Little Flower always welcomed the altar boys warmly and promised us a donut when Mass was finished. They didn't know it but she could keep the donut and we'd still be very happy.

On the better of the two trips a student, wearing the well-known maroon uniform of Little Flower, took us to the back of the auditorium so Forest Forester and I could put on our cassocks and surpluses. I noticed that this girl had a medal and yellow ribbon on her uniform.

"It's because I'm on the Student Council," said the girl before I asked.

"Here we are Forest and Bill; I'll be back to show you the cafeteria where you can have some juice and donuts after Mass and Communion," our hostess told us in the manner of a perfectly programmed robot. The girl was between short and medium height. She had blonde hair. If you liked older girls, you'd say she was very pretty; a perfect big city version of Tammy.

"I didn't get donuts the last time I was here, Forest; this is great," I said.

"She said donut, not donuts plural," Forest reminded me.

"No, she said donuts. I bet you my pick of your Yankee cards she said donuts," I challenged Forest.

"Hi guys, thanks for coming there so early. Which one of you will carry the book across the altar? And you are?" asked the good priest.

"Bill, Father, Bill McCaffrey," I answered.

"Ok then, you, what is your name?"Father wanted to know.

"Forest Father, Forest Forester," Forest replied knowing it will lead to a joke.

"I'm Father Hugh McHugh. I'm only kidding Forest. You will ring the bells at the right times. I am the chaplain here. Do you have any questions? I hope that you don't rush through the Latin responses. God appreciates being able to understand what we're saying. I do too; no Confiteor racing or loud, long bell ringing," Father gave the ground rules.

We quickly knew our roles and what we could do and not do. We couldn't touch Father's chalice. We couldn't go anywhere near the wine. We had to hold the Communion plate six inches below the person's chin. It had to be straight because the host was for real. It was Christ's body and blood and it could never touch the floor; this is God. Altar boys shouldn't read the Lectionary. Priests did penance if the host hit the floor. If the Host fell, the floor had to be covered immediately with a sanctifier, which is a clean white cloth, on the spot where the Sacred Host fell. Forest had to ring the bells when Fr. McHugh holds his hands over the chalice to pray to the Holy Spirit. Priests dressed for Mass in a separate room. Fr. McHugh took everything seriously and he kissed each vestment before he put it on. Forest had to ring the bells when Fr. McHugh holds the host up, after the Transformation into Christ's Body and Blood. Forest rings the bells when Fr. McHugh holds up the chalice, after the wine is transformed into Christ's Body and Blood.

Let's see, there's the amice, stole, cincture, maniple, alb, and chasuble. I know I missed one. The vestments were red, which meant that Father was saying this Mass in honor of a martyr, whose feast day is today. I don't know which martyr. St. Stephen, the first martyr has his feast day on December 26th. I think that the relic under Little Flower's altar is one from St. Teresa's cell at the convent.

"Forest, no competition with the Confiteor, we want to enjoy the juice and donuts (she said donuts, plural)," I reminded my partner.

"Sister gave a single donut last time," Forest remembered.

"The longer we stay here the shorter the class day," I told Forest.

"I definitely agree. But you're the one famous for speeding through the Confiteor," Forest reminded me this time.

"You OK with the bells, Forest?" I checked.

"OK Bill, I have the bells and you pour the water when we wash Father's hands and you move the book," Forest summarized.

"That sounds good to me Forest. Is there a dish on the table for the water?" I asked because it is a detail frequently forgotten.

"I saw Sister put one there a minute ago. We're ready," Forest gave the final OK.

"Was that girl angry or something? I just asked what the medal meant. We didn't get her name. We'll get it after mass I guess," I wondered out loud.

"Yeah Bill, she did look angry when you asked her about the medal. Maybe she did 'bad' on an English grammar test. Let's go. How can the host be the Body and Blood?" Forest took control and asked a tough question about our faith.

Mass went very well. It was amazing to walk out and see thousands of high school girls. Father seemed pleased as he walked out behind us carrying the chalice with a pacificator in it covered by a paten, a cover the same pattern and color as the chasuble covered everything the priest was carrying. A burse with the Father's pacificators inside was on top of everything. Father McHugh didn't miss a beat. His Latin was clear and his sermon on martyrdom was scary. Father thanked us and went to his area to prepare to leave.

Father's chalice is plain. He must be from a poor family or he is humble. He talked about the need to be ready to die for our faith, though he assured the girls that they will never be put in a position to be a martyr. He said that the United States isn't like a Communist country where religion is not accepted. I know that because we studied Cardinal Mehzenty, of Hungry, who is in a Communist prison. We know that Stalin and Hitler hate Catholics even though they were once Catholic. How can that happen? Sr. Gabriel never said anything about being a martyr or being in jail. She just wanted us to be perfect and like saints. Sr. Prophetess sounded like we could be having a tough time staying Catholic. I would do what the Communists asked; I always want to be with my family. Father made it feel like it was worth it to be

a martyr. Why do we have to have blessed candles at home in case we need Extreme Unction?

"Why are you rushing, Forest?" I asked Forest who was about to leave.

"We gotta go right away. Sister will kill us if we're late. She keeps time and knows how long it should take here," peeped a worried altar boy, who didn't even get his donuts and juice and he wanted to leave.

"Just listen to the girls sing Dear Lady of Fatima; we come on bended knee... Forest, here comes the student council's most unpleasant member. Let's not rush or anything, it's only 8:30 now. We'll be back before 9:30. I'm ready for the spelling test, are you?" I asked Forest.

"Yeah, I'm ok!" Forest settled down and said.

"Thanks Forest and Bill, the Mass was well done. Do you want donuts and juice Forest? Follow me. Bill, you follow too," invited our hostess.

I asked, "What's your name?" to the hostess. I tried to make amends for asking about the medal.

"My name is Maggie Clancy and I live in St. Joachim's parish, near Frankford Avenue and Orthodox. You know where it is?" Maggie replied.

"I do, my brother Fran is going there for his freshman year at North Catholic. He plays football for North," I bragged about my brother Fran.

"Here's a gift from the student council," Maggie offered.

Thanks to the Student Council. Forest, bring your Yankee cards to school and don't take the best ones out.

Maggie and I are on speaking terms. I thought she liked Forest and not me. Next time I come here Maggie will not greet us because they rotate. Lady of Fatima wants a rosary said each day. We say the rosary in May and October. This Immaculate Conception or Miraculous medal is a good gift. A gift, donuts, time away, high schoolgirls all around, what more can I expect? This is my day. Why did the girls sing to Our Lady of Fatima and Maggie give us a Miraculous medal when this is a high school dedicated to St. Teresa. Sister Assumption told us that the miraculous medal came from Mary directly to a girl in France, Lourdes, France, I think. That's got to be the reason; this medal

is higher than any medal to any Saint. I wish she gave me at least four medals; I'd give one to Mom, one to Grandmom so she can pin it on her apron, which is already loaded with medals and small saints' pictures that are laminated, one for Maureen and one for Theresa.

"That's my house, the end of the row," Forest said.

"Forest, you live here, next to Little Flower and Huntington Park? If you have a football, we still have time to throw it around for exercise," I told Forest.

Forest got the football without too much urging. He probably thought we were doomed anyway. Forest had a good arm and it was fun running out for his passes. We didn't pay attention to time and it quickly became 11 o'clock. I don't remember if Forest took the ball home. I don't think he did. We ran down Broad Street and up to our second floor classroom. We hardly straightened up when we walked into the classroom at 11:25am, one-half hour before lunch. Sister Helen saw the mess we were in with shirttails hanging out, sweat all over, and the looks of soon to be condemned serial killers. Sister never smiled; none of the Sisters smiled unless you got 100% on a test or all A's on your report. Even then, the smile was brief and ineffective. A smile was a sign of weakness to a Sister.

"Where have you two been? Did you get lost? Why do you two look like you do? William, comb your hair before you go to lunch," Sister insisted.

Forest was a very bright boy, but he stumbled looking for the right words this time.

He didn't have the advantage of knowing big time excuse makers like some of the big guys I played stick ball with or Terry Campion, who got out of playing hooky from school many times using a different excuse each time.

Think, what would Terry say?

"Sister, Forest and I served four masses because there were visiting priests who I guess needed to fulfill their obligation to say Mass every day. There were no sermons at the three special Masses, but one of the priests was home from the missions in Africa and his mother was there," I piled it on thick.

Forest was stunned. So was I. So was Sister. The boys in the class – I was in the all boys class in eighth grade – looked at me with their "you're pretty clever Bill" look. Sister looked at me assured that I wouldn't lie to her in any way.

"Sister, we ran all the way back because of the spelling test. We're sorry if we missed the test. I didn't know when to quit. It was my fault Sister, Forest wanted to leave but I felt that you'd want us to stay and assist at the Masses, especially during the Consecration," I rambled on.

Why did I get into the missions in Africa? I was thinking about Father Fitzgibbon's mother in "Going My Way". Father O'Malley was a good priest. The Consecration is too holy to use in a lie. What am I doing? The spelling test; I must be crazy to bring that up. This must be how Phil's friend was; speeding for the thrill of it until he was killed. This is the lane with many turns if I don't watch it. Now I'm worried.

"Don't be sorry boys; you performed a Corporal Work of Mercy. The Little Flower will tell all the saints about your thoughtfulness. I know that you both can spell; you don't need the test. Pray inwardly on your way home for lunch; think about the graces you just received. Be sure to offer up any pain or inconvenience you endured this morning to the Souls in Purgatory. Have a wonderful lunch and don't forget the Souls," Sister said as Forest and I breathed a sigh of relief.

At lunchtime, Forest and I led the other students out of the room. We both felt the icy stares we were getting from the other guys of the lesser graces. Sunny and Joe were not in my eighth grade so I remained silent as I smiled as we walked all the way home, a trip I made in record-breaking time. I was crossing Broad Street at Clearfield when Sunny and Joe were still at Allegheny. I was planning how I was going to brag to the Tioga T's, the big guys who enjoyed living on the edge, like I just did. I wanted to join the T's and this could get me in.

The Tioga T's might be friendlier to me when I tell them about my sharp thinking. Forest is telling his buddies what we did. Sister will now give me more Masses with Bishop McCormack. The Sisters are talking about Forest and I over their lunch. We will now be looked upon as potential martyrs. Sister Assumpta told me that we have a secret. I'm sure she thinks that I'll be a priest. Little does she know where I'm headed after the stint with the Yankees. I'll invite her to my installation if the cardinals don't take too long voting for me.

"Hello Bill," Pop lilted to me, "did anything exciting happen in school? We had leftovers so I made my famous 'from many, one omelets."

Pop found out; Sister Helen called. Why else would he want to know if anything exciting happened? He'll bring it up and I'll have to lie. What a mistake. Now I have to tell Sister the truth and Forest and I will be in big trouble. I can't go back to school. The guys all know I was faking Sister out. I will run back to school to find Father Curran or Martin for Confession. They can't rat on me. I can't pray, because I'll be told to be truthful if I do. This is the biggest mess I ever got into, including breaking Soremen's store window. I don't want to run into Doc the Clock and his silly singing. I won't answer any hellos; I'll just keep running like I don't see or hear them. I think Sunny and Joe will go without me; they've done it before.

"Nothing exciting happened really. Forest Forester and I served mass at Little Flower, that's all," I lied to Pop.

"You looked like you wanted to tell me good news when you came in, like you did something special in school this morning," Pop asked in a I tone I couldn't figure out.

Fran came in right behind me and Maureen and Theresa weren't far behind Fran.

"Pop, I have to run back so I can help Pete the Cop because he's got a broken foot," I lied again.

Why did I lie about Pete the Cop? Pop might drive us if it rains very hard someday soon then he'll see Pete the Cop and ask about his foot. I'll go right to the Rectory. I can't ask the Bishop to hear me. He'd destroy me and he'll tell the other bishops about me when I'm closer to being the Pope. I will never do this again. Sister would give us detention for not coming back to school. Now this!

10

School in the Afternoon

Sister Helen seemed to forget that Forest and I gained such an abundance of graces by serving four masses at Little Flower in the morning. Forest Forester and I served one mass at the local girls' high school. We played football afterwards and got to school late. I lied to Sister and told her we served four masses. She treated Forest and me as if we were martyrs. In the afternoon, she immediately got into the normal flow of things. "Here is a piece of paper. Fold it in half length-wise and print your name of the top of one of the sides. If you received your Palmer Method certification, you can write your name. If not, print your name at the top of the paper. Write the numbers one through twenty-six on the lines from top to bottom. We will now begin our spelling test," Sister was more ready than her students were.

"Authentic...barbarianism...complicity...zeppelin. Place the papers on the right side of your desks so that Eugene can pick them up," Sister instructed.

Eugene picked up the tests and a few snidely looks to boot.

I don't remember what else happened that afternoon, except that the cops came to take George Keebler away. We prayed for George and his parents as Sister requested. Forest didn't look concerned or different in any way. Sister Helen was irritated when she scanned the spelling papers. She asked who wanted to get up and quote the poem, "Gunga Din." Nobody raised his hand and I had the poem memorized, but was feeling weird. Sister made Forest and I feel like saints in the morning.

"I'll say it Sister," I stood up assuming an OK was on its way.

"Ok. Do you feel up to it William? Maybe the Holy Spirit will give you the words to say. You are full of the Fruits and Gifts. OK William, Gunga Din".

I started by saying "Half a league" then I remembered that it was "The Charge of the Light Brigade" that I knew by heart. I half-heartedly started "Gunga Din," which I only knew in parts. "..You're a better man than I Gunga Din"

"Wonderful William, you recited the poem with just the right cadence."

"I did? Oh yes, I did….thank you Sister. Rudyard Kipling is my favorite along with Paul's letters to the Corinthians." I lost my mind. I didn't know any of Paul's letters.

"William, you must know that Paul's letters to the Corinthians are a favorite of mine too. If there is time, I'll ask you to recite your favorite passages"

Thank you Blessed Mother for not having enough time. I never heard of Rudyard Kipling and I heard Bishop Sheen say something about the letter or letters to the Corinthians. I never read a letter from Paul or anyone else, except the pen pal from Scotland that I had for about two months and two letters. What am I doing? I'll never have a Halfball opponent from this classroom. They hate the way I try to impress Sister. I just want to go home and start all over.

"Now boys, some of you were talking while William was reciting. For that and for the poor spelling test results, you will stay after class for one half hour. Forest and, of course, you too William may leave. You two have made enough sacrifices for one day. I hope that you remembered the Sisters at one of your four masses. Get some rest."

"We did Sister. It comes natural to pray for Sisters and vocations." I couldn't stop myself.

Forest looked at me as if I was running for a political office or trying to be a comedian on TV. I was back on the roll of lying to make Sister think I was holy. I promised the Blessed Lady and myself that I would never do that kind of stuff again.

I must say that I got myself out of a big hole. I must have my great grandfather's brains. He was smart, made a lot of money and sent metal to Ireland to make bullets. My father's maternal grandfather, something Souerlander, was brilliant too and his son, my father's uncle became the president of the largest shoe company in the world. Fast with street smarts thanks to my ancestors, that's me. George should have discussed stealing cars with me before he attempted it himself. The Tioga Ts and I almost pulled off the car robbery of the century.

11

Horse Head Lady

Fran and I took turns carrying out the ashes from our furnace, which was down the stairs, the squeaky stairs to the basement. Mom and Pop took the ashes out of the furnace and put them in large buckets with handles. On alternate Tuesday nights, I carried the ashes up the stairs, through the alley to its end, where I would turn right and put the heavy buckets on the pavement in front of our house 3044. This was in addition to taking out the trash once a week and taking out the garbage once a week. The garbage buckets were the worst. They were heavy and filled up to the top with our garbage. The Garbagemen popped the lid off the buckets and dumped the garbage into their truck. They wore shiny rubber aprons and some wore rubber gloves that came up to their elbows. The gloves were the same kind that the Fishman wore in his store. These men sweated and the handkerchiefs tied around their necks didn't seem to absorb much of it.

I think the trash man took the ashes as well as the trash so maybe it was two trips in one night; really not so bad, but still dangerous for me. The work was not too hard, but it took time away from studying and playing or preparing for our local Olympics. Actually, I didn't mind the ashes, it was the trip through the alley that I dreaded and, I think, for good reason.

About half the time that I took out the trash, I heard the barking of dogs, big dogs, too many big dogs. A fence in the alley to my left was weak and low so that when the dogs ran and tried to jump it, I saw their huge heads and watched the fence sway back and forth stretching its limits with each jump. The fence was about to go and if the fence went down, I was sure to follow. The dogs were always drooling and their drool was hanging from their mouths with the yellow and dark yellow teeth. It was usually getting dark out when I took out the ashes. I saw at least two German Shepherds. I was certain that there were hundreds not yet released. When I put the ashes on the pavement in front of the house, I ran into the house and quickly closed the door. I kept hoping that the next time the dogs would be in their house. I knew the dogs' owner; she was the woman from Clearfield Street who visited our next-door neighbor, Mrs. Kleinmeister. Nobody knew her name, but she had artistic talents, which we all saw time and time again.

The woman could draw a decent horse head. She should be able to draw a horse head because she spent hours a day, at least two or three days a week, drawing horse heads on Carlisle Street. Horse Head Lady used different colored chalk, which was the only difference among her countless drawings. The horse heads were all the same size and shape. I often wondered if she could draw any other animals or birds of different sizes or poses. Drawings of horse heads of different colors cluttered our street. The only way out of this dilemma was to pray for rain. The Horse Head Lady staked out a sizable portion of Carlisle Street and warned us not to play in "her" (?) area. She didn't live on our street, but she owned some of it, according to her. Mrs. Kleinmeister, Horse Head Lady's best friend, didn't come to our aid. She could have because she was certainly big enough and strong enough. She stood at Carlisle and Clearfield Streets during a record-breaking hurricane and never budged an inch. The rugged customers from the Clearfield Bar had to hold on to telephone poles or street lamp poles to rest before they went the next twenty yards to the next pole on their way home. She stood on the corner with her arms folded in front of her like an Indian chief in front of a cigar store just as if it was 65 degrees and sunny.

Why doesn't Horse Head Lady draw dogs? I wonder just how many dogs she has in her yard. She should not have too many because her yard is small and her house is too small for dogs to walk around. She keeps at least a hundred somewhere, but I don't know where. I wish that a dogcatcher could come with me down the alley. We can't pour water over her horse head drawings because she would tell her dogs to get us. I still want to call her Junkyard Dog Lady. I think she's more famous for her vicious dogs than the horse heads.

Maureen, Theresa and their friends had to play hopscotch down the street or on another street because the colorful horse head drawings were everywhere.

O'Toole's parents said that the Horse Head Lady was very beautiful, and it was a shame that she wasn't rich. Albert's mother said that Horse Head Lady could be like a championship trophy wife for some rich doctor or lawyer. She could live on the Main Line, where the rich and beautiful people lived.

She didn't get a break when she was born, except her looks, I admit that. No rich man would marry her now; she's too strange. None of the people in this neighborhood are rich. At least she's beautiful.

Maybe rich men like strange women because they take them out of their stuff-shirt neighborhoods. I'm not going to ask her to keep the dogs in the house when I take out the ashes. She could set up a trap for me by loosening up the fence so it will break exactly at the time when I am taking out the trash. I can't talk to Mrs. Kleinmeister because she and her sister are stranger than old Horse Head Lady. They are all friends and I'd be turned in.

Nobody ever saw Horse Heads Lady's husband. He didn't exist in the minds of the neighbors.

Sunny, Joe, Richie, and I went to the Carmen movie to see two double features, twenty-five cartoons, a couple newsreels, a juggler, and trapeze artists. The price was reasonable, I thought: ten cents. Walsko couldn't go because he had sun poison and his father's famous remedy for it made things worse: his father pulled off the dead skin from Walsko's back. We saw "Twenty Thousand Leagues Under the Sea" with Gilbert Roland and a Red Skelton/Esther Williams movie. I can't remember the name of the movie, but I do remember coming out of the movie astonished at how much Ester Williams looked like the Horse Head Lady. Before I had chance to comment, Richie said that Ester Williams was the Horse Head Lady and Sunny replied, "Do you really think so; I think she is too".

Horse Head Lady, now called Esther Williams II by the four of us, should swim with us at the fireplug, and then we'd have some idea of the truth of her identity. Uncle Dan damaged his ear diving for sponges off the coast of Greece. The Paddy's Taproom heroes probably have injuries from their service days. Leahy and Bertello enlisted to serve our country. They are emotional people who would go to any lengths to preserve this country and Notre Dame. Uncle Dan fought in WWII and Korea; so did Buggy. I

will be brave like Pop, Uncle Dan and Buggy. I hope we aren't at war anymore though.

I used to think that, if Horse Head Lady was Esther Williams in disguise, we could get free tickets to her movies and meet movie stars. Nothing ever happened. She got her old name back. The horse heads looked the same and the dogs had the fence on its last legs. She never swam with us at the fireplug. Nothing changed. It was a shame for all of us. We could have used a change. Horse Head Lady probably needed a change too.

12

My Philadelphia Bulletin Paper Route

My older brother Fran had a friend, Johnnie Flynn, who was giving up his paper route. I needed money for baseball cards and fudge. It seemed like a perfect fit. I took over the route, which had the largest daily and Sunday circulation in the branch: one hundred and forty-five dailies and ninety-five Sundays. The branch was the building where we picked up the papers and folded them. The route covered a large area, maybe seven or eight streets square. It started a half mile from the branch, about the same distance from my home. If nothing else, I could expect some good exercise and sleep. I could not carry all my papers on my bicycle, so I carried them in a canvas bag. The bag was heavy and I looked forward to 16th Street and Allegheny Avenue, the halfway point of the route. The rest of the route was a breeze; the bag lightened up at this stage. My customers were great, even if they paid only on an every now and then basis or a "when my check comes" basis. Most of my customers paid up before I finally left my route. Some weren't in the position to pay up. Their missed payments to other people were a bit more serious. I was last on many of my customers' lists to be paid.

Some of the women on my route were clever, nice, or very farsighted. One called me "Sugar". I was not the sugar type but I seemed to be more sugary the closer we got to Saturday, payment day. Another told me that I was adorable with my jet-black hair and black eyebrows. The sugar lady always eventually paid and gave me a tip. The eyebrows' lady always paid too, when she was paid. I knew I wasn't adorable due to an unusual head shape and an imbalance of the ears. I remembered the women at Paddy's Taproom though. They thought that I was adorable with jet- black hair. They didn't owe me anything, but they liked Uncle Dan and probably thought he was kind to take me with him and be in front of his friends. The average bill for my paper customers was about fifty cents, by the way, and that included dailies and Sundays. I forgot what portion on the fifty cents went to me, but I remember many weeks when I couldn't afford baseball cards and fudge, sometimes cards or fudge. There was a Crazy Lady on my route, who never paid me. I never collected or even tried to collect from her. I didn't wedge her paper between her door knob and her door like I did to my preferred customers.

When I passed this Crazy Lady's house, she would wait until I threw the paper on her steps, then come running out of her house screaming at me and chasing me down the street with a broom. She wore a robe and a long red dress or something like a dress, which I could see from the bottom of the robe to the top of her shoes. The shoes were black and high enough to cover her ankles. Her hair had a green tint to it and it usually looked scary, especially when she had huge curlers sitting on top of her green, sometimes purple, hair or when she had a shower cap on top of the curlers. The Lady didn't wear glasses. Once or twice, she wore sunglasses. The sunglasses had a missing lens; it didn't bother her. It bothered me though.

She reminded me of the mother who stood at the top of the steps with a knife in "Psycho," only she came across more frightening. Her front door had a huge handwritten sign in red. The sign said, "I'll take the trick and keep the treet (sic) for myself. Get lost kid". I told Pop about her. He said that I should stop worrying about it, just run fast, and he knew I could run fast even though everybody beat me in races. Pop never suggested that I stop delivering her paper. He thought that the paper was her only source of entertainment in life. That was Pop. Mom would suggest that I stand firm, not run, and ask for my money, I'm sure of that. Mom was the most generous person you could ever meet, but to her fair is fair and you shouldn't walk away when someone was being unfair to you or your family.

"Billy, pay your bills and be respectable. Don't let people steal your money, no matter how they try to do it. If everybody took other people's money, we'd be in a sad shape. There would be no need to work hard to earn money and that destroys life."

Be a man. How can an old lady scare you? The other crazy lady killed at least five husbands and she was very little. Pop

knows I'm slow, he must know. Vince gets down the field faster than me and he's four years younger.

My manhood and business acumen were tested by the Crazy Lady and on other occasions on my paper route.

One day, a kid about three inches shorter than me approached me with an interesting request: "Give me all your money, and don't tell me you don't have any".

"I don't have any," I said.

"Pull out your pockets or jump up and down so I can hear if you have coins," demanded this experienced elementary school crook as he held a knife up to my chin.

I had change, forty cents, which I planned to use to get some baseball cards.

"Give me the forty cents," demanded the tough guy with a foot long knife.

I hope that he gave the forty cents to someone in need: only kidding. Mom would say something like that if we lost something. I told Fran what happened. This was a mistake because Fran was not just a good listener; he was the toughest kid in the neighborhood as well.

Fran went nuts! We both hopped on our bikes to scour the neighborhood for the thief. I kept praying that we didn't find him because there was no telling what Fran would do to him. Fran couldn't care if the kid had a knife or a machine gun; he wasn't going to get away with stealing from a McCaffrey. He had a lot of Pop in him. Uncle Dan told me many stories about how Pop had to fight to keep his money or for other reasons.

Thank the Lord the bandit escaped. I'm not sure that I would point out the villain if I saw him because I saw Fran's face. I am convinced that Fran would have more than avenged the crime. Crime, by the way, was always in the air and on the streets on my paper route.

I can remember more than once seeing one of my customers when I was folding my papers and stopped to read the first page above the fold. Once I saw one of my customers on the first page, not accepting the Nobel Peace Prize like the other person on page one, but getting into a red car. The cop escorting my customer had his right hand on my customer's head. He seemed to be pushing the head down. I was counting on this customer, who was in arrears to me for about five weeks. He promised to pay me on Wednesday. I needed the money to pay my bill to the branch manager. I assumed that he wouldn't be available to pay me for quite a while.

Things did not look good when I got to his house that day. I found that the place was cordoned off by the cops. He, my customer, met a sudden death earlier in the day. I don't know why he was murdered, but the word was he spilled the beans about someone when the cops took him in the day before. The word was out; he talked too much. He got the dailies and Sundays and he would have signed-up for the quarterlies and the "yearlies", if they existed because he never paid. Spilling the beans was the apparent cause of most of the heinous crimes in the neighborhood. I wasn't insured against these catastrophes and I could ill afford to be losing customers who were in arrears. The Bulletin did sell life insurance, not non-paying customers' insurance, life insurance. I only had one insurance customer, and he was not even a customer on my route.

Our branch manager, Phil O'Malley, had a friend who was a very crazy driver, a daredevil who constantly searched for opportunities to satisfy his thirst for excitement. Phil took out a life insurance policy on his friend – I think his nickname was Daring Damian. I was the insurance agent; I guess you could say, because Phil bought the insurance from me. Daring lived on my route. He was not a customer and he lived on the same block as the Crazy Lady with the broom and weird colored hair. After several months, the branch manager cancelled the policy saying, "He's too lucky; He'll never die. He's like a cat with nine lives".

The cancellation took effect on a Thursday.

Daring Damian died in a car crash in North Carolina three days later. He drove down a country road going fast; too fast to control his car. He tried to pass a car where the lines were solid, not broken up, which is legal. A truck was coming the opposite way and Daring was daring. He tried to pass the car and quickly get back in his lane. He passed the truckr and turned in very close to the truck he passed. He tried to sway off the road but couldn't. He somehow, according to the truck driver, lost control and went off the road right into an immovable tree. Daring's passenger confirmed the story. Daring died immediately. His passenger, a hitchhiking waitress, ducked down under the dashboard and survived without a scratch. Daring Damian had Phil's phone number in his wallet. The police called Phil and asked him to describe Mr. Damian. Phil wasn't aware of any family of Daring's. Phil was probably Daring's best friend. Phil didn't want to put the police in contact with some of Daring's friends because they might be on some wanted list. Phil wanted to pay me off to say to the insurance investigators that I accidently cancelled his policy and that Phil never stopped paying me for his policy. I was too scared of the consequences of lying to a judge to accept Phil's offer of five hundred dollars so Phil worked on another approach. I never found out what happened.

All these problems would be easier to deal with if I made money on the route, but I was lucky if I could pull in enough money to pay my weekly papers' bill to Phil. I worked hard on my paper route. I really did try to be a success.

I won several contests for signing up new customers or adding the Sunday edition on to existing customers accounts. There was a contest for signing up new life insurance customers. I usually won tickets to the Phillies game or money for a milkshake at Cicolli's or a new canvas paper bag. Once I won a ticket to an Eagle's game. The Eagles played the Browns at Municipal Stadium in South Philly. I sat on the edge of the cement/brick wall that surrounded the top of the stadium. I could see Philadelphia up to Market Street and City Hall. I can't remember who won because I was busy trying to save my life.

Jerry, the Misguided Brit, as he was named by the G's, a rival to the T's who have no association with the letter G, but who wanted to torment the T's, came to the game and roamed the stadium. Agnes, the social worker-type assigned to watch Jerry, found an old boy friend in the stands. He wanted bygones just to be bygones. He wanted Agnes to sit with him and to be at a certain place after she droped Jerry off to his family. Agnes agreed to every request of the old boyfriend. Jerry had challenges mentally and he was not British. He lived with his brother and mother. He was about twenty-five but acted like an out of control four year old. Jerry saw me sitting in a precarious seat and he got giddy. He saw the big "T and me" on my sweatshirt. The T stood for Temple though I told everybody it stood for the Tioga Ts. Jerry roamed over to me and pushed me as hard as he could. I can still see that laugh; like a gargoyle's "smile". I grabbed the edge of the wall and hung on for dear life. Jerry continued to laugh and push hard. He let go when the crowd roared. I don't know what happened on the field but whoever did what was done should be in Canton, Ohio for his timing. Jerry didn't know where he was sitting. He was lost. Agnes was not around.

Why does this insane person scare me? I can't hit him; I'd destroy him, I think. I gotta get outta here. Pop would be proud of Fran. Men like Fran and Pop take care of their families, no matter what. Real men, like the patrons at Paddy's Taproom and the WWII vets fight for their families and country. Some angels aren't real man, but they will fight if necessary, I'll bet on that. St. Raphael, Michael and Gabriel are tough angels. My Guardian Angel better be tough. He is tough. He saved me from being pushed over the stadium wall. St. Joseph was no slouch either. Should a real man have a deep love for the Blessed Virgin? Why can't I just admire Michael the Archangel for his toughness or St. George, who killed dragons? The Notre Dame first-string football players love Mary, I'll bet on it. This stadium should have better safety measures so no kid could get pushed over the wall. Agnes should get fired.

I remember when Sister Gabriel told the boys to treat girls like we'd want our sisters treated. I vowed that I wouldn't let anybody harm my sisters. I want to get to anyone mistreating them before Fran does. I'd beat them up a little; Fran would have to be pulled away by several cops, if they got there in time.

Sister also told us to respect the sixth grade girls even more because someday we could be marrying one of them. She's crazy. No way will I marry one of the six graders. I'm a seventh grader and younger girls wouldn't like Notre Dame or the Yankees. Besides, I'll be the Pope after a ten year career with the Yankees.

Let's be honest the real reason I sign up so many new customers is because they're late paying me. They want to help me win contests and they plan to pay, but they don't always do. I wonder what the Crazy Lady does during the day and at night. She has the long robe and black high top sneakers on every Saturday morning and at about 6:00 pm during the week. I think her sneaks are Chuck Taylor Converse All Stars sneakers. Doesn't she ever change? I can just see her now: looking in the mirror and asking it if she wasn't the fairest in the land. The response had to be a resounding "no!" MGM could use her to make horror movies with Bella Lugosi or biographies of people like Mrs. O'Leary of Chicago fame or some wicked witch. Thank God Violet is on my route; she's different in a fun way.

13

Violet

Near the end of my route was a whole city block of big row homes four stories high – some were five stories high. The houses were apartment houses and there were two apartments on each story. I served about ten customers who lived in these apartments. Violet lived on the fourth floor of the next to the last building I served. She never insisted that I deliver to her door, but I did any way. I delivered to everyone's door. Violet was an actress or a dancer, or just plain nuts! I don't think she was very sane and she tended to deviate from the norms of society, but she fit right in on my paper route.

She wore wild multi-colored clothes like blue robes with orange slippers and a bright red scarf. How about a bright yellow robe with purple pajamas and no slippers? Her hair changed from time to time. She never had brown, black, blonde or normal red hair. She had blue hair; bright blue, not the light blue that the Crazy Lady had at times. One time she had red hair that looked like she painted on to her hair with fire engine red paint. She had a metal Studebaker logo nailed on her door and she tied some old socks to her front door knob that were on or off from week to week. She wasn't very old; maybe twenty five, maybe sixteen for all I knew. She always answered the doorbell, which was not the case for many customers, and smiled prettyly while she told me she wasn't going to pay me. Her teeth were the whitest I had ever seen. She once answered the doorbell wearing sunglasses and fighter's green robe, marked on the back with "Pretty Boy O'Neill" and a small hubcap sized white shamrock.

"Do you have an eye infection and you have to wear sun glasses? I hope that Pretty Boy O'Neill didn't hit you," said I as the Lancelot in me came out.

"No, no, I fell while I was practicing a new number" quickly rebounded the Broadway dancer, who probably never saw Broadway, "my face hit against a table and I cut my chin. Pretty Boy is a friend and he's too nice to hurt anyone."

Somebody hit Violet. Sunglasses aren't made to cover up a chin. Where'd she get the Studebaker logo? I want a Packard and a Cadillac one. How can Pretty Boy be so nice when he's in the "knock-you-out" business? I bet the socks are a secret message to her close friends. When they are on the doorknob, she's there but not to be disturbed. Irish fighters don't hit girls. It wasn't the Pretty Boy, I'm sure. She won't squeal. Actually, her chin looked perfect.

Music was always in the background when I collected and sometimes when I delivered. She never opened the door more than six inches. Nat King Cole, Bilie Holiday, and Ella Fitzgerald were her favorites, I bet; they were always playing. She told me that she likes jazz and asked me if I did. I didn't know too much about high brow music. I knew Eddie Fisher and the Uptown, Ferko, Dick Crean, South Philadelphia, and Polish American string bands. Violet said that string bands don't count as music and Eddie Fisher sings terrible songs.

"Jazz is true music and your girl friends will love you if you play it on the radio or phonograph. Do you have girl friends?" Violet asked me, a seventh grader.

"No," I answered as I thought that girls wanted boys with money and courage; not a paperboy who's afraid of hard ground balls. The odd shaped head didn't help me either. Violet showed me a different side of her as she spoke to me for a long time. "Sugar, with that black hair and that Irish face, you won't need money. Get yourself a convertible and play Dizzy Gillespie, the Count, and Nat King Cole. Sinatra fits in there as well. The car has to be red and the seat covers white. The best places to drive are in Fairmount Park. Girls really don't like sports; they pretend to because they think they have to do what the boy wants to do. Flowers are a waste of money, so are candy and clothes. Just be nice, act like a gentleman at all times, always be on time, don't curse in front of girls, open doors (even car doors), and only go to movies where actors and actresses treat each other like diamonds worth millions. Be a brave hero; lay your coat out over a puddle if you have to. Be sure that your girl's shoes won't get wet. If you can't afford a nice dinner at a nice restaurant, that's ok. Make some sandwiches and have a picnic, but not at Hunting Park. Valley Forge has good spots. No hoagies or cheese steaks; they are oily and make you uncomfortable after you eat them and while you're eating. Bring nice napkins and soda; find out her favorite flavor. Going for walks is the best unless you decide that you don't like your date. Downtown is a good place for walks. Take the C bus on Broad Street right to downtown".

"Sugar, do you think I look like Dorothy Dandridge?" Violet asked and she was serious.

"I don't know because I don't know what Dorothy Dandridge looks like," I told her.

"Wait, I'll show you a picture," Violet said in a way that made me believe that she didn't want me to leave until I saw the picture.

The door opened halfway. The socks were not on the door. I could see that she had a glass table and white chairs.

The picture could've been Dorothy Dandridge but it had to be Violet. The resemblance was amazingly close. Violet looked much younger and healthier though.

"What do you think; is it close?" Violet wanted to know.

"Exactly like you Violet, except that she has normal hair. I'm sorry but your hair is different than her's," I informed my prettiest customer.

"Oh Sugar, this isn't my hair. I use wigs for my shows; a different color for each song. See?" Violet said. She took off her bright red wig and held it up for me to see.

"You're prettier Violet but you do resemble her a lot," was my honest assessment.

"Oh thank you Sugar. What's your real name?" Violet asked as if I just asked her to dance.

"Bill McCaffrey," I responded to this easy question.

"That's Irish all right. A lot of Irish fight for a living, like Pretty Boy O'Neill. Don't you fight for a living Sugar. Be a doctor or a lawyer or something big. Will you bring some Mummers' music next time you collect? I want to hear what you like about it" the jazz fan commented.

Her hair looked normal again, like any young persons, after she took off the wig. She could be Dorothy's double though Violet was younger and prettier. Violet looked relieved that I thought she looked like a star. She got a little silly.

Violet wanted to look like Dorothy Dandridge. She's better looking so why go backward in looks? College guys should deliver her papers. They'd take her to shows and lovestory movies. Bob Can-of-baloney will get me a poster of Dorothy Dandridge from the Strand and I'll give it to Violet. Maybe nobody tells Violet that she is beautiful, except her parents. She and the Horse Head Lady, Sophia and Maria from Second Street all are similar: beautiful, smart, young, and not movie stars, which they should be. I'll stop at Cicolli's before I go home today. It's my turn again to get the bottle caps. Violet reminds me of the bartenders at Paddy's Taproom, young, intelligent, talented and at dead-ends in their lives.

I'll see what I can do to get Leahy to look at Paddy's Taproom's bartenders. Uncle Joe has some Mummers' music records. I can ask Bobby Ronan's father who is the captain of the Uptown String Band. I'll get some 45's from Bobby.

Violet rarely paid on time, but she always paid. When she paid, she closed the door behind her and handed me the exact amount. She always called me back after she paid as I started down the steps to give me a nickel or dime tip. I knew she was going to call me back, but I acted as if I didn't know. I always gave her the "you gave me the <u>exact</u> amount, did I do something wrong look? " This was a better look than the poor boy who is trying to help his mother make ends meet begging look.

I'll bet she is a good singer because she has a soothing voice, like Mary Welch's when she recites poems in class. Violet is my best customer in many ways. Adults are cool as far as I am concerned. They give what they can to help people. Some even buy me A's tickets in the bleachers.

"What's the news today Sugar? Who's on page one? What times do you deliver the Sunday comics section on Saturday mornings and the Sunday paper on Sunday mornings? Will you knock on my door when you deliver the Saturday and Sunday morning papers if I sign up for them? I want to be sure to wake up and get going. What grade are you in? Do you have homework on weekends? Why do you wear t-shirts with college names misspelled on them? Do all your brothers and sisters have black hair? Are you an altar boy? What Masses do you serve? Do your priests hear confessions? Which priest is the best one to go to for confession?" These are some questions that Violet asked me. They have stuck with me even until now.

Violet must work night work because she is usually wearing pajamas and a robe during the day. She had better have an escort with her when she comes home from work. Violet is self-made, I can tell. Nobody was going to force her to finish high school if she didn't want to. She's like the bartenders at Paddy's Taproom, like a movie star but no one will ever know her. She always knows what she owes me. I have to remind my other customers, who never add the current week's amount when they finally pay me. "Last week you said I owed you one dollar and 25 cents, well here's one dollar and 25cents," is a typical comment.

It's a shame that Violet can't sing and dance at Paddy's Taproom. Sister Clare gives too much homework on weekends. I hope that Mom has her chicken and fried tomatoes tonight. Pop would like Violet's taste in colors. He likes to paint purple mountains and greenish skies. Maybe she can sing *My Buddy, my Buddy quite so true* or *Mother at Thy Feet is Kneeling, one who loves you very much.* (Pop's favorites). I miss Buddy and Helen and I never even met them. What must Pop feel? When I'm old enough to go see Violet sing, she'll be six or seven years older than now. It probably won't be the same.

I have wonderful memories of walking around my route and on the way home listening to beautiful music, especially on hot, humid days. All the windows were open in all the houses. There were no air conditioners and there was no air to be felt. I guessed that some houses had fans, but I never saw one. Coming through the open windows was the beautiful and powerful voice of Eddie Fisher, a Philadelphia boy who was a neighborhood hero. His music was great; a very special voice and beautiful words and musical backgrounds. Eddie was not from our neighborhood, but he was a Philly guy. He was famous and a real hero to the people on my paper route and on Carlisle Street. He was also in the Army for a while. I tried to sing *I'm Walking Behind You* like Eddie, but it was clear that playing street sports and planning for my future with Notre Dame, the Yankees and the Vatican were the current priorities in my life and they were going to stay that way. I couldn't sing let alone compete with Eddie Fisher or Mario Lanza, another Philly guy. Mario's a South Philly choir boy who caught the attention of one of the Sisters in his school. She set him off to an incredible career. Sisters were amazing; they can do anything.

Sister Assumption Marie told me she'd tell no one about our little secret.

"What's our little secret, Sister?" I asked.

"That you want to go to St. Charles seminary after eighth grade. I can see all the signs; I know you're in touch with the Holy Ghost. I taught five Jesuits and many secular priests and I saw the same signs. I'll pray that you will listen closely as the Holy Ghost whispers in your mind," Sister Assumption said as if she just had an epiphany.

What signs does Sister Assumption see? She never taught me, except to teach me how to sell candy in the classroom. She'll be very old at my Pope ceremony in Rome. What if Mario's school didn't have a choir and he sang like all the other boys who fooled around trying to mess up the hymns at the Stations of the Cross? What if Mario's Sister didn't like him because his family didn't give enough to church? Eddie is Jewish and he sang in the shower or on the corner, like Frankie Lyman; he had to; how else would he be famous. If I'm lucky, Mantle will be retiring just when I'm used to fast curve balls and hard grounders to third. Casey will remember that I am a Yankee fan when he signs me to a contract. I'm a A's fan and I like the Phillies. Casey probably told his wife about me when he got home from his trip to play the A's in Shibe Park.

Pop can sing and paint, why can't I? I can see the ball coming out of Frog-face's hand when he pitches. I can't see anybody else's. Frog-face has won some games at the park. I don't know how. He has perfect control and his pitches are just the right speed to clobber.

"Hey Bill, my best friend Karen O'Hara lives on your route at 16th and Allegheny. Does she get a paper from you?" Maureen asked hoping that I said yes.

"Is she in your classroom or the other classroom?" I responded in a less than hopeful way. "I never see sixth grade girls, except when we walk to school and you and your friends keep up with us. I have no one named O'Hara on my route. Does she walk to school with you? I know all the Irish people. 16th and Allegheny is where St. Joe's home is and I don't have anyone on that corner," I came back with a lengthy answer.

The last thing I needed was a friend of Maureen's on my route. I would have to see her parents on collection days. Who

knows, maybe they couldn't pay or maybe they aren't tippers. Karen couldn't face Maureen too easily if her parents didn't pay and she would have to stop coming to our house. Her parents would want to know all about the seventh grade Sisters. They would want to know which one would be the best one to teach Karen the next year. They'd want me to tell Karen about seventh grade during the summer and give her some study tips. Besides, I never look up when I'm on my route, except to collect money and buy fudge or cards on the way home at Cicolli's or when I'm in the crazy lady's area. I wonder if Karen is the girl who Maureen meets up with at Allegheny Avenue.

I just want to get home to Carlisle Street before it gets too dark to play stickball. The older guys choose me in sometimes. I can't tell who I see on the route. The St. Joe boys like Michael McFadden, Billy Reilly, Pegleg, the speedster, and Goose can't come to our block, I don't think, because it's too far away to get there and back before dinner and after their study hours. They live at 16th and Allegheny.

The best part of my paper route is the interesting people, except the Crazy Lady who chases after me with a broom as she screams about late deliveries. I'm never late and I don't collect any money from her. Violet bothers me but at the same time I consider her my best customer and a good friend. I hope that she doesn't stay in her apartment all day until it's time to go to work. Pretty Boy shouldn't be her boyfriend because she's afraid of him. That's why she said she fell. She didn't fall and Pretty Boy probably won his first fight!

14

Our Lady of Venice

"Do you guys want to play tackle tomorrow at Huntington?" asked Raymond, a Nicetown guy in my class.

"Yeah, I'll play; what time? which field? Who else is playing?" blurted out a couple other Nicetown guys, who could be on the field ten minutes after they walked out of their houses.

"I can't, I have a test on Monday," volunteered Terrence O'Brien, the "studious one" who never did well on tests or in class. He always had to study for tests but never passed any of them. He was "too frightened of his own shadow" according to Raymond the one inviting everyone else. Terrence could always be counted on to have his book open on his desk, which was just where Sister Rose Carmel made us recite poems and history lessons. We read right from Terrence's book when we had to recite poems or history lessons. In my opinion, Terrence was a lifesaver, many times for many students. If he closed his books, we would die and we'd have to start memorizing things.

Bobby said, "I'll go if Bill goes. It's an hour and fifteen minute walk for us, I'll play".

"What time you guys getting there?" I asked as I calculated the hours (it was more like an hour and forty-five minutes) and I needed to complete my plans for the day.

I stopped delivering papers due to a lack of profit due to a sudden lack of payment and profit from some customers, like Quick Draw Paul. He had the same outrageous excuse whenever I tried to collect, "Come back next week, my Vertigo is back and I can't see. He scanned the headlines when I handed him the paper. He always held a wet towel on the back of his head. He told me he was a political cartoonist named Paul. That's why I named him Quick *Draw* Paul. I needed to know everybody's plans for the day.

"Early, say eight-thirty, meet at Forest's house, across from Little Flower" Raymond said as if he was the coach. Bobby and I talked about playing football on a good field and how we should do well. Bobby didn't play on our Temple's Dentistry Frat Field. He did play on our Johnson's Wax Field with its rocks, stones, trash, and whatever else was lying around and building up in the abandoned field. Of course, we cleaned up as much as we could prior to a game of tackle. Some rocks were too big to move; they were like an extra defensive back to get around if you were running with the handmade ball, made from newspapers rolled up in a silo shape.

"Bobby, did you play at 29th and Allegheny?" I asked Bobby.

"Just once, it was too dangerous with all the black stones and glass" Bobby reminded me.

"It was safer than playing on Carlisle Street where equipment was not allowed" I reminded Bobby, who played in the street all the time.

"My mother was finding those little black stones in my pants' pockets for days," Bobby complained.

"Where's the Nicetown guys Raymond?" I asked when Bobby and I arrived.

"They'll be here, don't worry. They stopped at Forest's house to get a football" retorted Raymond with confidence.

Some of those Nicetown guys were good, really good. Spider Webb could run like a deer and he wore cleats. Butch Broadneck thought he was Ramar of the Jungle; I think he'll be the next Steve Van Buren. O'Donovan can catch anything and he doesn't go down easily even though he's skinny. He has cleats and he has his cousin's helmet from Frankford's team. Raymond told me about O'Donovan's cousin.

"Curry, Ronnie O'Donovan's cousin volunteered to help cleanup Temple stadium after a Frankford/North Thanksgiving game. He snuck into North's equipment room and stole a helmet and a jersey. Those helmets are like the Eagles, I swear. Curry was like that; he enjoyed stealing. Even adults paid him to get things like cigarettes, car mats, and food, anything they wanted. He volunteered to help clean Reading station in preparation of Cardinal O'Hara's coming to Philadelphia. He walked home with a Red Cap's cap and a beautiful pocket watch. He's crazy and he's bound to get caught" Raymond told Bobby and I.

Raymond was right, Curry was crazy and he would be caught some day. He bragged too much. Too many people knew about him.

Curry had some baseball players' hats. He leaned over the guardrails at Shibe Park's right field, near the visitor's bullpen, where the players loosened up before their games, and grabbed their hat and took off. He collected hats like I collected autographs and bragged about whose hat he had the way we brag about whose autograph we have. The ushers were helping people to their seats while Curry ripped off the players' hats. He had the process down pat.

"Here they come, twelve of them; that's great," I blurted out because I saw a good game brewing.

"Seven on seven, that's good. I'll choose you Raymond, "heads or tails?" I gave him the choice.

"You call it Bill" he gave the choice back to me.

"Heads!" I always choose heads.

"It's tails. Raymond chooses first," said the coin "tosser," Broadneck I believe.

"I take Ramar" Raymond quickly asserted.

Now I had two picks because Ramar Broadneck had shoulder pads and a helmet. When your opponent chose someone with equipment, you got to pick two players. I think I chose Bobby and in a little while, we had two seven-man teams.

"Sig-gulls, set down one, two…." I heard the quarterback from Our Lady of Venice screaming out signals. He always yelled sig-gulls for signals.

Our Lady of Venice school is nearby; I'd know that signal calling in Korea, during the war, if I heard it. They must always play football in their uniforms. They wear their uniforms even when they are messing around playing or practicing. I heard that quarterback barking out sig-gulls for signals for a long time. The uniforms are great and every player is fully equipped. They must be in the CYO league. St. Edward's CYO team is supposed to be the best team. Our Lady of Venice guys tackle low and hard, like you should. I'm going to try tackling low today. Right now I just grab guys around the neck and pull them down. Welshie has an Our Lady of Venice uniform. Maybe Curry got it for him. Welshie walks around the neighborhood like he's on the Eagles. Now I'm embarrassed because I know that they'd kill us in a game because they are a real team with real uniforms.

I gotta come here more. But it's an hour and a half to get here. I can't come here too often. The Italians, like the Venice team, are strong people and fast too. O'Donovan's head is lost in the helmet. North uses the same style and quality helmet as the Crimson Tide wears.

"We got this field for practice," said number fifty-five for Our Lady of Venice as he waved to the rest of the clad players to come join him. "We use it every Saturday 'til we want to leave," continued the round mound of a center.

"You guys can watch or go to another field," summarized their eighth grade, Chuck Bednarek-like, dark skinned, soon to have to shave, team spokesman.

Another Our Lady of Venice player, number seventy-six, came running over yelling, "Get off our field or we'll get you off".

"Do these guys wear their uniforms to bed?" I asked myself.

"You don't own this field. We're staying; you go. Which goal do you want to protect Bill?" Ramar Broadneck asked as he totally disregarded the Our Lady of Venice guys.

"Hey, I'm telling you guys to get out. This is our field; we're here every Saturday" came a loud, confident voice from a loud, obnoxious eighth grader with black marks under his eyes, like the North guys.

"Get out of our way punk. Let your team find a high school field to practice on," yelled Eugene Bitterman, a red headed bull of a boy, who looked like he was angry enough to rip old number fifty-five to shreds and enjoy the process.

I never knew that our class was so tough. O'Donovan told the other guys to ignore the Our Lady of Venice team and get started. I'm not the toughest guy in class like everybody said I was after punching Frankie. I think Ramar is the toughest. We're right on this one. They are trying to push us around and intimidate us with their helmets. Seventy-six looked surprised that O'Donovan fought back. Bif would fight back. Fran wouldn't just talk; he'd go after the whole Our Lady of Venice team. Uncle Dan and Pop would not let these guys butt in.

"Hey Antonio or Rocco or whatever your name is, get off the field and take your buddies with you. Go to the Sun Ray and buy some Gillette razors for yourselves and your girl friends" was my contribution to their challenge. Ramar was surprisingly silent but he stood next to everybody who was talking.

I'll tell the Tioga T's what I said, but not Pop. He'd have no problem if I punched these guys, but he'd get angry with me if he knew I insulted their heritage. Italian girls don't have mustaches. Gina and Sophia tie for the most beautiful with Grace Kelly and Maureen O'Hara.

Terrence O'Brien ran over and asked if we needed his help. "Go back to your knitting Terrence; I'll need a new sweater this winter" mocked Raymond as O'Donovan and he laughed to each other. Terrence was big; it was a shame he avoided contact sports from what I knew.

"If we get into a fight Terrence, go to the office and get some bandages and make sure they match the Babies of Venice's uniforms," O'Donovan wouldn't give up.

Eugene Bitterman ended all discussion: "Just get out of here and stop bothering us". Our Lady of Venice left. We finally got started.

"We won the toss so we'll receive," I yelled as the rep for the team that lost in the selection process, lost big.

Raymond kicked off to us. The ball went about ten yards. Spider picked up the ball and ran fast as he could to about their twenty-five yard line. The Our Lady of Venice team and their coaches left us alone and we were having fun. Barrett's big brother was steady the quarterback. He pointed to areas on the field where we should go so he could throw to us. He couldn't run with the ball because he was sixteen. We were going back and forth and no one scored. Barrett's brother stunk out loud. He couldn't throw worth a bean. We couldn't get rid of him. Defense was more fun. I was Wild Man Willy McCaffrey after the Eagles defensive star. A middle-aged man who was standing on the sidelines kept telling me what to do. He was huge and he watched our argument with Our Lady of Venice without a comment.

"Get further out. Go around him. Go inside him. It's a pass, go back! Tackle that quarterback" he would say. He coached me on every play. I couldn't tackle the quarterback because all we had to do is grab his jersey and yell, "caught!"

"Hold up guys," somebody yelled. I think it was Raymond.

"Who's your coach?" asked a wise guy in a wise guy way.

"I am," said Raymond.

"You are? What do you know about coaching?" was what came back from a high school-looking kid with an "Our Lady of Venice Holy Name Society" t-shirt. The kid needed braces, a comb that worked, and a mentor to tell him to shut up or expect some broken teeth.

"You guys 'wanna play us. We won't hurt you; we'll hold back. We could use the practice and it looks like you guys need to learn how to play," a pudgy kid, number seventy-eight. They were all big shots but they could probably back it up.

"Play 'em; you'll be alright. They're not that good" my personal coach assured us.

"You guys 'wanna play 'em?" Raymond asked. With one exception, Swifty-Shifty Neal, everybody wanted to play them.

"You keep score Terrence. Can you do that?" Ronnie O'Donovan asked.

"Sure!" Terrence said although I doubted that he could.

"We'll be back after lunch, say twelve-thirty?" laughed number fifty-two and their agent with the Holy Name shirt.

I never played on a grass field and never one hundred yards. Raymond shouldn't mock Terrence. Spider is the smallest guy and he wants to play. Terrence is as big as Raymond. This will prove that I'm a tough guy even though I love the Blessed Mother, vanilla fudge, and light blue colors for Notre Dame and Blessed Virgin Mary. Otto the Outrageous played for North's JVs. It's about time I find out if I can play tackle on a real field against a real team.

We kept playing our game until twelve-twenty when Our Lady of Venice came, complete with fans and cheerleaders. Even the cheerleaders had uniforms. They were all girls and Ronnie O'Donovan suggested that Terrence cheer for us since we didn't have girl cheerleaders. Terrence said he'd do one or the other; keep score or cheerlead, not both.

"I get tired, you know. I'm tired even now," Terrence complained. Terrence was big enough to knock O'Donovan's block off. But Ronnie and some others on the team wouldn't get off Terrence's case.

All I think about now is Fran on North's JVs and the veterans from Paddy's Taproom and Lattner and Lujack and Leahy. I'm not worried. Pop thinks I'm fast enough. He played

left tackle semi-pro at about a hundred sixty pounds soaking wet. I'm really not fast. I never won a race or came in next to last, always last.

"O'Donovan, Ramar, Bitterman, Barrett, Spider, Bobby, O'Neill, O'Brian, you too Davidson: let's win one for the Gipper," I called out to the team.

"Did I say that?" I asked myself. I was so excited and I didn't know why.

McCaffreys are tough people, just think about it. Terrence has a neck like Butch Broadneck. He never laughs. He tries to make everybody like him with the poetry book and all.

I think that I'm a scaredy cat when things get rough except when I'm angry. Then I want to fight for it. The Ts gave me that and so did Pop, the vets, the Ragman, the Iceman, the Moving Man, the Pretzel Makers, Uncle Dan, Bif with one F, and so many really tough guys. I wish Leahy was here to scout us.

"Tails, you lose. We'll receive." was the dialog among the referee, who had an Our Lady of Venice shirt, and some massive Our Lady of Venice player, number seventy-eight, their captain, and Spider, who said he'd bring us luck if he called heads or tails. The ref's t-shirt had "Pray for the Conversion of Russia" on the back. Another man from the sidelines volunteered to ref. The volunteer came from the Our Lady of Venice crowd and his shirt advertised a South Philly pizza shop that delivered. The back of the Holy Name shirt advertised Venice's Friday night Bingo. Two or three dark headed girls clapped their hands and jumped up and down while standing next to Venice's high school agent, crooked teeth.

"Bill, you're quarterback because Forest says you can throw fifty yards. He saw you do it outside Little Flower". Raymond assigned positions to all our players. He knew most of them and what they could play. Bobbie and I didn't know what any of them could do. In fact, some of the players from St. Stephen's surprised me. I thought they never played sports, like Eugene, Swifty, our center and Len Lewandowski and Arty Henson, two impressive looking linemen from Nicetown, one in my eighth grade, Arty.

Raymond kicked off and he got some lift on the ball. Swifty Neal, who couldn't wait to play, was burning with a desire to "flatten the pizza boys to pizza looking boys". He yelled, "Kill the pasta boys". We all ran down the field. I was mentally practicing tackling as I ran right into number sixty-three, who had a bar across his helmet. He blocked me off balance a little and he tackled me from behind when I got going.

The Our Lady of Venice speedster, number five, a little bigger than Spider, took the ball and took off. Nobody touched him and he went all the way to score a TD. The extra point attempt missed by a mile; it got up just enough to go over the center's head. Their center centered ok and a Sal Mineo look alike held the ball correctly, but seventy-six couldn't kick. Six to zip; they kicked off. Sal's look alike was out of sync with the others. His uniform was a different shade of purple and his football pants were green, not gold like the others.

I shouldn't be concerned with the color of anybody's uniform. Sixty-three doesn't know it but he was the first person to block a future Notre Dame All American.

Seventy-six isn't going to kick for more than a few yards. Everything looks strange. The Nicetown guys did this before. Bobby doesn't look lost. Bitterman looks like he wants to kill somebody. Raymond keeps yelling, "Let's go, they stink, just catch the ball and run". Broadneck doesn't need a helmet; Lenny does. Maybe I don't look lost. I'm not lost; I'm an Irishman.

I didn't know where to go or what to do. I watched many kick offs but was never in one let alone on the receiving end. The ball might come to me. I never played a real game. I don't think I ever played a tackle game with a real football at Temples Dental School field or on Carlisle Street; we always used the wrapped up newspaper. Our Lady of Venice looked like Roman Catholic's varsity to me when they lined up to kick off. They all had cleats, helmets, pads, jerseys, football pants, purple socks, numbers and two coaches on the sidelines. Even the referees looked like real referees. Our Lady of Venice had a tee to hold the ball while seventy-six kicked off. The ball came dangerously close to me. Raymond got hit by an Our Lady of Venice guy. Spider picked the ball up and ran for quite a gain.

"Keep quiet everybody. Let Bill call plays," Bobby cautioned the Stepheners in our first huddle.

"Ramar, I'll hand it to you. Center the ball on signals two", I called my first play. My personal coach was still on the sidelines telling me what to do on every play, especially on defense.

"Set down, signals one, signals two," I barked out like I did at 29th and Allegheny. The ball came to me in a snap. I turned around and gave it to Ramar Broadneck, who sure did have one. He ran into the line and kept running after being hit by number forty-two. Back in the huddle, we all felt great. I wanted to be Chuck Bednarek at first, but now I was thrilled to be Ralph Guglielmi, without the number three. I started to give directions and the ball to different players.

"Ramar, when I give you the ball, run around Henson's end". "Hopalong (Corey Cassidy, in my class), pretend you're Neil Warden and go between Raymond and Eugene" I directed.

We made progress every time we ran the ball. I wanted to be the quarterback forever. Our Lady of Venice was winning six zip and their quarterback kept saying "sig-gulls" at the line of scrimmage. The speedster who ran back the kickoff kept getting the ball and going nowhere. My personal coach kept at it during the game. "You 'gotta throw these guys off, they're soft; I've watched them many times". With his advice I was able to make a few, just a few, tackles and it felt great. I went from a college player to an All Pro, Wild Man Willy. Raymond told us during one of Venice's frequent time-outs that he wanted to be called Big Tree, like his father when he played for the Frankford Yellow Jackets. This was fun.

I'm feeling better about my chances at South Bend. I can see big things happening. I wish Leahy was here to watch me. None of the T's except Fran made North's JVs. I hope that I can run a play or two. Spider is so small yet he gains all kinds of yards every time. I can't see anybody here that could go to Notre Dame.

"OK, Spider, you go around either end, you decide," I told our speedster..

"Bill, pass the ball. You can throw, I saw you. They won't expect it," Spider responded.

I never threw a real football in a game. I just play catch with Richie's football on Johnson's Wax lot. Number three of the Irish practices every day. I can imitate Ralph Guglielmi; I'll try that. Big Tree can't block.

"I'll run this play and pass to Ronnie or Henry on the second down. Ok, I'll get the ball on signals four and run past you Henry so keep that big guy out of the backfield. Ronnie, I need your helmet". I felt that I needed a helmet to run since the other runners had one.

"Use mine; it's a Wilson I think," volunteered Ramar.

"No, I want to wear North's helmet," I replied as I thought about next year when I'll be the quarterback for North's JVs until the coach recognized my talent and brings me up to the first string varsity for North's final four games.

"Remember, signals four, not two or three like usual". "Set down, signals one, signals two, signals three, hurry up signals four".

I got the ball and started to run past Henry when number fifty-two grabbed me from behind and pulled me back for a loss. He mocked me and said that it was a giveaway when I came to the line with a helmet. There was no problem for him to run after me. He ran on signals three and the ref didn't call off sides. Next play.

Swifty centered the ball on signal one to throw Our Lady of Venice off a little. I ran backwards and saw O'Donovan all by himself. I threw him the ball, which did not spiral, but got to him. Him caught the ball and ran for a big gain.

"I told you I'm Pete Pihos, just throw it to me every play," Ronnie O'Donovan shrieked.

Actually Ronnie wanted to be Leon Hart but he was too small and skinny and we forgot how big Pihos was.

I want to pass all the time. Wait 'til they see my spiral. I'm getting a Notre Dame helmet like Guglielmi's. Leahy will probably want to give me number three when I get there. Being Pope is out of the question right now. Replacing Mantle could still work. Pop will understand and agree for me to put the Vatican off for a while.

We were in scoring position. I could have easily scored at the dental field with this situation. "Ramar, I'll give you the ball and you run straight up the middle, like Van Buren and try to score. On signals three, team, let's go" I instructed as I enjoyed this more and more.

"Signals three". The ball came to me and I challenged Ramar to break free and score.

Ramar took the ball and ran like a wild beast right up the middle. Swifty and Eugene blocked their men very well. Eugene, Swifty, Henson, and Lewandowski, our interior linemen, watched the Our Lady of Venice kids practice blocking. They tried to imitate them because they didn't really know how to block. When the Our Lady of Venice coach was yelling at the linemen, our linemen tried to listen to their coach for some advice so they could try what the coach said so they could know what to do. They all were perfect on this run. Ramar Broadneck bullied himself to the two-yard line. Our Lady of Venice guys were pulling at him and grabbing his bull neck and pulling at his waist. Two Our Lady of Venice guys held onto Ramar's legs. I pushed Ramar forward; Big Tree pushed me into Ramar. The entire Our Lady of Venice team was either pulling Ramar backwards or jumping on top of the pile Ramar created.

"You're over the goal line Ramar, just go down," yelled Lewandowski.

"Who's this kid?" someone yelled from the sidelines, "he's an animal".

The refs didn't have whistles so one of them, the one with Venice's Holy Name Society shirt, whistled the two finger whistle, as if he was trying to get someone's attention or calling a dog. Ramar wouldn't stop and he went clear through the end zone and stopped. Everyone got off him or let him go; he never did hit the turf. Big Tree, of course, missed the extra point. It barely got over the linemen. Score tied, six six.

Ramar is tough. He and I will probably be on North's varsity next year. Nobody on our team is tired or wants to quit. Bobby needs more action. Sig-gulls is easy to tackle. Big Tree stinks; he can't block.

"Five minutes to go," a friend of the ref yelled on behalf of the ref, who lost count of how many minutes were left. Big Tree kicked off and Venice's number five grabbed it and started down the field. Spider tackled him before he went too far. Spider made a nice ankle tackle.

"Call time out," cried my personal coach.

"Time out ref," was about all I could do at the time. The guys with helmets took them off and knelt down. They wanted me to say something since I called time out. My coach signaled for me to talk to him.

My coach advised me, "Number five is tired. He's holding the football like a baby, vertically and up against his shoulder. Hit the ball when you tackle him, he'll fum-ble".

"Try to hit the ball from number five; he's tired," I told the guys. After two bad throws from "Sig-gulls," it was third down and ten to go.

"Stop a minute, I 'gotta go to Confession today," screamed Arthur Henson, who is a good player.

"One more play Art. There's less than five minutes to go and we need you. Go to Confession next week" Ramar begged.

"I can't wait, it's late now," was Arthur's quick response.

"Time out," it was our second time out and I needed to think – Big Tree turned over the responsibility of the team to me when we kicked off at the beginning.

How did Art know what time it was? He's running in the opposite direction to church. No substitutes are around. One left a long time ago.

Knowing how important this play was, I asked Terrence if he'd come in and play. Most of the other guys went ballistic and complained that Terrence would rather play dolls or Hop Scotch than play football. They claimed that Terrence likes ballet and never plays street games during the school year.

"What did you say? I didn't hear you. Do you need an extra player?" asked Terrence.

"Yes, hurry up. Stand here and stop the person with the ball if you can," I implored Terrence.

"Third down and about two minutes to play" signaled the ref.

"Sig-gulls hut-hut" railed the QB with the spotless uniform, who took the ball from center and tried to run himself. He got nowhere except in Len's arms.

Last down for them; we need to hold them. They'll run to Terrence because our guys made a big deal of not wanting him to play.

"Terrence, this play, you go behind the line and tackle the ball carrier if he gets past us," Big Tree said. Terrence knew that we were keeping him out of the play and he didn't seem to care. Number five got the ball and ran to his right, trying to get around end. He was smacked down and he fumbled. I could hear five's pads get hit. Terrence whacked him good. Terrence recovered the fumble. Terrence made the tackle and the recovery all by himself. There's about a minute to go. We didn't have time to congratulate Terrence. We ran a few plays and made a couple first downs.

"Call time out. Time out" the voice wasn't a seventh or eighth graders. My sideline coach was on the sideline crying out probably as loud as he could.

"See the back part of the end zone in front of where the dog is standing? Throw the ball to either O'Donovan or Barrett in that area. Can you reach it?" coach wanted to know.

"I could if I was just having a catch, but I don't know about here in a game. I'll try," I retorted. I was thinking about playing catch with a football every Christmas with Richie Cione.

"I will throw the ball to the left rear section of that end zone to you or Henry," I instructed.

"That place is full of stones and glass. Don't throw to me," sobbed O'Donovan.

"Me neither" echoed Henry.

"Ok, Spider, I'll give the ball to you and you can try to go around Terrence to that section. Ok, let's go" I directed Spider and the whole team.

This field is much better than Johnson's. Why do they worry? They're not used to our fields. They live too near Hunting Park. The Our Lady of Venice guys probably don't want to ruin their uniforms. It is worth a loss to them not to get holes in their uniforms. Spider is tough. Terrence amazes me. He's our best player.

I whispered to Bobby as we broke from our huddle to go to the left rear section of the end zone as fast as he could. I knew that Bobby played at Johnson's Wax a couple times and didn't complain about the glass, rocks or stones. I got the ball from center and ran to Terrence's side. Spider blocked somebody after I let him pass without giving him the ball. Terrence blocked seventy-six and fifty then stood next to me like a bodyguard. He stopped before he tackled me. I threw the ball to Bobby, who caught it right in front of the glass and stones. He didn't even get into the mess. No one was near him and no one came over to congratulate him except Spider and me. Everyone else was too shocked to do anything. The Our Lady of Venice guys left the field with their coaches. Seventy-six came over to wish us luck in high school next year. Art was there.

"What happened to you Art? Why'd you leave the game? You couldn't have gone to Confession. You're a good player," Eugene asked.

"I had to go to the bathroom; I couldn't wait any longer," Art was being honest.

"It's ok Art, Terrence made three beautiful plays for you," Ramar joined in.

"Terrence, you played great, we couldn't have won without you," several players said in unison.

"Terrence, why didn't you start out playing? You've played before, I can tell. Good tackle and recovery Terrence; you have to come every time we play; Terrence be sure to try out for North. Terrence, I'm sorry for misjudging you," each team member had something to say to Terrence.

Terrence was getting all kinds of accolades and he didn't seem to care.

"Raymond told me not to play because the game was for men, not girls and sissies. He wanted me to be a cheerleader like the Our Lady of Venice girls. He didn't know that I play football every week with the Nicetown Red Legs," Terrence informed us.

The Nicetown Reds are a Pop Warner team that traditionally plays for the regional and state championships. They brag that so many players from their team end up playing college ball. Raymond and Broadneck looked like they just squealed on a friend.

"What's your last name?" some kid asked me.

"Me?" I wanted to be sure he was talking to me.

"Yeah, you," same kid, different question.

"McCaffrey, why?" I questioned the obvious sixth grader.

"I thought that your father or brother was coaching you. I think your coach is Bucko Kilroy and I wanted to get an autograph," he said looking like a kid who was afraid to ask for an autograph.

Terrence is a Nicetown Red and Bucko Kilroy coached me. I'm not sure which is more incredible.

15

BIF with One F

My friend and an older guy had a standard, well-rehearsed response to anyone gutsy enough to ask him for his name: "B-i-f, not B-i-f-f, like the guy from Fishtown who only beats up smaller guys and wears big rings on his fingers to put nicks on the guys face and neck".

Bif with one F prided himself for beating up anybody, big or small, mostly big, except when the smaller guys won't quit bothering him or refuse to pay his boss' bills on time.

Bif with one F drove the annoying little guys against a fence where he promised to punch them and their best friend until they both had to walk with canes and eat only liquids. He wore a big ring, given to him by the owner of the Pawn for Dollars shop if he, Bif with one F, would stand watch outside the shop on busy days. He was a strong man, and about twenty years old. His arms were huge from working out in the gym and working the docks. He always wore T-shirts, the kind that look like basketball shirts with no sleeves and skinny shoulder covers. He was another Ted Klusewski. During winters, he wore a Navy Pea coat and a Navy Watch cap. His hair was black and thick, so thick that it looked like heated tar. I'd say he was seven feet tall, but he really was about six feet. He wore the kind of shoes boxers wear in the ring everywhere he went. He alternated between bowling shoes and boxing shoes; the bowling shoes wore out faster. The men from the industrial bowling league gave Bif with one F their old bowling shoes. There were many shoes and Bif with one F took all of them but could only wear size thirteen and above. The boxing shoes felt like his for the first time; he earned them by boxing Tommy "the Boss" Taylor at the Cambria.

Bif with one F's boxing shoes once belonged to Kid Gavilan, who gave them to a guy Bif with one F knew in high school because

Kid lost to Bobo Olson and the shoes lost their special powers. Bif with one F's friend proposed to barter with Bif with one F. If Bif with one F tells his friend's business partner to stay away from his friend's wife then as a reward Bif with one F gets the famous shoes.

Tommy "the Boss" was a seasoned pro with many fights and an occasional win. He was a bull of a man, about six-four and muscular; he worked out at a gym and at a condemned place called Jim's Gym and Pool Hall. Bif with one F had to learn what to do in the ring about two hours before the fight if he agreed to fight the Boss. The guy that the Boss was supposed to fight, "Shamrock" Tony di Franco, the Irish guy with a totally Italian heritage, who "likes Guinness over Gratz or Schmidts, shamrocks over pizza and James Joyce over Lil' Abner," couldn't make the fight. He had to take his wife to the hospital because she got hit in the eye with an umbrella when she fought his part time girl friend over some jewelry, which Tony stole from her to give to his part time girl friend. By agreeing to take on the fight, Bif with one F amazed everybody who didn't know him but not anybody who knew him from the neighborhood. Shamrock wasn't missed at all. Bif with one F was now the one to watch.

If Bif with one F can do this, even if he loses, I can field hard ground balls at Johnson Wax's lot or anywhere else. If Bif with one F wins, he'll probably start training for more fights. I hope not. Bif with one F might not be too scared. He doesn't seem to care about things. He only laughs when someone asks him about his tattoo or the bowling or boxing shoes.

Everyone who went to the Cambria said that Bif with one F held up his hands over his face for the first two rounds, swinging out of control a couple times. The Boss laughed and pounded Bif with one F as hard as he could. The Boss told his manager in between the second and third rounds that Bif with one F takes every hit as if it was a massage. He'd probably have to just fight it out until Bif with one F got tired of being punched, then pow!

"The big famous right hook is on its way this round, the kid is done," so said the Boss to his manager, Scotty MacDougal, who wanted to play a bagpipe in the Mummers' parade. Every string band refused to let him play, not because they couldn't see where he'd fit in but because he made the bagpipes sound like an overworked bellow.

Bif with one F told his manager that he's ready to fight now because the Boss gave him an insight into his weak spot, his nose.

"When I hit his nose, he flinched and shook it off. His jaw is too hard to break and his body wouldn't be hurt if a train ran into it. So, watch me this round" Bif with one F told his manager, the legendary Rory Caldwell, who had a flat nose, which he said came from years in the ring. His friends said it came from years in the South Street ginmills. A ring announcer once labeled him legendary and it stuck.

"OK what's your name, get it over with," mumbled a pessimistic Rory Caldwell, who was chewing on some gauze as he tried to patch up a small gash on Bif with one F's iron-like chin.

Caldwell, who was a long time member of the Cambria, saw them all: Dempsey, Sugar Ray, Jersey Joe, Joe Lewis, Marciano, Basilo, Giardello, and the rest of the best. He, Rory, said that Henry Armstrong was the toughest guy he ever saw and Dempsey came across as a nice guy, but he could hit like a Mack truck. All this came out in the Bulletin the day after the fight at the Cambria. Caldwell told Bif with one F to keep the hands up and don't worry about the Boss' nose.

"Go on out dare and pretend you're tired and hurt. Keep close to the ropes and keep your hands up over your face like you've been 'doin' so far. After two minutes, go crazy, swing with everything you have. It's a gamble, but you're never going to get hurt anyway; this guy can't hurt you cause 'yeer' a truck and don't just look for the nose. Hit him anywhere you can".

Bif with one F paid no attention to Rory and he walked up to the Boss at the beginning of the third round and looked him straight in the eye as if to say, "Can't we be friends?" The Boss thought that it could be that Bif with one F was trying to tell him to play along with him so nobody gets hurt. The Boss nodded ok and started to back off. "Whack!" Bif with one F smacked the Boss right in the nose. The Boss went down and didn't get up until he arrived at St. Christopher's hospital, a children's hospital, but the only hospital that the Brinks security guard knew how to get to. Bif with one F smiled at Rory. The Brinks guy got free admission for "borrowing" the truck for the night.

Rory swung his towel down to the ring and said, "I'm ready to go God. You can't give me more than you just did". Bif with one F got one hundred and twenty five dollars and his picture in the

Bulletin's Sports section. He took his money and split it with his mother "60/50" cause she deserves more than me for my being sometimes bad". Rory got to keep his job. Bif with one F was a fixture at the Carmen theater and his fame grew. Everybody had the Bulletin picture – some probably still do – and Bif with one F never wavered from who he was and would always be, Bif with one F.

Bif had a tattoo on his right shoulder that said, "Angels, St. s (Saints), and Me". Below that line was the devil with a sword going through his body and an angel standing over the devil smiling with a look of pride. Bif with one F designed that tattoo right after he came back to the church for the third or fourth time. Bif with one F had a hard time with Confession. He thought: "Since the priests know my mother, they won't know what to say to her if they ask her, 'How's Bif with one F?'" Bif with one F was good at Poet and Picture Study when he was in St. Stephen's and that he could recite several poems by memory and he could describe all the pictures in the Picture Study book much better than any other student ever could. The Sisters made Bif with one F feel good when they told him that his commentary on the poems and pictures were distinctive and extraordinary. Sister Theresa went so far as to tell Bif with one F that she would work with him to get him to a good Arts school, where he could write poetry and paint, if he had any skills as a painter. Bif with one F said that he appreciated Sister's comments, but that he hated homework and "All school, except Picture Study and Poem, which we don't do as much as Spelling, Arithmetic, and other stuff, like Catechism or singing songs that make no sense like, 'Oh So Cool' or you know".

Sister couldn't get Bif with one F's parents to come to school to discuss his gifts. She asked Bif with one F to write a poem for the Bishop's Easter Mass. He said he would and he did. Sister actually cried when Bif with one F read it. Bif with one F was too nervous to read it to the Bishop or to the other Sisters. The poem wasn't read at the Bishop's Easter Mass because Sister didn't want anyone else to read it. Sister kept the poem and told Bif with one F that she will read it every Lent to her class at that time and to all the Sisters she was living with at that time. Bif said, "That's good, thanks Sister Theresa".

Bif had a great voice, but refused to sing in church. Then he saw "Going My Way," and heard Bing Crosby's choir. After that, he sang louder than anybody did at Mass and at practice for Confirmation and the May Procession. You could hear him singing "Danny Boy" or even Sister Rose Carmel's "Oh So Cool Was the Deep Green Pool" above the fifty-five or so students in his class in seventh grade. Father Fitzpatrick asked Bif with one F to sing "Going My Way" at the Bishop's St. Patrick's party. Bif with one F stopped singing all together.

Father Fitz should start a choir like Father O'Malley did. Callahan's brother Ian knows everything about Bif with one F. I still don't know if the priest can bless candles at the house when he does Extreme Unction. Our candles are for decoration, they're not sacramentals. I shouldn't let the candles bother me. I'll get blessed candles when I serve the 6 (6am mass).

Bif with one F wandered aimlessly up and down Germantown Avenue, never going too far, maybe a block or a block and a half. He got to the Carmen at 1pm and left after the last kid left. He wasn't paid to hang around and the area around the Carmen wasn't very dangerous. Kids were safe because Bif with one F was nearby. One Saturday at movie time, Bif with one F hadn't showed up and nobody would go in the theater or even buy a ticket.

"Where's Bif with one F?," all the third, fourth and fifth graders wanted to know.

"He'll be here; Bif with one F didn't go anywhere".

Ah, but he did and nobody knew where. Nobody knew where he lived or if he had brothers and sisters. There were all kinds of rumors.

"Bif with one F went to New York with a real trainer to fight in the Garden". "Bif with one F became a Buddhist monk and moved to Burma". "Bif with one F and Deafy started a tomato pie shop in California". The best was, "Bif with one F is at the Jesuit seminary in Rome. He'll stay there after he's a priest to show the Italians how to sing or box or do the yo-yo". Who knows what really happened?

Usually Bif with one F watches over us like a hawk or a cop, maybe he is an FBI agent and undercover. We have too many people who just kinda come here from nowhere and leave. I'll check out the trash cans for Bif with one F's bowling shoes. Maybe someday I'll get a tattoo of Bif with one F's victory; one of Deafy on his motorcycle; one of Otto the Outrageous and two more: Violet with her normal look and Maria with an As baseball cap. I'll let the Horse Head lady draw a tattoo of a horse head on my forearm.

Bif with one F isn't coming today. This is a good movie too, staring Grace Kelly, from Philadelphia, and Cary Grant. He's funny; she's serious, but I haven't seen her movies. She is Catholic and must've gone to Catholic school. How did she learn acting? We don't teach acting. Mario Lanza sang at school and a Sister helped him like Sister Teresa wanted to help Bif with one F's poems.

To Catch a Thief was the second movie of the double feature. Most kids finally went into the Carmen to watch some movie about the ocean and sponge diving. Uncle Dan dove for sponges off the coast of Italy. Cary Grant was a thief and Grace Kelly was a rich girl who lost some diamonds in the second movie. Grace Kelly was walking and moving around in a smooth manner. She didn't look like anyone on my paper route, but between her and Rosy the Riveter I could see the Horse Head lady. Her clothes did not come from Big Hearted Sam's or any shop on South Street. Cary Grant walked, talked and acted like he was rich and famous, which he was.

Mom has black hair, Grace has blonde; Mom is short, Grace looks tall; Mom wears glasses, Grace doesn't; Grace is Irish, Mom's Scots-Irish; they're both Catholic and that's the only similarity. But Mom reminds me of Grace Kelly by the way she seems to be: gracious, polite, polished, and very intelligent.

Mom works in crummy factories where people lose fingers a lot. Grace has directors and beauty specialists to fix her up to look good. Mom starts her day by waking us up and fixing us breakfast, then going to the factory, then cleaning the house and making us dinner, then watching us do our homework, then ironing for us and herself and Pop, then going to bed if we are all being good and not messing around. Grace couldn't handle Mom's schedule. Both Mom and Grace are great ladies, but Mom has the edge to get to heaven quickly; Grace has less of a chance than a giraffe does to go through the eye of a needle because she's rich. I'm betting that Grace will make it. Mom can walk or run through the needle!

Pop is Cary Grant more than Cary Grant is Cary Grant. Pop gets to wear a suit on Sundays. His suits cost from ten to eighteen dollars, including alterations, and he can buy one every six years or so. Pop's shoes are always spit polished because he learned how to spit polish in the Navy. The tie store next to

Amigo's shop has good ties for good deals. Three for three for three seventy-five. Pop's ties are beautiful, not the ones we buy with Mom for Christmas, which Pop wears just to please us. He and Cary could double for each other if Pop didn't wear glasses and Cary had white hair. They are both debonair. Nobody in the movies acts kind and generous as well as Cary; Pop doesn't act.

Pop's father was debonair, like Cary and Pop and rich like Cary, until he started to drink after one of Pop's brothers or sisters' Baptism party. How can we be sure to have a priest with us when we die if we just wear a brown scapular? Can it be a different color? Sister said that Hitler could be in heaven if he begged God for forgiveness at the end of his life, but the little boy who missed Mass and was hit by a car had too much black on his soul with mortal sin if he couldn't get to Confession. Mom and Pop couldn't commit mortal sins. God, I hate mortal sins.

16

Our Lady of Mercy Have Mercy on Us

I sometimes stopped off at Simon Mueller Public Elementary schoolyard to play basketball. There were two rims, not baskets because they didn't have hooks to put nets on at Mueller. Somehow, the same two big guys were there whenever I was there. They always took the better rim, the one that didn't shake and make noise whenever a ball hit it. I didn't have the nerve to ask if I could join them because they made it a point to station themselves in front of me with their backs to me when the other big guy was shooting. About half the times I was there, a peer of mine would show up with a basketball. I retrieved his missed shots and eventually wiggled my way to start shooting every second time I retrieved the ball. The next step was as a full participant in shooting 'em up. It was such a disappointment when the ball was like a beach ball, large and smooth. The ball didn't go in the direction you shot because the wind took it in its direction. Very few shots went in, even layups, because the ball's circumference was about the rim's circumference. It would be hard to put the ball inside the rim standing over the rim. On the other hand, what a joy when an accommodating elementary school kid, who didn't know me, asked if I wanted to shoot a few, and the basketball was legal size and almost brand new. I was not too good but I enjoyed playing. The big guys, about seniors in high school I guessed, just kept shooting. They never played games.

Some kid started to talk to me as we were shooting with his ball, "I just got this ball, my other ball finally busted when I hit the bubble on the ball with a hatchet. I hate when the ball has a bubble. You have to try to figure out which way the ball will go. You can't dribble or play a game".

"Most of the time I go to Mueller, I play with a ball with a bubble. It stinks, I know," I said. And I did know it stunk. The same kid asked me, "Wanna play one-on-one or H-O-R-S-E?"

"Play horse? What do you mean?" I wanted to know.

"If one of us makes a shot and the other one misses the very same shot, the guy who missed gets a letter until H-O-R-S-E is spelled out on the loser. One-on-one is where we play a game against each other. Choose odds or even to see who goes first in H-O-R-S-E or one-on-one; which is it?" The kid let me call odd or even.

"H-O-R-S-E," I said in a whisper.

"Odds," I said with fingers crossed.

I chose odds although I didn't know what was to be odd or even.

"Odds it is, you go first. What's your name?" He didn't do anything, yet he said I won. Maybe he thought of a number.

"Bill".

"Ok Bill, take a shot".

"What's your name?"

"Julius".

"Julius what?"

"Julius Peartree".

"Not bad Bill. You were close".

"From the right side, no backboard," Julius called before he shot.

Julius told me that if a player calls his shot and makes it, the other player must duplicate the called shot; like no rim and no backboard.

"Your shot Bill".

"From this corner Julius, no rim".

"Close. Behind the backboard, can't hit the rim Bill".

We played H-O-R-S-E for at least a half hour and the score was: H-O me, zero Julius.

"We have to stop now; I have to get home to do some work. My name is Sylvester, but I like Sliver for my name," Julius said abruptly.

"Just as well because I should go home. I got here by volunteering to pick up my Grandmom's new glasses at the eye doctor's office, near Mueller but nearer to the Carmen movies," I didn't want him to feel bad for calling off the game.

It was then that I realized that I got sidetracked and forgot about the glasses. I ran to the Optometrist's office and got the glasses. I know that Mom and Pop had to sacrifice something to buy these glasses and I was determined to get them home in good shape.

I thought his name was Julius Peartree. He's a good player and he thinks he doesn't need a backboard.

"Where you gone (sic), punk? Give me that bag. What's in it?" said a good-sized bully as he stood in front of me.

"My Grandmom's glasses," was my weak response.

"What's an old Gizzer like Grandmom doing with glasses? Can't she use beer bottle bottoms like every Gizzer should," continued the bully, especially since he detected my weakness.

"I'm late; I gotta run!" I tried to come on a little stronger.

"You run Faggot and don't forget to pick your Pansies on the way home," said the major smart-aleck.

"You nuts Buzzard, he's Fran McCaffrey's brother," interjected a high school girl with a Little Flower uniform and saddle shoes.

"Tell Fran that Buzzard thinks he was lucky making North's JVs. I was sick during the tryouts and he moved into my position on the JVs".

"Buzzard, Fran can beat up seniors, even the ones on North's varsity; he'll kill you if his brother says something" the girl warned.

"Hey Morning Glory, are you gone to tell on me to your big bad brother?" Buzzard was mocking me."Don't worry; I won't say anything to Fran. You do look like a Buzzard, though, but that doesn't make you tough. It makes you ugly". I think I surprised Buzzard. I know I surprised myself.

I passed by a house with a basketball rim with a net. The ball came rolling down the driveway.

"Here's your ball," I said hoping for a couple shots.

I put the bag with the glasses down and took a long shot. The ball came right back to me after it hit the backboard with a thud. I picked the ball up and started to dribble as if I was in a game. It was all right until I dribbled on top of the glasses, which were in a flimsy case marked, "Do not mishandle. These glasses are very fragile." I knew that I had to hustle home and make up a good excuse for smashing Grandmom's glasses. I was getting close to home, passing The Clear (or The Field or the Clearfield) when I thought I spotted Bob Can of Baloney. It was Bob, Mr. Campalonie, I was sure of that but he looked different than he does at the Strand. He was bald. He had hair before. He was all messed up when he was the perfect dresser most other times; even his Santa Claus outfit was always clean and pressed. He needed a shave badly and he looked much shorter than when he is with a bunch of kids. The customer's at The Clear were tall. He was drinking beer and he preached against it to little kids as a Cub scout leader and usher at the Strand. I think Bob was more Bob at the Clearfield; the other side was on the outside of the Clearfield Bar.

"Hi Mr. Campalonie, remember me?" I was sure he would.

"No, should I?" he didn't appear to know me.

"I go to the Strand sometimes".

"Yeah, you do look familiar. Are you one of the guys who sneak in and sneak friends in?" he asked telling me that he really knew what was going on at the movies.

"No," I said although I did sneak in the door and crawl one time to impress Eileen McDermott.

Bob probably works at the Clearfield Bar on weekends only. A tall fourth grader could be close to Bob's height; Santa (Bob) can't let little kids sit on his lap. When Bob's at work, he's on stage, pretending to be somebody different than he is. Even the little kids know he's not Santa. They say "thanks Bob" when he is dressed as Santa handing out candy canes and gifts. I pray that they never make Bob an Elf; the kids would destroy his pride. Why did I call Buzzard ugly? He's ugly alright, but I feel bad about it. I started to get angry with him and I remembered that I gave Joey Ryan a good fight and I beat Mousy even though it was a draw.

Mom, Pop, and Grandmom let me off the hook. They said that everybody makes a mistake and not to worry about breaking the glasses. I went about my normal life, except that basketball started to replace Halfball as my third favorite sport.

I talked to some of the guys I played football with at Hunting Park to see if they would like to challenge St. Henry's or Our Lady of Mercy to a game of basketball. Ramar Broadneck, Ronnie O'Donovan, who thinks he's Leon Hart, Gene Bitterman, Charlie MacDonald, and Mousy wanted to play. Spider Webb wanted to play too but he couldn't practice and would meet us at OLM's gym. By the way, I called "Leon Hart" O'Donovan the Neil Johnston in basketball. I can see Ronnie getting many rebounds. Ramar had to be the best rebounder anywhere. No one would dare to mix it up with him.

We scheduled a practice at Hunting Park after school on Friday. Then I walked down to Broad Street to Our Lady of Mercy (OLM). I knocked on the rectory's door and hoped that someone other than a priest would answer.

"Yes, what can I do for you?' said the priest, whose Roman collar was minus the starched white part.

He wore a medal; I could see the chain. He looked like what a priest should look like, skinny, thick glasses and a long, hooked nose like Pius XII. Frankie Lyman was singing "Why Do Fools Fall in Love" in the background, which made me think he was younger than he looked. He looked to be about Zeke the Madman Barber's age, maybe thirty. He wasn't a Jesuit like the Michigan guy I met; he was too young to have spent fourteen years in the seminary after college. I never saw a priest with an unbuttoned Roman collar before. He let me in as far as the foyer. I saw an old room to my left with dark furniture and with pictures of Angels and the Stations of the Cross. There was a large leather-like chair, perfect for watching the replay of the Irish football games on Sunday mornings. Next to the chair was one of the ashtrays that look like the holder for the big candle we use at Easter time. The floor was wooden and shiny. The door to the room was dark, like the furniture, and as thick as the front door. There was a small table – one like I once saw at Maria's store on Market Street – with holy pictures and an ashtray on it. An umbrella holder was behind the open front door. It was empty but it looked like it could hold about five umbrellas. Using my Boston Blackie techniques to find bad guys, I deduced that there were five priests assigned to the parish.

"Would your school like to play St. Stephen's in basketball?" I sprung on him.

"I don't see why not, but I'm not the coach, Fr. Farley is the coach and he just happens to be here. Father, this young man from St. Stephen's wants to challenge your team to a game of basketball," said the hooked nosed priest.

"Who's your coach?" Fr. Farley asked.

"I guess I am," I replied thinking that I never thought of being a head coach.

"What's your name, coach?" old hooked nose wanted to know.
"Bill McCaffrey".

"Bill, I don't know if we can compete; I hear great things about St. Stephen's team".

"We didn't have a team father until two days ago. Some of our guys are pretty good, I think, though".

"I'll see which of our guys wants to play you. Next Saturday OK with you, if we get five or more players? I'll call your bishop to let him know if the game is on".

"Fr. Farley, could you call me instead of the bishop at SA- 2- 9065?"

"Sure, we can play downstairs, in our gym".

Fr. Farley called before I got home.

"We're on guys and we're supposed to be at OLM on Saturday at 9:00am sharp. Don't miss Friday's practice. It's the only practice we'll have. We can discuss how to get to the game after practice," I acted like a coach talking to his team.

Friday's practice was revealing. I was hoping that at least one of these guys knew how to play basketball. I didn't myself but I could dribble a little and shoot when there's nobody to guard me. I never played a real game with teams. All I knew was shooting like Paul Arizin by bending my legs when I shot. All the players but Mousy and I played on a court, a cement outdoor court with chain nets. Charlie could dribble pretty well and Ramar dared people to out rebound him. Neil Johnston O'Donovan could just run up and down the court scaring the Mercy guys from what I saw. After the first quarter, they wouldn't be scared. They could see that O'Donovan had no idea what he was doing on the court. Gene made three or four beautiful shots from at least ten feet out. The practice lasted about a half hour because no one thought we needed any more. O'Donovan wanted to take the last shot. He went to the foul line and threw up a shot, a bullet that banged against the backboard.

"Nice shot Ronnie; just a little softer next time," was the only response he got. It came from Ramar of all people.

"Thanks, I think I'll be good tomorrow. I'll get up early and shoot for about ten minutes or so; so I think we can win," volunteered our own Neil Johnston.

Oh my God, we have no idea what we're doing. They felt that this half-hour practice was more than enough preparation.

Mousy didn't even practice; he just sat there and blew those things off a dead flower when you say, "She loves me, she loves me not". Charlie was OK but Ramar stole the ball from him every time he tried to dribble. I will never play basketball at Notre Dame. Football and baseball will be enough. I don't want to be the Pope. Pop might've been kidding when he said I'll be the pope. I can't learn enough Latin and I always take too many bottle caps from Cicolli's. The Venango Street kids use bottle caps to play their version of Dodge Ball, called Cap Attack. They throw bottle caps at the kids in the middle of a circle. I made a mistake. None of us knew anything about basketball. I hope the people at OLM understand.

We all agreed to meet at the Broad and Susquehanna subway stop at 8:30 in the morning, which will allow us to get to the school by 8:35. Mousy wanted to walk part of the way home from practice with me. He was very talkative about everything except our game in the morning. He heard about Buzzard and me and the name-calling and threats and had some things to say. Mousy actually looked like a mouse. He was small and dark with black hair and a face that kinda came forward and formed a V in the front.

"You think I look like a mouse, don't you?"

"No I don't Mousy; of course not".

"You were looking at my funny shaped face and small ears; everyone does".

I didn't answer, but I realized that Mousy and I lived with the same problem: Odd shaped heads.

Mousy got my attention and started to talk seriously, "I heard about you and Buzzard and the threats and wise guy stuff. Buzzard's a cool cat, trust me. His Dad hates him and his mother. Buzzard talks about his Dad in glowing ways. Buzzard has two sisters and one brother. His sisters make him happy because they love Buzzard and are not afraid of their Dad when he's around. Buzzard's Dad wants his daughters to study hard and, mostly, look good so they can marry rich guys with money and fame so he can be well known. He, Buzzard, is very handy with wood and wood tools. He makes model planes and boats from scratch without models to copy. He finds odd pieces of wood, any kind of wood and uses that. His scooters are the best. He takes old wooden milk boxes and some wood and he borrows nails and tools from his

Dad's basement. His scooters look nothing like ours do and you can ride them like real scooters. Rich kids come from the outer parts of the city to buy his scooters. He puts bottle caps on the sides of the scooter and charges more money. Some rich kids bring the wood and milk cartons to Buzzard; their parents pay for everything. One kid from the Prep called Bradford wanted to stay around here to make scooters and play Halfball and Buck-Buck. His mother said OK, but his father insisted that he 'leave this filthy place of next generation's factory workers'. The father noticed me noticing him and turned his head the other way".

"Buzzard thought that he could have made North's JVs if he didn't get sick and my brother Fran would get cut. Did you see him play football? Is he good?" I peppered Mousy.

"No, he hates hitting and getting hit. He wasn't sick during the tryouts. He was afraid of not making the team. His Dad played for South Catholic and was a starter. Buzzard is bigger than his Dad was in high school and his Dad thinks he should be a better player. Buzzard is afraid of football. He wants to build houses and buildings like the Empire State Building. Once Buzzard's Dad took a hammer and destroyed a building Buzzard built with an Erector set. Mr. Friel, Buzzard's Dad, fought the Germans in France and he told Buzzard that the French were like little girls. He calls Buzzard Frenchy sometimes when he's at the New Garden of Eden Tap Room. He screams at Buzzard's mother and calls her very bad curse words in front of Buzzard. Mr. Friel blames his wife for Buzzard's athletic ineptness".

I felt bad for Buzzard, especially since I called him ugly to his face. I think that Dr. Ida was right to leave school in the seventh grade. If your family hates you, it's better to quit and start working in Atlantic City. Otto the Outrageous left school in the tenth grade saying he wasted the last two years. Buzzard's father hates him. How can he live like that? Pop loves me though I'm afraid of the crazy lady on my paper route and Horse Head Lady's dogs. I hope OLM gives us a few breaks. Ramar will scare them. Basketball players are real babies compared to football players. Gene doesn't even run up and down the court. Charlie looks at the ground when he dribbles. I only know how to shoot but the ball rarely goes in since I just started. What made me want to challenge them? I wish I was playing Halfball or

anything but basketball against OLM. What if we beat them? Oh God, that would be great.

I wish Buzzard could teach us how to make scooters and benches. Our benches never stand up without leaning against a telephone pole.

"You guys are ten minutes late; let's run to the school," I commanded as the self-appointed coach/captain.

There were a couple players from OLM to greet us and show us where to dress. We didn't know you had to dress because I never saw a grammar school game.

"We'll play like we are, thanks".

"You're gonna play in those clothes? Don'tcha guys have uniforms?" asked OLM's tallest player.

"Most of us have sneaks on, is that enough?"

The Mercy guys came out of somewhere to the court. I didn't see them come out and when I turned around, they were in two lines running one at a time to the basket and shooting short shots. We couldn't get two lines with just six players – Mousy wanted to keep score, so make that five players. O'Donovan's ten to fifteen minutes of practice in the morning didn't do much good; he continued to throw the ball against the back board. Broadneck Ramar kept staring at the Mercy players. After about several seconds of staring, Ramar told me that he wanted number nine.

"I'll run next to him the whole game and he'll never get a shot". It sounded like good basketball strategy to me. Number nine looked like he played for North's varsity.

"OK Ramar, but you have to get the rebounds when we shoot". I wanted Ramar to know his role.

Gene Bitterman went to the bathroom three times while everybody else was shooting and throwing. Ramar had a strange shot. He jumped and bent his legs like Paul Arizin, then landed on his feet and then threw the ball as if he was in a panic. His shots go in more than any other's do somehow. Spider came to the gym at the sound of a loud horn-like alarm. Maybe it's an Air Raid was the thought of three of our players, including me. Mousy thought it was an alarm to alert everyone that the pastor or the cops were coming. It was a warning that the game was to start. It wasn't a warning to the OLM guys; to them it meant "good times".

"Ok, St. Stephen's, who's jumping center? Son, I'm sorry but you can't play with shoes on. This floor is new and we can't get it smudged up. You can put your shoes over next to our bench. Coach Bill, who's the center?," the referee priest asked.

"I don't know what a center does Father," I replied, ashamed of myself.

"St. Stephen's asks for a brief delay to the start of the game. Come over here boys. Do you understand basketball?" Father asked.

"Just taking shots and playing H-O-R-S-E Father," is all I could say.

"Stand here. I'll bring Fr. Farley over," offered the ref.

Fr. Farley spent about a half hour teaching us the basics of basketball. He lined us up by height and O'Donovan was now the center. Charlie had to be near the basket because he was playing with socks that had identical holes on each big toe. Ramar roared for some still unknown reason. Fr. Farley placed him under the basket and taught him how to jump and get the ball. Gene was to play on one side of the court and Ronnie O'Donovan the other. Spider and I were to be something called the backbone or the back something or another.

We were told that we couldn't hit the other team, which pretty much took Ramar out of the game. We couldn't "walk"– move the ball without dribbling. Father waived some rules to another day. We were ready; we got psyched up. O'Donovan stood next to OLM's center and the ref tossed the ball up in the air. The OLM guy jumped and tapped the ball to his teammate. Ronnie forgot to jump.

Ramar had nine fouls in the first half. The entire OLM team had two. Mousy couldn't keep score because the game was too fast and he didn't know you get two points for every regular shot you make and one point for every foul shot that goes in. Spider and I played defense using the windmill style Gene's cousin taught him. All you do is swing your arms like a windmill and the other team can't shoot. O'Donovan outran all the OLM players but he didn't know what to do when he beat them. The OLM guys let us shoot by not playing tight defense. Gene came close twice; O'Donovan brought the house down with his baseball throws at the basket. Spider took a couple shots that almost hit the rim and backboard. The guy assigned to guard me pretended to fall and I took my famous Paul Arizin, Mueller School, shot. It went in and you'd think we just won our third straight World's Series. At halftime, the score was OLM thirty something; St. Stephen's two.

The game got worse in the second half and only the parents of the players and the cheerleaders remained. We lost by many points. OLM stopped keeping score, thank God. We ended up scoring six points. Ramar broke the OLM gym's *team* record for fouls, twenty-one. As the OLM guys went to the shower, we started to leave the gym. Gene had to go to the restroom and Spider lost his PTC subway token. While they were fixing their problems, I looked around the gym. It was dark and cold looking, much like the Ragman's innermost part of his storage area. There was a copy of The Angelus painting and a picture of Cardinal Dougherty and Cardinal O'Hara. There were no images of Our Blessed Mother. I wanted to see what Our Lady of Mercy looked like.

The windows were high up and useless as far as I could see. The priest that first greeted me at OLM's door came over to congratulate us for finishing our first basketball game.

"You fellas will play many more games of basketball and you will thrill your audience with good playing," he assured us.

I think we thrilled our audience already. None of us ever has money so we have to find Spider's token. I've now played my first football, baseball and basketball games and I will never look at those games in the same way. I like all the games and I'll probably stop playing street sports.

An adult in the crowd gave Spider subway money and Gene returned from the bathroom. We started out of the gym when out of nowhere we heard, "Give me an S, S; give me a T, T"...until Steven was spelled out. We spell Stephen with the ph in the middle, not the v. A couple of OLM's cheerleaders cheered for us. Ramar said to O'Donovan that we were close. O'Donovan said that OLM wasn't that good. Spider said that we'd a won if we had the right shoes. Gene agreed with Spider and vowed to try out for North's basketball team so they could play these guys again in high school. The OLM guys will go to Catholic High also called Roman Catholic High. We'll go to North Catholic.

"Thanks for the cheerleading," Gene said.

"We enjoyed the game, St. Stephen's," answered one of the girls who had to be kidding.

"Call us by our normal names," Mousy asked.

"Ok, Ramar, is that your name?" asked the prettiest cheerleader.

"Yeah. Ramar Broadneck."

"I'm Spider".

"I know you're Spider; you're my favorite player for today," responded the shortest cheerleader.

"I'm Lorene and this is Nevada," said the shortest introducing the prettiest.

"I'm O'Donovan and Ronnie at the same time".

"We know Mousy. He spent the entire game sitting next to the cheerleaders' bench," squealed Lorene.

"I'm Bill McCaffrey and I'll be at North next year. Where will you girls go?"

"The rumor has us at Maria Goretti's," answered Nevada.

"Is Nevada your real name?" I inquired as if I never heard strange names.

"It's as real as McCaffrey is your real name".

Nevada was very pretty and very nice. Our team stayed around to talk to Nevada and the other cheerleaders. Ramar, Spider, Gene and O'Donovan had a longer ride than I did. Mousy wanted to walk home and save the dime, his parents gave him for carfare; he didn't need to be bailed out. I had to ride the subway because I had to deliver my Saturday afternoons. My branch manager, Phil, got his friend to deliver my Sunday supplements on the morning of the game. His friend was studying something at Penn where he had to do a real life study about some aspect of people's lives. I was hoping that there were no major disruptions on the route, like stabbings or fights or even the Crazy Lady in one of her dangerous moods. Seeing the Crazy Lady in action might be good information for a researcher.

"What's your last name Nevada?" I asked.

"Nevada".

"What's your first name?"

"Reno".

"You're Reno Nevada?"

"No, call me Butte Montana," Nevada came back with.

"Yep! I will and I know a girl named Paris France".

"I'm only kidding, my name isn't Reno, it's Sierra. My brother's name is Vegas".

"Can I call you Sierra?"

"No, call me Butte. Of course silly, you can call me Sierra. That's my name isn't it?"

I told Sierra all about Carlisle Street and all our games. She told me that her Dad, who worked for the Department of Sanitation, told her many stories about street games. She said that she would ask him about Carlisle Street. Sierra talked about her family and friends. She's the only girl on her block that goes to OLM and, in fact, hers is the only Catholic family on her block. Most of her friends go to Reverend Devine's church. She cheerleads but doesn't like sports. She reads a lot and actually goes inside the library rather than jump from the library steps all day when she is there like we do. Her nuns are like our nuns, except they aren't Sisters of St. Joseph and she never had a visiting nun like Sr. Prophetess. She, like me, found it hard to believe that people in our country could be snickered into taking drugs. She didn't understand the abortion part of the discussion and I didn't push it; this topic was for men to understand and do the right thing. Sierra likes nice clothes and would someday like to live on a ranch in – you got it – Nevada. She was kind enough not to mention our game too much although she did say that Ramar would make OLM a better team if he was on it.

"None of our players are tough; they all like to shoot and pass the ball like Bob Cousy," Sierra said with a look of disgust. Ramar didn't shoot 'til near the end when OLM stood there and literally watched him shoot.

I told her about our football game with Our Lady of Venice and how their concern for their beautiful uniforms cost them the game. I had to leave but I didn't want to. Sierra had to leave also. Maybe she wanted to. I hope not.

"Maybe I'll see you again Bill," said Sierra.

"OK Sierra," was my very unromantic Bif with one F-like reply.

Sierra is as beautiful as Violet or Sonia. Her skin is like Violet's but a little lighter; like coffee with two creams. She is as tall as I am. I hope to see her again. I wish she didn't say maybe. I hope her father knows our block on Carlisle Street. Horse Head Lady and Maria are older versions of Violet, Sonia, and Sierra. Sierra will be a movie star, like Marlene, the husband killer, only saner.

I got home at about one o'clock in the afternoon, served my papers, and collected. I usually collected on Saturday mornings. This unusual collection time was the perfect excuse for customers not to pay me on time.

"I had the money this morning, but had to use it for essentials. I wasn't going to give a stranger your hard earned money so I put it in the bank until next week," Violet, my movie star-like customer left a note taped to her newest door ornament, a leprechaun.

"Bill, don't let that guy be your collector again because he wanted to ask me so many questions about this apartment complex, the neighbors, and other things. He even started to get into my own life and boyfriends. It was none of his biznes (sic). Anyhow, I had to go to work, see you soon. Violet. 'PF' (sic) how did you like my ~~leap~~ new thing on the door". (No "?" was used in this sentence).

Violet usually works on Saturday nights; I guess it's getting late. Hardly anybody paid me. Phil didn't tell me that his friend was going to ask a lot of questions. Ramar and O'Donovan will tell the guys at school that the game was close. Bitterman won't deny it but he won't agree either. Spider will say nothing, as is usual for him. If it wasn't for meeting Sierra, I would want this day to start all over. I wouldn't be worried if we didn't win and I'd spend more time with Sierra.

The guy just wanted to get a date with Violet, I'm sure. Violet wouldn't know when a boy liked her; she probably never had a real boyfriend to go to walks and movies with. I have the six (6 am Mass) tomorrow. Last time it took twenty minutes due to no sermon and very few Communions.

I arrived at the branch at about 6am to pick up my Sundays. Phil and the other guys were reading the front page, which was unheard of. I got my pile – twice as many as the kid with the second most Sundays – and looked to see what was so interesting. Some kid stabbed his father to death.

"Hey, I know this kid, his name is Buzzard," I spit out, "his Dad hates him and his mother". I was picturing Buzzard in a striped uniform on his way to the gas chamber.

Reggie "Bugs" Reynolds, who had forty Sundays, said, "His real name is Mike Friel and he's in my home room at Joachim's. He's real quiet in school. Knobby - North's disciplinarian - caught him smoking on the football practice field a couple times. He's not on the JV's but he hangs around until their practice is over. I think he told his parents that he made the team or why else would he hang around?"

"I thought he was sick during the tryouts Bugs," I said.

Bugs said, "Coach Gillespie wanted to give him equipment to tryout since he's always there; he always said no".

"I called him as ugly as a Buzzard on time. He hated Fran because he wanted the slot that Fran got on the JVs. He looks sad in the picture on the first page, no less; not like he looks when he's at Mueller," I told the guys.

"He's gonna fry, I'm 'tellin you. You can't kill a priest, a cop or a parent even if you're a freshman," Phil added.

"I hope the jury hears how mean Mr. Friel was to Mike and Mrs. Friel," I also told the guys.

If I knew this before the six, I'd ask Fr. Melley to pray for Buzzard's Dad and his family and Buzzard. Buzzard just couldn't take it anymore; he's not a machine that just keeps going. I'll visit him in prison to apologize for calling him ugly. Wait'll I tell Fran. I want to tell Sierra. Maybe this is a good excuse to see her again.

"Mom, his Dad hated him as he always teased him. His mother is gonna crack up and his sisters will never feel fun again," I let Mom know.

"We'll pray for that family at mass this week. Where does the family live?" Mom asked and I saw her sadness.

"I don't know Mom. I see him at Mueller all the time. He's a wise guy but Mousy said he is great with building things like model planes and scooters. Fran knows him; he goes to Joachim's and North".

Mousy, Buzzard's best friend, never came back to Carlisle Street. He only hung out in Sonny's garage, our clubhouse. Mousy and Sonny became good friends and Mousy would not even talk to other people.

Sister Helen told me that she considered asking me to serve Mr. Friel's funeral mass, but I was already committed to serve on the altar when Tommy Milligan says his first mass, the next day. Tommy was a neighborhood favorite, who lived two short blocks from the church. At least three or four altar boys who lived within a few blocks asked to serve Tommy's mass. Sister said that she wanted certain altar boys to serve this mass because there would be Bishops, and priests from all around the diocese. Bishop McCormick supposedly invited his uncle, Cardinal Dougherty. Sister whispered something in the other altar boy's ear right before the mass. He was related to Tommy and lived in another parish. She walked over toward me as if she wanted to whisper something in my ear. I braced myself and looked at my shoes to see if they were shiny. I soaked my hair with Vitalis so that was probably ok.

"William, don't rush through the Confiteor. I hope your shoes are mended because you had holes in them two weeks ago. Sister Assumption tells me that you and she have a secret. I'll pray that I'll be assigning altar boys for your first mass someday".

Tommy's first mass went well. I had my picture taken coming out of the church and with the other kid, Mr. and Mrs. Milligan, the Bishop, the Dean of St. Charles' Seminary and Fr. Milligan. Sister Helen suggested that the other kid and I stand on opposite ends of the line of people, holding candles. It sounded like a good idea to me, but I had no vote. It was six, no's; zero, yeses – the other kid got a vote.

The choir was at its best. I almost forgot my cues when they sang, "Hosanna, Hosanna..." Tommy's so happy today and yesterday, the Friel family was so sad. Fr. Milligan and I are so lucky that our parents love us and let our failures be chalked up to being a kid or being human. Buzzard probably wanted to go to a Trade School and learn carpentry. Mr. Friel would drive Buzzard crazy if he went to a Trade School. Candles represent Angels just like flowers represent all the graces stored up by all the Saints in heaven and earth. I think I made up the flowers' part – maybe not.

Mousy said that Buzzard got As in Algebra, Latin, and Religion and his Dad wanted to know why doing well on the tough courses he didn't get As in History, English and Biology. Fran remembered a day when Mr. Friel came to JV practice and tried to convince the coach that his son, Mike, should be on the team. Coach agreed just by seeing Mike's size. Mike faked a headache or a toothache. Mr. Friel refused to drive Mike home and Mike curled up like someone hiding behind the bushes.

I hope that Mr. Friel is in heaven. Mrs. Friel can't miss and God will listen to Buzzard's side of the story. Lord, help Julius Peachtree or Sliver find his way and his real name. I think he's messed up in some ways.

17

10th Street Corinthians

McDonald and Neville told me to meet them at Hunting Park on Saturday morning, after the eight 8am Mass. I was serving the six (6 am Mass), but I could kill time because I wanted to play baseball on Hunting Park's field. Mom gave me money for pancakes at H&H's and I could shoot baskets at the park if anyone had a ball that they were willing to share. It was in spring, right before Pentecost Sunday. The priest gave his sermon about the Tongues of Fire to the four regular people who I saw frequently at the six. Five times as many Sisters as regulars joined us to made up the congregation of twenty-five. He was a young priest, recently ordained and a product of the Sisters of Saint Joseph's teaching in Bayonne, New Jersey. He told the congregation all that before he started his sermon and after he read the gospel. "A tongue burned miraculously over the heads of each person in the room where the Holy Ghost entered," he told the congregation. He said that we should be on fire for Jesus all the days of our lives.

I saw a painting of the tongues of fire and the disciples in the room at the Art Museum so I could picture what he was saying. The painting had a white dove over the tongues of fire and the people. The painter saw the Holy Ghost this way.

Why tongues of fire? Why not flames of fire? I hated that part of the painting. I like the white doves because it makes more sense. Being on fire for Jesus is a good way to put it. I don't know why I can't adore Jesus like the sisters, priests, and other good people. I appreciate that He died on a cross so we can go to heaven. How can I adore a host? How can the Host be His body and blood? This is hard to listen to and believe.

The Sisters were nodding their heads in unison and the four other members of the congregation kept each of the four corners of the church occupied; that seemed to be about the extent of their interest. Either the regular congregation's heads were already on fire or they preferred an easier way to receive the Seven Gifts and Nine Fruits of the Holy Ghost. I was the only altar boy this day. Ray Albanese was a "no show". Ray was usually a "no show" for the six. He was always ten or fifteen minutes early when the Bishop was the celebrant at the seven.

Ray probably assumed that the Sisters wouldn't be at the six on Saturday morning. Otherwise, believe me he'd be there ahead of schedule checking out the altar so he would be visible and he'd be well groomed – slick hair (his godfather was a barber), shined shoes, and as phony a smile as a human can conjure up.

The young priest came into the altar boys' room after Mass – something I never saw – and started to talk school and sports.

"What grade 'yin?" he inquired.

"Seventh; Sister Rose's class," I answered with some pride.

"It seems so long ago when I was in the sixth grade," Father said as he looked at the ceiling.

"Seventh, Father," I corrected a priest.

"Let's see, two, four, four, and fourteen. That makes twenty-four, twenty-four plus twelve, that's about right" Father calculated after not hearing a word I said.

"You're thirty six, Father,?" I calculated. He added the two years after the sixth grade to the four years of high school to four years of college to how old he was in the seventh grade, twelve. I understood that part but I didn't get the fourteen.

"Just about," he said with a lilt.

"What was the fourteen for? That's a long time," I grilled for information.

"Seminary. I'm a Jesuit and it takes a long time for us to get God's Word through our thick heads," Father said as he tapped his forehead with a half fist.

"Jesuits are the smartest priests from what everybody tells me; you must be smart Father," I assured Father what's his name.

"Do you know anything about the Jesuits?" Father wanted to know.

"Yeah, Father Feeney was excommunicated because he said that only Catholics could go to heaven. Francis Xavier was a Jesuit martyr and Ignatius Loyola formed them with the Pope. They are to be at the disposal of the Pope. The leader of the Jesuits is called the "Black Pope," I went on a little too long I thought.

"Wow, you know most of what there is to know about the Jesuits," said the young priest in an effort to make me feel good.

"Our history book had a chapter on the Jesuits, Father so I read about your order," I replied thanking God that I happened to read that part of the book.

The Sisters clearly are in awe of their products or maybe it's just pride in priests overall. He's twice the age of the big guys yet he looks like one of them. Fourteen years in the seminary. That doesn't seem possible. I'll bet he could tell me why Jesus let the Holy Innocents die. And he probably knows why Jesus told the apostles that Judas was going to betray Him. It's not like Jesus to squeal on anyone. Judas HAD to betray Jesus; he was set up because Jesus already told people he would betray Him. Jesuits have all the answers, bishop Sheen and the Jesuits. Otto the Outrageous said he went to the Jesuit seminary in Gal-o-leo for a few years. I knew where he was for that time period, in elementary school.

"Did you go to Notre Dame?" I continued to grill.

"No, but we played them in football. I went to Michigan. We waited all year to play the Irish so we could beat them. Why did you ask about Notre Dame?" he wondered.

"Isn't Notre Dame a Jesuit school?" I didn't think I needed to ask because I was so convinced it was.

"No, the Holy Cross Fathers teach there. They're a French order," Father corrected me.

"Did you play football at Michigan?" I always ask college men that question.

"Yeah, but I don't think I was very good," Father surprised me because he wasn't very big.

"What did you play?" I always ask if they did play.

"Halfback and defense backfield," he made sense because he couldn't be a lineman.

"Did you get in the Notre Dame game?" I continued grilling.

"Yeah, I played against Notre Dame three times. They were always the best team to play against. They were always challenging and fair," replied a good priest, I could tell.

"I'm going to play for Leahy after high school," I bragged.

"If you do, and I think you will, you will be taught to play hard and practice hard as well. Leahy is a real stickler," Father boosted my confidence.

"Do you like the Yankees?" Father got on to baseball.

"You bet I do," I responded. I liked this priest.

"I'm from northern New Jersey, not too far from Yankee stadium. I've always been a Yankee fan," Father sounded like me.

"I got the 1954 team's autographs, mostly at the railroad station. I met the Mighty Mick. Did you play baseball Father?" I asked thinking I was a big shot with the autographs.

"Yes I sure did," Father said as if he liked baseball more than football.

"Who'd you play for?" was again one of my standard questions.

"I'm glad you asked; the Yankees! The summer after college, I played for my favorite team. I played in the minors for three months and in the big leagues from about the 15th of September until the season was over. I played baseball for Michigan too," father informed me.

"What position?" I asked.

"Centerfield!" he answered.

"Did you really play centerfield for the Yankees?" I exclaimed.

"I was on the team for one season, yeah. DiMaggio was the centerfielder so I had to wait to play," Father told me.

"I'm meeting some of the Nicetown guys after the eight. We're playing baseball this morning. I'm going to H&H for pancakes until after the eight," I said though this wasn't like playing for the Yankees.

"I'm having breakfast with the good sisters, who invited me to say Mass this morning. I'll watch for you at Notre Dame and Yankee stadium. Sister St. Theresa was my seventh grade teacher and I'm visiting her. She actually taught me how to play baseball. She managed our CYO team and she knew what she was talking about. She could catch a long fly ball. She taught us how to listen for the crack of the bat and get a jump on the ball. You guys should ask her for some pointers. She'd be happy to help your team," Father finished our conversation with the hope that I play for Notre Dame and the Yankees. He followed the good sisters out the side door, genuflecting in front of the Blessed Mother's altar.

He's a foot taller than the tallest sister, Sister Clare. He's too old to play punch-me-as-hard-as-you-can with Bif with one F.

Priests are good athletes sometimes. Why does someone become a priest? Sister said it's a calling from God. He could have been on the Yankees all those fourteen years. I'll learn from him not to get out of the Yankees and go into the priesthood. I couldn't tell him that I'm planning to be the first American Pope. He wouldn't understand how the McCaffreys think.

I waited in the altar boys' room after the eight. Neville and McDonald said they were too tired to play ball. Actually, I never saw these two play baseball. McDonald said that I should go to Hunting Park anyway because many teams needed players when some of their players don't show up. Neville agreed and said that we could do this another time. McDonald was known as the biggest talker and the shortest doer in Nicetown. He was very short and he had a round face and arms longer than they should have been. His rosaries always fell out of his pocket when he served the six and the sisters happened to occupy the front pews. He'd have them hanging out of his pocket then pull at them when we knelt down for the opening prayers. His Latin made no sense. He didn't know the responses. He followed the other altar boy's motions. One time a priest asked Neville who McDonald was and what grade was he in. Neville said that he was in the fourth grade even though he was in Neville's seventh grade classroom. Neville knew his Latin but he never told the truth.

Theodore Neville claimed to have had dates with several college juniors and seniors. He couldn't remember all their names but he could always describe how beautiful they were. It might have been true but if it were true it would have been the first time. Every Monday morning, rain or shine, Theodore told about his weekend parties at Temple, Penn, LaSalle, Haverford and he even spent a weekend at Prince town (sic) in New Jersey.

I'm glad they're not going to the park. I'll find something to do. Horse Head Lady and Joan the diving diva promised to play double-dutch jump rope with the girls. I guess I could go and do double-dutch with them. I never got the priest's name or autograph. I wonder if he had a Topps' card.

I debated whether to go home or go to the park and play on a real baseball field for the first time in my life. I went to the park. Bikers, runners, basketball players filled the park and all the baseball diamonds were taken. Most of the games were underway. However, I saw kids about my age just standing around waiting to start, I guessed. There was total silence, like a moment of silence for some important person's death.

My glove gave me away as I walked towards the muted field. They could see that I wanted to play baseball. I had the kind of glove that infielders used, not catchers or first basemen mitts. At Johnson Wax's field, a glove was a glove but I noticed that one catcher's mitt and one First basemen's mitt hung from the batting cage. My glove looked brand new because I polished it with Vaseline or Noxzema. Both teams had uniforms and gloves. A few bats were on the ground or upright against the batting cage. The area behind the plate was all dirt and coke bottles were standing up in the back of the cage. The coke bottles became targets for BB guns or stones, I could tell. I saw many broken coke bottles surrounded by stones and little black BB's. There was a natural dirt line from the plate to the pitcher's mound – where the grass was trampled on many times. The bases were real bases, not rocks or old t-shirts all rolled up. There was no wall around center field. A long drive to center could end up being an easy inside the park homer. Ten yards past where the left fielder would play was a road. The leftfielder or centerfielder would have to run a long way if somebody really got hold of one in his direction. There were benches and picnic tables behind right field. The apparent manager of one of the teams, the one that clearly lacked substitute players had a Phillies Whiz Kids hat on and a pencil going up it right between his right eye and his right ear. The pencil said something that was unreadable; there was no eraser left and there were teeth marks all over it. He looked like a person who would chew on a pencil, untidy and disoriented. Nine - I counted - players for his teams, the 10th Street Corinthians, were waiting with their manager for a couple of no shows. I guessed that at least one of the nine guys didn't play or couldn't play.

"How old are you kid?" the manager wanted to know.

"Twelve until September," I hoped it would be ok.

"Can you play today?" he asked as if he had no other option, which he didn't.

"Yes, sure, where?" I accepted.

"Right field," My first real manager assigned me.

"Ok," I assented.

The manager explained a few things, "We're the 10th Street Corinthians as you can see from our uniforms. You'll bat ninth.

We're the visitors so we're up. My name is Mr. Smalley and I'm the manager. What's your name?"

"Bill".

"Bill what?" he needed to know for the scorecard.

"Bill McCaffrey, from Broad and Clearfield and St. Stephen's parish," I thought he'd like to know.

"Keep the St. Stephen's thing to yourself". We're missing two players. We have nine but one kid doesn't want to play because he is afraid of hot grounders on this field," said the manager as if this was a bad field, which it was not.

Right field is Elmer Valo's, Hank Bauer's, and Dick Sisler's position. It was the Babe's too. I hope that it all looks like it does when we're hitting them out on Johnson's Wax's lot. I never batted against a pitcher in a hardball game. I see the mound close up. I just want to make contact with the ball. I don't feel at home on a Protestant team. The manager is talking too much. He might be the pastor or the lead singer of the church. I'll get Fr. Martin's blessing to play for a Protestant team. If he says no, I'll ask him why we don't have a team. This can't be a mortal sin; I hope not anyway.

"Joey, Larry, Tom M, Greg, Bob, Tom B, Dick, Rufus, and Tim will bat last. Rufus, keep a towel on your right shoulder and arm. Tom J, do you have the catcher's equipment? It's all here Smiley, er Mr. Smalley. Joey, you're up. Don't swing on the first pitch. Larry, get on deck. Tim you get the balls if they go foul on the first base side. Put the balls we used for practice in the bag. It's over there near the big tree. Bring the bag over here when you put the balls in order Mr. Smalley.

I'm lost already. I didn't know what he was doing calling out the names of the players. I never played with a catcher with catcher's equipment on my team. I'll have to wait to bat and that's good. What's 'on deck' mean? He said Tim but he meant me. The 10th Street uniforms look like the Reds with their cut off sleeves. The players have their names on their gloves. I didn't think of that. Joey has number 7. Why is our street so famous for Wireball and Halfball that kids come from other neighborhoods sometimes? Who cares about Wireball and Halfball? This is baseball. This pitcher is slow; I'll kill his pitches. I'm not too scared. These guys are my age.

"Joey, I said not to swing at the first pitch. This kid would walk you if he throws a ball on the first pitch. Larry you're up now. Tom M, get on deck. Let the first pitch go by. Tim, move that bag with the bats closer to our bench," directed Mr. Smalley, who got messier every minute.

Larry heard the same instructions as Joey; do not swing at the first pitch. Larry swung at the first three pitches and struck out. Tom M imitated Stan Lopata by crouching down as if he was half sitting. He was mocking a major league catcher. Our team made progress though; it took Tom M four pitches to strike out. We went to the field; me for the first time in my life.

I positioned myself behind first base by about twenty-five yards. Our centerfielder, Greg I think, and our left fielder, Larry, were having fun throwing the ball to each other. They'd throw pop ups or grounders or line drives to each other. They caught about half of them. Rufus was throwing pitches to warm up. He looked good and fast too. The problem was that Visitation, our competitor, could hit fastballs and it was two zip at the end of the first inning. Greg, Bob, and Tom J took a little longer than Joey, Larry, and Greg did in the first inning, but the results were the same. Visitation kept going. At the end of the second inning, the score was five zip.

I came running off the field worrying that I'd make a fool of myself at my very first time at bat with a real pitcher, on a real field, with baseballs with covers and bats that weren't broken, nailed and taped with electric tape to prevent batters from getting cut by the nail or splintered by the bat.

This is so strange, like playing against Our Lady of Venice in football with their uniforms and techniques. Greg doesn't stop. He's throwing stones at Larry as he leaves the field. He doesn't run to the bench like the Yankees and As do.

Visitation put in a new pitcher. He was faster than the first guy and much bigger. He laughed a lot and picked up dirt on the mound to pretend he was using resin. Dick held the bat vertically and leaned his body forward, but not too forward. He could never get that bat around to hit a fastball the way he held it. Mr. Smalley didn't care; neither did Dick. Mr. Smalley stopped telling guys to wait it out. Dick actually hit the ball foul to right field but struck out two pitches later. He looked at his father – or some older man near third base –

and smiled after he hit the foul. The father smiled back and gestured to let Dick know he was proud of the foul ball he hit.

"Rufus, you're up. Tim come over here," ordered Mr. Smalley.

"Tim, try to get hit by a pitch. It won't hurt. The other guys, who can hit, will drive you in. OK?" said the manager trying to spoil my debut.

"My name is Bill, Mr. Smalley," I calmly let him know.

"I know that, you told me. Now try to get hit by the pitch, Tim," Mr. Smalley acknowledged.

"Let's go Rufus, knock it out of the park" was my contribution to the team's energy. We cheered for the As and the Yankees when the game was tight. Rufus looked at me and laughed. He looked at Joey, Greg and Tom J; the four of them laughed at me in unison. Mr. Smalley was talking to Joey, probably telling him that I'll be hit with a pitch so be ready to bring me in. Rufus stunk as a batter (and pitcher to be honest) so the new pitcher notched two quick outs. Rufus pointed to center field when he came to bat much like Babe Ruth did to signify that he was going to hit a home run to center field. Of course, this was an extension of all the joking and mocking that had been going on so far. Unlike the Babe, Rufus hit a grounder, a weak grounder, to the pitcher, who threw him out.

"Bill, remember what I told you. We'll bring you in," lied the manager. Then, in a whisper he said, "Try to get hit. It won't hurt and we can win if you do".

I'm not taking a dive for anyone, especially Mr. Smalley and this team. Pop and Mom never deceived anyone, never. Uncle Dan would never take a dive at the Cambria. Even Bif with one F didn't take a dive at the Cambria and he could have made good money if he did. Paddy's Taproom people don't take dive. The Irish don't give away points to anybody; Leahy would drop them from the team if they did. Mantle and Zernial wouldn't stop swinging hard even if they were well ahead. All the A's hustle all the time. I can't dive; I can't dive, Mary Our Mother, remind me not to dive when I'm at bat.

This at bat is one I'll never forget because it's the first one. The sky is blue and very good for a baseball game. The clouds are golden. How can that be?

Thanks to the people who influenced my life – none who would take a dive - I started to feel confident and very anxious to get up to bat for the first time in my life. I went over to the bat pile and looked for one with a thick handle, like Gus Zernial's.

"Take any bat, Ted, it won't matter; you know what I mean," peeped impish Mr. Smalley, who was bad with names.

I chose one that I liked. It had a red dot with a "#36" sticker on the bottom of the handle.

"Batter up; let's go" screamed the umpire, who stood behind home plate and wore a mask and a hefty chest protector.

"That's our slugger," yelled out Joey in as sarcastic a tune as there ever was.

I went into a batter's box for the first time ever in my life and I started to get worried that I'd make a fool of myself. "Savior of the world, save Russia" came to mind, as did "Bless Us O Lord and These Thy Gifts"; "O my God I am heartily sorry" and "Crown Thee with Many Crowns". I tried to line up with the plate and move away from the plate until I thought the bat's sweet spot would be right over the plate.

"You're too close to the plate, move back," screamed the ump.

If the ump said so, I did it. Visitation's new pitcher started to show off. He picked up some dirt and let it trickle through his fingers, signifying, I think, that he's coming after me. The sky was what I call Blessed Mother blue, so light that it easily could be mistaken for blue tinted white. The pitcher bent forward and acted as if he was getting signs from the catcher. He shook off a few pitches like the major leaguers do then he went into some Vinegar Bend Mizell exaggerated wind up. He threw the first pitch I ever saw from the batter's box of a real field. The ball looks like a beach ball. I see it like Ted Williams sees pitches. I'm 'gonna knock it 'outta the park.

"Swing Bill, swing," somebody said.

I swung with all my might and I connected. The ball went over the left fielder's head into the street area. I ran as fast as I could but it occurred to me that I didn't know where second base was. I touched first base and ran out towards center field. Somebody yelled, "Where are 'yaw gone; run back to second and keep going to home plate".

I turned back and kept running even though I remembered that even Ronnie could beat me in a race. I was too slow to go all the way. People kept yelling for me to go home. I touched second and saw third. The coach at third yelled for me to get going, run. I touched third and headed home. The third base coach thought I could make it, so I felt good. I touched home plate and proudly thought to myself that this was going to be a fun summer.

None of my teammates greeted me and Mr. Smalley came over and said that he was proud that he told me how to hold a bat and swing at good pitches. When we got up again, Joey struck out and, again, he swung on the first pitch, a high and outside fastball. Back to right field. I had no action in the field so far. That was short lived.

The first batter hit a routine grounder to first. He was out on a good play by Joey. The second and third batters walked. Their slugger, Bison Byron, was up and he nailed one, foul. Bison grabbed his bat and slammed it on home plate. The Visitation runners on base both stole bases. Second and third, one out. Bison hit a short pop up to the area between half way from first to second and right field, a Texas leaguer. I made the catch and stood there wondering what I was supposed to do.

"Throw it to Bob," hollered every Corinthians in North America, I swear.

I threw it home with all I had. I learned to throw beat up baseballs from out of bounds near third base at Johnson Wax. Sometimes the ball had no cover or electrician's tape around it and it unraveled by the time it got to first.

"You're out!" The umps words meant everything to me.

The next batter stood at bat while three strikes went by him. Our turn again. I can't wait.

I wished that they would yell the position; I didn't know Bob or that he was our catcher. He's not the catcher, I don't think. It's like somebody telling you to turn west and you not know which way is west. I'm sure that I'll be invited back to play next week.

"Nice throw! Good homer. What's your name?" I heard all these nice words as I was running toward our bench. The Visitation players and parents were the ones with the complements, not the mighty 10th Street crew.

An inning or two later I was going to get on deck. When I went to the pile of bats, I couldn't find the one with the red dot and #36. In fact, the pile of bats became three or four skinny, ugly, sissy bats. I grabbed what looked like the best of the lot and repositioned myself in my favorite batter's box. No more mocking, no more fake resin, no instructions to take a dive, no more yawning; the Visitation people watched. My teammates were sitting on the bench kicking dirt on to each other.

Things are different this time but I can't always get a lucky pitch like before. The left fielder doesn't want to go back but his manager makes him. Mr. Smalley has the top of his fingers in the cage. His Phillies hat is way back on his head. His well chewed, eraserless pencil is on his ear and he's yelling, "Do it again Tim". I'd like to tell him that I'm not Tim but it doesn't matter. He wanted to impress the mothers with his big time show off tough guy stuff.

First pitch, "whack," a single between third and shortstop. I ran to first and stopped.

"Take a lead, about six feet," whispered our first base coach, who had a t-shirt that said, "10th Street Atheists vs. 9th Street Hypocrites".

The pitcher looked angry at what he just did and started to talk to himself – he saw Ryan Duren do that. He quickly stopped talking and threw the ball to their first baseman, who tagged me.

"Out! Yerout! Take a seat," screamed the ump at first base as he put his right hand behind his right ear with the thumb of his right hand dominating the picture.

"Why'd jah stand there? You were picked off," screamed the first base coach as if I was suppose to know you can be called out if you get picked off.

I stood there because he told me to stand there, six feet from the base but I kept quiet. I didn't know about pick offs. I saw this scene many times at Shibe Park; now I know what it means when the runner dives back to first. Manager Smalley shook his head as if he just lost in the numbers game by one number. "Go sit down" was his best response to my negligence. The first base ump asked me if I felt embarrassed or ashamed that I got picked off.

Why is our coach wearing a 10th Street Atheists vs. 9th Street Hypocrites t-shirt? I'm learning about real baseball. That's good because I can't stay where I am long. I have to progress quickly. I'll make the mistakes now. I'll never get picked off again when I find out what I'm supposed to do.

The seventh inning didn't come too soon for the big hitters.

"Smalley, when's the next game?" asked Greg, I think his name was Greg.

"Refer to me as Mr. Smalley from now on. Didn't your parents teach you manners? Next Saturday, same time, field C" Mr. Smalley said so that all the players could hear him.

Everybody had to pick up the bats and balls and put them in Mr. Smalley's duffle bag. One or two guys helped. Tom J, again, I think it was Tom J, picked up a handful of dirt and put it in the bag. We lost. Nobody cared. Losing was expected. Mr. Smalley didn't call a practice session. The mothers weren't happy and the fathers promised their sons that they would teach them how to hit.

"Who 'dwee' play next week, 8th Street Buddhists?" Joey wanted to know.

"I think it's the Germantown Cubs; and they're good," said one of the coaches, not the one with the t-shirt.

"They must be; they have Ernie Banks. Am I pitching next week?" asked Rufus who could be a good pitcher.

"We'll see Rufus; you messed around today and you didn't even pick up the equipment," Mr. Smalley noted.

"Wait Mr. Smalley, I see a bat under that bush," said Rufus.

I wondered how he could see the bat in all those weeds. How did it get there? I wondered.

"This is my son's favorite bat. He has #36 stuck to it because Robin Roberts is his favorite player. Thanks for finding it Rufus," said Mr. Smalley.

That's my favorite bat too, I said to myself. Rufus knew just where to get it; he must be the one who hid it. The walk home was longer than usual because I was very tired.

"Bill, you didn't get to Confession. When can you go?" Mom was like an alarm clock that rang when we had to get up, take out the ashes or trash, watch Bishop Sheen or go to Confession- twice a month.

"Maybe today," I hoped I could.

It was Saturday, one week after my first real baseball game. I had the six again and Albanese didn't show up. The Jesuit was back to where ever he came from. Father Visitor, a visiting priest from a Catholic college in West Virginia, almost broke another visiting priest's record of a fourteen minute mass. He said thanks to me twice; once when I poured water over his hands and at the end of mass. He packed his chalice in his black box, which was like all the other black boxes I saw, black with red lining. I always took notice of the priest's chalices. Most were beautiful and many were sentimental. One priest told me that his father made his and melted his wedding ring with the gold to make it. His mother didn't want to melt her wedding ring, but she contributed a couple precious gold coins to the effort.

I took off as fast as the priest said mass and headed home to touch base and eat Cream of Wheat, then go right back to where I just came from to play ball – about four miles in total. Doc the Clock and Uncle Matt were on Broad Street, near the Allegheny Avenue subway stop. It was somewhat early, like seven-thirty or there about and I had time to chat, but I wanted to get to the park and find field C. I tried to get a couple of the Johnson's Wax guys to join me. They didn't want to play in front of people. Renaldo the Purloiner got a box of hardballs, brand new with the hide and stitches looking like the National League ball Granny Hamner hit to me. There was a new sign on the wall at Johnson' Wax, which was the target for double hitters. The sign said that trespassers would be prosecuted and fined. There was never a security cop or a regular cop anywhere near Johnson's Wax. The games were played as if the sign didn't exist. I planned to stop in Temple hospital for water. I went into the hospital's west wing even though the east wing had nicer nurses and doctors. I had to cross Broad Street to get to the east wing – it wasn't worth it, I thought.

"Who are you to tell me that I am not having a heart attack? I'm a doctor too and I know when I'm having a heart attack" the voice was familiar. "I should be in your Intensive Care Unit not in your Insensitive Care Unit".

God, I hope that's not Dr. Ida.

I hadn't seen him for a long time. I heard he was a doctor now at fifteen and with no medical training. He called himself Dr. Ida from what the word around the neighborhood said.

"There's someone I know; a former patient. Young man, tell these people who I am," asked a fifteen year old with a lot of guts.

"He's Dr. Ida, a doctor to the people who live around my neighborhood," I provided a witness for him.

The good doctor and I walked out of the west wing on to Broad Street. He actually looked like he could be eighteen, but not a real certified doctor's age.

"Didn't I cure you of something? I'm sure I did," inquired Dr. Ida.

"Well Dr. Ida, before you were a doctor you did tell me that the best things for my sun poison would be cold water with ice and a drop of blue ink. The ink has an ingredient in it that 'makes hot skin not so hot', you said," I answered the doctor.

"Where are you going young man?" inquired the good doctor, my age superior by maybe two years.

"To Hunting Park to play baseball Dr. Ida; you know my name. You're just a couple years older than I am".

"I played baseball in medical school. We played other medical schools and Catholic seminaries".

"What position did you play?"

"I knew you were going to ask me that. Is there a second center player?"

Dr. Ida's Story

Dr. Ida told me what I think is just about the whole story of his life.

In my last ever confession, the Cardinal, Father Something or other, wouldn't forgive my sins. He said that I didn't 'Promise to go and sin no more'. I couldn't make that promise. I had plans for that day that required sinning. I had to sin to get something, a job. I knew I had to tell the person that I had experience-painting houses. I was broke and I needed this job real bad. I was 'gonna steal Tasty Kake lemon pies and hoagies when Gatemouth wasn't looking. I wish that I had the 'firm purpose of not sinning', but I get hungry and thirsty. I wish I was an altar boy again. I wish I stayed in St. Stephen's school then go to North. I used to like First Fridays and not eating meat before Communion. It was when I knew that I could never agree to sin no more that I left the Catholic faith. I think I was in seventh grade".

Dr. Ida continued, "Before I left being a Catholic, my Dad stopped going to church after he had a fight with the reverend father over the Communion being a real body. He hated the Catholics after that; he would kill me if he knew I was an altar boy. He didn't know that I was going to St. Stephen's because he never asked me and didn't seem to care about it. My mother went to the early masses when my father slept or didn't come home until late the next day. I preferred it when he didn't come home; so did Mom".

This was sad and I didn't know what to do, except listen, "I quit St. Stephen's when I saw my father go crazy on Mom because she gave a dollar to the priest at the block collection visit. Before that, I stayed in St. Stephen's as a non-Catholic student. Mom worked at The Undenter's Body Shop. She was a taper and painter. She loved the job because all the people there knew her from St. Stephen's grammar school and they told her how smart she was and that they rated the girls for prettiness and that she always won by all the votes. My Mom was Blessed Mary in her fourth grade Christmas play. My mom has eight kids and we all adore her. Mom was on Little Flower's student council and she sang a duet with a senior at North in North's annual musical. Her name got mentioned five times at her Little Flower graduation for academic achievements. She did all this, by the way, while she worked on weekends at H&H's on Broad Street. Hey, I forgot, a committee of women who looked for beauty contests' contestants approached my Mom to ask her if she could represent Philadelphia County in the Miss Pennsylvania contest. She could have gone to Atlantic City for Miss America. Singing was her talent. Her beauty was visible to everyone".

Dr. Ida really loves his mother like I do my Mom. I wish his father was nicer to her.

The story kept going and Dr. Ida was on a roll, Of course, Mom had to say no to the ladies because she had very few clothes and she wasn't a college student. The committee agreed to help with the wardrobe and college tuition – Mom had at least three full academic scholarships to good schools, including Penn. One of the committee's women taught singing at Temple and Swarthmore. Mrs. Hemp, this teacher's name, wanted to 'rope' Mom into going to either school. Nothing could convince Mom because she knew that, underlining all of these scholarship offers was the income that her parents counted on. Mom could never ask to be relieved of this responsibility. If Mom didn't bring home an income after she finished high school, her family wouldn't have survived. I don't know what work she did after high school but it wasn't anywhere near what she should have been doing. Mom never told me things about her: my father did! He truly loved her and wanted to work so she could go to college, become Miss America, climb mountains, sing at the Met, visit a hundred countries, sing the Mass at St. Peter's in Rome, and raise about ten or twelve kids. My father could have made these opportunities available for Mom because he was a graduate, with highest distinction, triple E Engineering from Fordham".

Ida went on, "My father went to work for IBM as one of their developers of Electronic Data Processing in Endicott, New York. Mom told me about my father. She was as proud of him as he was of her. My parents dated when my father worked in Endicott. They talked about marriage, but Mom could never leave this area. She advanced to the primary breadwinner for her family with some added responsibilities, like caring for her baby brother. My father loved working at IBM and asked for a lower paying job in the Philadelphia area so he could marry Mom and stay with IBM. IBM just happened to have a Customer Engineering position open in Philadelphia, where he would fix IBM machines for some very important accounts: Defense Supply, RCA in Camden, the Navy Yard and several smaller, but not less important to IBM, accounts. When he came to interview with the IBM manager, Mr. Larson, he not only got the job, but IBM paid to move him".

Ida didn't take a break, "Mom and my father got married at St. Stephen's on a snowy day by Father Goldfield, S.J., a Jesuit from the Bronx, New York. They stayed in our neighborhood and lived in a third story apartment on top of the magic shop".

"Not the magic shop on Broad Street, near Tioga?," I interjected.

"Yes, that one" he answered and continued without missing a beat.

"One of my father's teammates at Fordham was their best man. He had an Italian name like Lombard or D'Umbardy. My father played for the famous Leahy at Fordham, I think. Mom's little brother moved in with them and all was well. Mom got pregnant two months after they were married. All the talk about college for Mom, beauty contests, travel and everything else came to a halt. "Maybe after the kids get to college" were the words used by my father to soothe my parents' disappointment. Mom loved the living daylights out of my oldest sister, Veronica Macgregor McCauley (her words). She quit her job, a good job as a management trainee for the Philadelphia Mint, to raise her. My father wasn't too happy at this time and his personality changed. I don't know why. Mom and my father both took career hits, but Mom was used to getting hits now and then; my father wasn't. He went to Fordham on an academic scholarship combined with a Grant-in-Aid to play football. My grandfather, my father's father, was the president of a large shoe company. My father was starting to miss work and didn't even meet his friends at the Fordham-Penn or Villanova game at Franklin field or Municipal Stadium. I don't know which".

Ida started to get emotional, "At my younger sister's Baptism my father, who we called Dad up to this time, started to drink even more heavily. This led to total alcoholism and a total destruction of our family. He was mean and vicious all the time".

I interjected again, "Did you go to Simon Mueller when you left St. Stephen's?"

"No, I went there and they said I needed to bring my parents. I couldn't tell my father that I was in a Catholic school and I couldn't tell Mom that I left Catholic school. I waited 'til the next reports were handed out, then I took a bus to Atlantic City and got a job as a gofer in a huge hotel. I wrote letters to Mom and had a friend mail them from Trenton. There I met the girl of my dreams and then some" Ida smiled as he said this, thank God.

"She was a waitress at our hotel and she looked like Grace Kelly, but with a nicer attitude. She was going to Penn State and worked at the shore in the summers. She went to the ocean at 7 am every morning and rode waves until 9 am or so. She liked my poems and paintings. They were all about being home with the family at different times during the year. Kinda' like Rockwell in writing and a poet like the guy who wrote the poems in our Poetry books in sixth or seventh grade. When we went out she wore her finest clothes and put on some perfume designed to 'make the men in your life want to be with you and not their other girl friends'. That's the way I described her perfume. She said, 'Thanks, now I feel better'. Before our first date she was entered into "The Lifeguard's Dream Date for 1955".

"She wasn't crowned 'The Lifeguard's Dream Date for 1955' because her lifeguard boyfriend quit right before the contest, which she was told she already won. The lifeguards voted a week before they were supposed to settle some bets and to give them time to look over the contestants without having to judge them during the real contest. She had an invitation for two to the party and wanted the rest of the crowd to know she wasn't bothered by the betrayal of her lifeguard boyfriend. She thought that her boy- friend quit being a lifeguard because he couldn't swim too well and he would be caught eventually. She still expected them to go to the contest. When she found out he wasn't going, she invited me. The boyfriend's roommate at Slippery Rock State Teacher's College was on the swim team. He passed his own lifeguard test and the tests for at least four others, including her boyfriend. A local TV program, called 'That Man, McCann', was doing a special about the lifeguards and how well they are trained, tested, and retested throughout the summer. Her boyfriend was chosen to swim out for a quarter mile with a life preserver on his shoulder. The lead lifeguards choose him because he scored so well in the qualifying test. Her boy friend packed his bags and left without telling anyone. The truth always destroys lies. Ever notice that?"

I was becoming totally amazed by this guy as he continued, "We went out a couple times after that and we hit it off well. One night we were driving to the hotel, where she lived, and a cop pulled me over. Of course, I had no driver's license – he was fourteen or fifteen - and my car was in my friend's name due to being underage. It wasn't really my friend's name either. It was then that the truth came out".

"The cop wanted to see some identification, like a draft card, which I was three or four years away from getting. He looked at my girlfriend and said that he'd let us go if she had a driver's license. She did. She got in the driver's seat and stayed there until the cop drove away; then I drove again. She cried the rest of the way home. I felt bad too because I lied to her but she should've asked me my age when she asked me to take her to the lifeguard's party".

The story never ends, "My girlfriend now had questions like:

"How old are you Sean – I used Sean to protect myself – and why did you tell me that you were a junior at Fordham? Why Fordham anyway?"

"I'm fifteen and twenty-two I told her. Fifteen years old and twenty-two years experienced. Fordham is where I planned to go someday, when I get my GED," I said. I was almost honest all the way.

"I can't see you anymore outside work; you're too young. We'll be friends and I'll still share tips with you when you bus my tables, but we can't go out. How'd you get that car anyway?" she wanted to know.

"I know a good used car dealer who specializes in underage kids. He recommended that I buy the driver's license with the car, but I didn't have the ten dollars. Can you lend me ten until I bus your tables for ten dollars worth?" I tried to be funny.

"Sean, you are impossible. Is your name really Sean Devlin?" she wanted to know this too.

"No, it's Shane McCauley. I bought the car to take you to our first date. Are you going to give me back my poems, stories, and paintings?" I asked though I wanted her to keep them.

"No, they're mine and we did have some very good times together," she made my day.

"I didn't know your name, so I used Grace in my poems. Was that ok?" I was serious this time.

"I never told you my name; it's Shannon, Shannon O'Malley" Shannon too came clean.

"Are you related to Fr. O'Malley in the movie Going My Way?" I asked hoping she was.

"No, but my father is Frank O'Malley, who suggested to the big wigs in Hollywood that Victor McGleglan was a natural for 'The Informer', she said and she made me happy to hear that.

"I'll see you in work on Monday; I'll take your tables" I either threatened her or made her happy.

"Thanks for buying the car for our date. I'll cherish that thought as long as I live," Shannon wrapped up a special evening.

The crook specializes in underaged kids; what's that? This has to be true; Shane wouldn't normally lie to anyone unless he had to help them or somebody else. Why didn't they know each other's name is beyond me, but that's what happens when you try to fake somebody out.

Shane had more to say and I was spellbound, "Shannon O'Malley didn't come to work on Monday. I got a letter from her from Princeton University. She went there, not Penn State, and she wrote that she was an English Literature major and she showed my poems to her favorite professor, who encouraged her to encourage me to write more and more poems. The emotion and honesty I wrote into my poems was far more important to him than the numerous misspellings, she wrote. In fact, the professor suggested that I simply don't worry about spelling; just write my deep-felt, heartfelt emotions. I never wrote another poem or story. The misspellings were part of my style. She never wrote to me again. I joined the Navy at sixteen, lying about my age again. I told the recruiter that I was eighteen. You had to be seventeen, I think".

Shane made a big move in his life, "The Navy recruiter was a conman, like me. 'Well, you got good scores in the test; I'll write eighteen' he said. I was assigned to a Destroyer Escort".

"Hey Shane, guess what?" I interjected for the third time, "my Pop was on a Destroyer Escort, the USS Jacquard, in the Pacific".

"This was near Korea for me," Shane said as he kept going, "My Commanding Officer, stationed in Seoul, assigned me to his personal staff to write speeches, reports, and articles for the Navy magazine. The Navy wanted me to re-up, promising me that I could finish college, by-pass high school, and become an Officer some day. I wanted to be a doctor. The Navy had other plans. I left early with an Honorable Discharge. That's when I became Dr. Ida. I knew the patients I would have weren't hung up on degrees or fancy pansy offices. They needed help and I was the man".

"As a doctor now, I practiced downtown around the Race and Vine and South Street areas. My practice went all the way from 13th Street to and including the docks and from Vine Street all the way to South Street. The Reading Railroad station and the Greyhound station are in my primary area. Ignorant people referred to my area as the armpit of Philadelphia or Pigs-alley. My patients lived in empty icebox boxes, abandoned buildings near the river, police cellblocks, and outside, under old blankets or discarded horse blankets from the mounted police's barracks. One woman, who made smokers on one 3rd Street, slept in the building where they made smokers. Her movie name was 'Dora, the Little Rascal'. She wasn't a star and I didn't care. Once she paid me with a personal showing of her latest flick, "Memories Are Made of This". From that point on, I only saw Dora for colds and earaches, which are free. All my services are free".

Shane was where God wanted him to be. "Most of the time my patients had oozing sores or bloody mouths received from their friends, who wanted their blankets or their money. One of my all time favorites, I'll call him Cagney because he had swagger, got day jobs at a filthy employment agency on 13th Street, across from the Reading station that had ongoing needs for dish washers and blood donors. Every now and then, Jewels, the owner of the agency would have a pressing need for volunteers for a special study by some medical or veterinarians' school. Jewel's dishwashers and blood donors' ad was at least twenty years old. It was written on the back of a "Roosevelt

One More Time for President" cardboard sign. It was a disgusting yellow and almost unreadable from the marks and dead bugs on it. The 'Volunteers Wanted' sign was put in the window only when volunteers were wanted. It, too, had been around for years. The volunteers' sign was printed on the backside of a 'Temporary No Parking' sign. Jewels got money for each volunteer he brought in and the volunteers got lunch at Woolworth's counter, not to exceed $1.50".

"I never knew what Cagney's day jobs were, but he was proud of it and he, unfortunately, discussed his work with his closest 'friend', who I'll call Lucifer. Lucifer would wait until Cagney went to sleep to make his move. When Cagney started to snore, Lucifer went to work, stealing Cagney's hard-earned money. If Cagney stirred, Lucifer beat him unmercifully; to the point where Cagney couldn't see straight or move without severe pain. Cagney reached for his money, which was hidden under his icebox. He was glad he found it. This kind of crime took place more than two or three times; each time Lucifer acted concerned and vowed to get Cagney's money back, 'no matter what it takes, so help me Cagney'".

"I treated Cagney and my other patients with the band- aids and chemicals I stole from Franklin Hospital's emergency room. Unbelievably I passed for an intern (with some pimples) and walked into the emergency room. I followed a real doctor and a real nurse into a room with gauze, band-aids, white tape, bandages, and so much stuff that I had to pick and choose what I needed and could take with one try. Oh, I did steal a surgeon's cap, a stethoscope, and a doctor's coat, labeled Dr. Lefkovitz or something like that. Harry Chin took the lettering off and his wife, Xianling, sewed Dr. Ida with red thread. It was a perfect look. The stethoscope made my patients feel more confident in my skills, I think. I know that I felt more confident".

Shane talked about some of the people in his "doctor's area" as he called it. "Don't Call Me Tiny," the owner of the small taproom on Vine Street, near the Chinese Catholic church, let me get hot water whenever my patients needed it; sometimes several times a day. Don't was not tiny and Don't Call Me Tiny wasn't his name. He hated the mocking tone people had when they called him Tiny. I believe that his real name was Jeremiah or Isaiah, a prophet's name.

"I found white rags in a cut-open bale on the docks one time. I took all the rags I could at one time and came back for more.

Thankfully, the bale lasted for several weeks and through a few rainstorms".

"In my practice I met many kind Terrific Samaritans, like Don't Call Me Tiny and the Jesuits at Old St. Joe's church. Fr. Tim McSorley, S.J. left the side door opened on really cold nights. I took the most serious patients inside the church and they stayed until I asked them to leave in the morning. The patients thought they were going into a firehouse. One brilliant patient – I called her Ruth; she called herself Judith – wasn't fooled".

"Inside the church, Judith recited the first question from the Baltimore catechism: why did God make you? I said that I didn't know although I did know. 'To know, love and serve Him in this world and to be happy with Him in the next', Judith told me in a tone that said, you should know this so you can live in peace. I know the seven sacraments and the Gifts of the Holy Ghost. I know most of the Holy Days of Obligation because I go to St. Augustine's under the Ben Franklin Bridge and Old St. Joe's when I remember them. Sr. St. Catherine, an IHM sister from my grammar school, Our Lady of Lourdes and Fatima, made us memorize these things and much other Catholic stuff. I loved Sr. St. Catherine, she loved me because I carried my rosary everywhere I went, and I wore a scapular and I had a Miraculous Medal pinned to my uniform. I was in the girl's choir and my homework was always hanging up in the classroom.

Judith was in the May Queen's court in eighth grade. She was selected for the court because she got all As all year long. The May Queen got mostly As but her parents bought white dresses for all her court. Judith's uniform was tattered and worn; so the May Queen's mother took her and the others in the Queen's Court to South Street and bought them used, but good, white dresses. Judith's father made her throw away the white dress because he felt that he and only he could take care of his family. My old man was a proud person, but he quit every job he had after just a few months. He was convinced that the jobs were beneath him and that he could find a more suitable one. He'd go to Billy Ryan's Reading and Relaxing room to have a few, just a few, beers and think things over. He took the money that Mom earned waitressing and taking in clothes to be washed and dried. Mom had to put our clothes on the clothesline in the basement so she could hang her customer's clothes outside. Mom had to get a big washboard because her business was good. Billy Ryan's was a bar that the cops raided a few times for gambling. Dad went into Billy Ryan's in a bad mood. Dad usually came out of Billy's in a worse mood".

"My Dad didn't have to drink or play the numbers; he didn't like to do either one. He simply wanted fair treatment for himself and for his family to get all that was due to them. As a well-known Bookie, Dad saw all kinds of payoffs and people getting to high places because of cronyism; they knew somebody big. He wanted a hard worker to get ahead and a lazy person to fail.

"At the May procession, Dad refused to watch the procession because I 'was robbed; should've been the Queen'. He fell asleep in church and I could hear him snoring from the front pew. At the cookies and punch social after the procession, Dad told the Bishop that he looked like a fool with the pointed hat and cane. 'You're not crippled. Why do you fake it and walk around with a cane?' The Bishop laughed and Dad steamed. 'My cousin's Godfather's son is a priest in Rome. He'll hear about this', promised Dad. My four sisters and three brothers started to walk home. A neighbor offered to take Mom and Dad home. Dad and Mom agreed to go and Dad asked to be dropped off at Billy Ryan's. The next day, Dad took all of us out of Catholic school even though I had one month to graduate with high honors. I was never the same".

"The Sisters let me graduate from their school; I did homework and took tests for the last month. I even took the same final exam as the other students. My Mom registered us in the public schools. My friends from Our Lady's went to the Catholic high school, Mary Immaculate, in Morgantown. I went to classes for two months hoping that I would get used to the school and make friends. I brought my best friend from public school, #4171, home so I could tutor her in Biology. Dad was coming home from The Pit, a nasty bar near the mines, where Dad worked. It was October Fest at The Pit and 'a good time was had by all', said Dad. The mines were closed in honor of some made up union head as they were always closed for the union head during the three days of October Fest."

"Mom's diner wasn't closed – it never closed. She was at work, bringing black coffee and Alka Seltzers to the 'German for a Day' miners. Dad walked in the house wearing the German paper suspenders he won in the spelling bee, held at The Pit during the height of the October Fest. He was the only one who could spell whiskey. The Pit Crew, as the patrons called each other, were beer drinkers only. Whiskey was not in their vocabulary. Dad looked suspiciously at my friend, Xianling, and asked her if she was related to Annie Oakley. Xiam was Chinese American, the only one I ever met up to that time. She didn't look like Annie Oakley. Actually, she was the spiting' image of a china doll I saw at my other friend's house when her father returned from the Korea War. People looked at her as if they saw her beauty but couldn't accept her for who she was. What a shame, she was wonderful as well as beautiful.

Shane – he doesn't want to be a doctor anymore and wants me to call him by his real name– and I went to field C. Shane wants to get back to normal again. He isn't a doctor and he's moving on.

There were several cars parked nearby field c and many more people than the Visitation game.

"It must be like a parent's day, Shane. It wasn't this crowded last week".

Some of the guys on the team saw me and acted surprised.

"You can't stay here. You're not Protestant, you're Catholic. Go play for the Cardinals". Joey had everybody in stitches, including Mr. Smalley and, I assume Mrs. Smalley, because she timed her degrading laugh to be coordinated with the so-called manager.

A sign welcomed everybody to the Third Annual 10th Street Corinthians' Picnic and Ball Game. The Germantown Cubs were having hot dogs and cold Cokes. The minister began to address the audience. The following is a direct quote. I'll never forget his words:

"Welcome to all God's loving children and to anybody from St. Stephen's. Only kiddin, only kiddin. Is anybody here from St. Stephen's? You're in the wrong place; you need to be in a confessional on a beautiful Saturday like this. Only kiddin, only kiddin. This is our third annual picnic and it's going to be the best one because it's my first. I want to thank all the women from the Hospitality Committee for setting this up. Actually I was surprised when I watched them cooking; they weren't bare-footed and they didn't appear to be pregnant. Oh, St. Stephen's again. Only kiddin, only kiddin. I'll shut up and let you all enjoy some good old fashioned Nicetown cooking. One more thing, our building fund is close to completed. We need about ten thousand dollars more."

"I'll leave a box next to the stands where I can keep my eye on it. If you have the desire and the money with you, please drop it, not the desire, in the box. If you have the desire and don't have the money, drop in a piece of paper with your name and how much you desire to give. You don't want us to start Friday night Bingo, do you? Just kiddin; we'll start a block collection instead."

Almost no one laughed, which was a complement to the audience. Mr. Smalley and his wife roared the whole time. Maybe, Mr. Smiley *is* his real name.

"Mr. Smalley, am I out at right field again?"

"Not today. Our regular third baseman is back so we can fill right field with whoever played third base last week, I can't remember. Why don't you look around to see if any other team needs players? If you want, you can try out for our team next April."

"I walked two miles or more to get here Mr. Smalley."

"I can tell; you're sweating around the ears. Walking is a good exercise anyhow. I'm busy now."

He turned around and walked up to the pastor probably to congratulate the minister on his excellent sermon, only kiddin.

Jesus will greet Shane and welcome him into heaven some day by saying, "Come in, Dr. Ida or Shane McCauley, I've been waiting for you. My Mother has told me so much about you like Bishop Sheen says."

Mary will tell Jesus about my family, my friends, Bif, Otto, Zeke, Renaldo, Gerald Cummings, Lee Horn, Uncle Matt, Doc the Clock and all the "unusual" people with difficult lives behind them. The bartenders at Paddy's Taproom, Iceman, Pretzelmen, Ragman, the Movers, the women at Paddy's Taproom, Carlisle Street and Reese Street. Marlene the Husband Poisoner, the Crazy Lady on my route, and all the people I seem to meet by chance.

Jesus will have Mary with Him when Sonia, Horse Head Lady, Violet, Magdalene and Maria come to Jesus to welcome them and to tell them that they passed one of the toughest tests humans are asked to take; they stayed loving and caring despite being physically beautiful and a natural prey for fast talking creeps.

Shane and I walked to field D to see if I could play for somebody, anybody. I played a softball game for the Marcus Hook Crooks. We beat the Tioga Tremblers. I learned the hard way what forcing a runner out was – I overthrew the first baseman from third when I could have just tagged third because there were men on first and second. I also learned by the worst way not to stand in front of third base when someone was trying to stretch a double into a triple. I got hit by a grown man while he was running full speed. I watched "Puddn' Head Jones" after that to see where I should have stood. While we were playing, Shane met some of the Crooks.

He told them that he was a doctor, Dr. Ida. Some of the Crooks were pointing to the various aches and pains they had. Dr. Ida was making "professional' recommendations telling one guy that he saw his very same rash at Princeton, where he went to medical school.

"Use Noxzema and stay away from railroad sidings and friends with long, stringy hair. There might be cooties or other bugs in that hair," prescribed the good doctor. "My office is on the fifth floor of Temple's medical school if you want to see me professionally. I have an office in center city, near Vine and Broad and at Temple's medical school."

Shane is back to being a doctor. He really thinks he can help people; I thinks he's nuts but I also know that some of his patients living under boxes or horse blankets are thriving.

The 10th Street Corinthians players, coaches and friends were passing by. Mr. Smalley was carrying the equipment bag trying to keep up with the pastor. The pastor was laughing so aloud that people were turning around to see what was happening. The players were throwing stones at each other and the mothers and other women were apparently having great conversations as they walked. I dreaded the long walk home.

"So long Dr. Ida."

"So long young man. Remember what I taught you lad; study hard and follow the Ten Commandments. You have a promising career in medicine or accounting. Forget baseball, you stink!"

Fourth grade at St. Stephen's Catholic school.
I'm the 4th from the left, three rows down. ...

Halloween on Reese Street.
Theresa is at the furthest to
the right.

I'm in front of Grandmom
McCaffrey's house.

Maureen and friends.
Marie, Maureen, and Kathy.

Pop with the oldest three.
Fran, Maureen, Pop, and me

Thanksgiving at Carlisle Street.
Mom, Vince, Theresa, Grandmom
Maguire, Maureen, me, and Fran.

Mom and I in
Townsend's Inlet, NJ

18

Renaldo the Purloiner

I'm not sure where Renaldo the Purloiner went to school, but he didn't go to St. Stephen's or Simon Mueller or any other school in the area. He was always going to school at the same time as the rest of us, only in a different direction than any of us. He must have been in a special public school because he "had to wear a tie every day and it didn't make a difference what color". No matter what shirt he was wearing, Renaldo wore a tie. His tie was a different color every day, but the design was always the same, Davy Crockett. He was a favorite with the high school guys because he gave them cigarettes and Davy Crockett ties. Renaldo roamed the streets looking all around, up and down. He didn't, at least I never saw him, smoke but he carried cigarettes inside his school bag. In fact, that's all he carried in his school bag. He wasn't very good at drawing, but he sketched all the stores on Clearfield Street. He was most interested in how the stores connected to each other. He didn't work but he ate TastyKake pies all the time. In fact, he shared his TastyKake pies and TastyKake cakes with Doc the Clock and Uncle Matt. He never played sports but wanted to learn how to shimmy to rooftops. He always gave the best gifts to anyone celebrating a birthday. In fact, Renaldo got many of his gifts back because the parents felt they were too expensive. He always asked the guys who fooled around with cars, "What is the easiest car to drive?" He practiced driving a shift by putting his foot to the ground and simulating the shifts. He never talked about school and he certainly appeared to be content.

He said that his school didn't give tests because most of the learning came by way of field trips and movies. He was about thirteen and could fix old bicycles and paint them any color that a buyer wanted. He said that he found these old bicycles in the junk yard near the retreaded tires. The junk yard was not close. It was across the street from his uncle's house in Fishtown. He lived with his brother and parents somewhere on Clearfield Street or Toronto Street or near the train station, no one knew for sure. He used the abandoned garage next to Johnson Wax's lot to store his school supplies and tools. He covered the windows of the garage with cardboard and rags. He had some very good tools, like a set of screwdrivers, two hammers, several types of saws, and a 45s record machine, which he said he brought from a store in Kelly's Mart in Kensington. He asked us whom we liked as a singer. He offered me two Eddie Fisher 45s records. He asked for a nickel apiece, but would take a Baby Ruth or Hershey bar instead. I remembered my experience with Richie Cione's dad, when I took pies because I thought it was ok and it wasn't. Richie's dad didn't want anyone spending the money he won betting on the numbers. I declined the offer. Renaldo knew where to buy flowers and Whitman's candy cheaply and quickly.

He frequently left flowers and candy on Sonia George's steps with notes attached asking for a date. Renaldo asked me to write the notes to Sonia. His finger was sore, he said, because he hit it with a hammer when he was covering a garage window with cardboard. I tried to use my best Palmer method writing and these romantic words by Renaldo, "Dear Sonia, can I have a date with you? I am tall for my age and I think I can drive. Can I have an apple or Baby Ruth if you say no? Do you want a new pair of shoes? What size? What kind of car do you want me to pick you up in?"

Sonia was in high school and at least four years older than Renaldo. Renaldo might be older than thirteen, who knows. We didn't know him very well. He just happened in the neighborhood one day riding a cool bicycle, which we all admired. Renaldo sold this bike to Kevin O'Keefe, a North guy, for two milk shakes and a Zero bar. Renaldo agreed to paint the bike a different color for no charge. Renaldo got another bicycle right away. It was red for two days when he painted it green. Kevin gave Renaldo the Zero candy bar but forgot that he promised two milk shakes. Renaldo took it pretty well but wanted to know where Kevin lived and what the license plate number was on his or his parent's car.

Kevin and his parents came around to our street asking for Renaldo. Seems as though their car was painted overnight with the same white paint the highway people use to make white highway separators. Of course, none of us knew where to find Renaldo. Then Renaldo showed up right after the O'Keefes left and turned off Carlisle Street.

"What-id they want?" asked Renaldo moving his head up.

"They wanted to see you about their car, I think," answered a little kid who had a baseball glove on order from Renaldo.

"I didn't paint their car. I don't have black paint anyways," responded a crook with no sense.

Of course he painted their car. How else did he know what they wanted? Besides, Renaldo had white paint all over his clothes and fingers. For the first time that I knew Renaldo, I felt that I didn't know him. He actually looked different, more mature, angrier, taller and more inquisitive. It was scary.

Renaldo had black, thick, curly hair, which he could never lose; it was too thick. He was between Otto the Outrageous and me in height, maybe two or three inches taller than me. He must have athletic skills because he wants to shimmy up the walls and he can run like a deer. One time Renaldo looked down the street towards Clearfield Street and said that he had to go home; he was late for dinner. It was about three in the afternoon and two red cars were coming up our street from Toronto. Renaldo was out of sight like nobody could be. The police saw him but didn't chase after him because they knew that he had hideouts on just about every block in this and other neighborhoods. I knew that Renaldo had Converse sneaks on because he bought two pairs and he offered me one of them.

Sonia was tall and black-haired. She never talked to anyone and was never around the high school guys or girls. She wore what appeared to be expensive clothes. She had the same look about her as *Sonia* Loren, her "name alike" according to Renaldo. Sonia and her younger sister Alicia lived by themselves. Their parents stopped by occasionally but not for very long visits. Their mother snubbed the residents of our street. Their father told us to stop playing Buck-buck Come In on his pavement. He drove a big black or dark blue Hudson with a light outside the driver's side window. Sometimes he wore a white fedora ala Al Capone or Dick Tracy. He always wore a white scarf wrapped around his neck. I could see Otto the Outrageous wearing that scarf, but not this man, who looked like a cousin to

Howdy Doody. Opera music played loudly on their car radio. No doubt, Mr. George thought of himself as Caruso himself. There was no need to blast opera on Carlisle Street; it interrupted many a game of Wireball or Dead Man's Box. Heck, even Zeke the Madman Barber played opera music – the Texaco radio operas. He didn't blast it to show off.

Mrs. George was always dressed to kill, literally. Her wardrobe matched her unpleasant, lips downward smile. She always looked like she lost something, maybe her machine gun. I bet she couldn't even find South Street let alone buy from there. Both parents studied the horse head drawings on the street and the mother asked who did them. Of course, nobody knew anything about the drawings because it was obvious that she would give the Horse Head Lady a hard time. Nobody squealed about anything. Nobody ever did on Carlisle Street and anywhere this side of Broad Street. Alicia saw the Horse Head Lady at work and even she was mum. Sonia smiled slightly at us when we declined to squeal; she knew, I think, who the Horse Head Lady was.

We grew towards really liking Horse Head Lady. Don't ask me why. Maybe it was because she learned our names and addressed us by our names. I wished I had the nerve to ask her to keep her dogs from climbing her fence while I'm taking out the trash. The Horse Head Lady avoided the Georges and went home whenever she saw them coming.

Sonia's mother had a dark complexion and black hair but did not resemble either of her daughters. Alicia was a nice person; Sophia was a Prima Donna. Mrs. George was short; Sonia and Alicia were much taller. The seniors from North and Northeast kept their eyes on Sonia, even when she looked nasty and that was very often, like most of the time. The George parents seemed to have a problem with North and Northeast guys trying to make dates with Sonia. Trust me, they had nothing to worry about; Sonia paid no attention to any of them.

Apollo Jupiter, a senior at an undisclosed Greek military school, thought that Sonia was like the Greek goddess Irene, who was beautiful and rich. Apollo was the only Greek person I saw who had reddish hair and fair skin. I always suspected that he made up his name and heritage to impress Sonia. I also believed that the only Greek military schools in the world were in Greece. Apollo claimed to be the quarterback of the school's football team. Could be, I guess, except Apollo was about five-five and two hundred pounds and home early from school every night, even on the nights that North and all the other football teams had practice. Apollo walked around Sonia's house singing Greek songs in Greek. Most of the times when Apollo was singing, Sonia and Alicia would drive up to their house, get out of the car and literally run from the street to their front door. Apollo looked surprised that they were out when he was serenading Sonia in Greek. Apollo couldn't sing in English let alone Greek. He sounded like an auctioneer asking people to bid higher.

Apollo was singing to an empty house again. Apollo's name isn't Apollo; he's trying to meet Sonia. He thinks she's Greek and likes football. I think Sonia is Scots Irish like me. She could be Greek if Sonia is her real name, I guess. Sonia is popular with the bigger guys, bigger than Apollo, who don't live around here. They have nice clothes and long cars, usually Chryslers or Studebakers. Maybe it's her sunglasses or it's because she looks like Veronica, Archie's girl friend. She hates all of the North guys, I think. She's missing some good times with the North guys. Violet is like Sonia; they both go to dances and football games. The North guys would pay for the tickets and wouldn't ask her to sneak in if she went to the movies with them. Alicia will be better looking than Sonia in ten years, maybe five if Sonia continues to make faces as if she's bored when she sees high school guys. I think that Violet missed many chances to have fun with guys her own age. Sonia is on her way to a downward-sloped smile. Alicia wants to swim at the fireplug. When I invited her to swim with us, she said she had too much math homework. It was July and Alicia didn't have summer classes.

Renaldo knew that Sonia liked Whitman's chocolates because they were never left on her steps like the other brands he tried to leave for her. Goldstein's drug store had a display of Whitman's chocolates but they took it down right about the time Renaldo started to give them as gifts to Sonia and Alicia. Alicia, was in my grade, but in the public school. She was about as friendly and visible as Sonia was when Sonia was nearby. When Sonia was away, Alicia stood on her front steps to watch Buck-buck Come In played against her front wall. She didn't play any games, like the Old Black Cat or Baby in the Air, with the boys and girls. Alicia was a good dresser, like Sonia. She had to standout at the public school because the girls in public schools didn't wear traditional Greek dresses and head gear; Alicia did sometimes. Alicia wasn't pretty like Sonia. She had the black hair and the dark skin, but she had nothing to bring them out like excessively white teeth or the crazy baseball hats some seventh grade girls wore. Neither Sonia nor Alicia went swimming at the fireplug. Sunshine and fireplug water would do Alicia good.

Alicia looks out her window when we're playing the Old Black Cat or Buck-Buck Come In. I hope that she gets out playing because she might not have the number of boyfriends Sonia has; at least I think she has. Sonia too looks at Tackle and Buck-buck games. She should meet Violet. That fireplug water pressure cures a lot of sore feet and shoulders. We need more girls at the fireplug so the games don't get as rough as they sometimes do.

Mary Collins and Patsy changed their lives when they started to swim with the rest of us. They told us so. I guess that girls didn't feel right playing some games. I understood Wireball, Tackle, and Buck-buck Come In, but swimming could lead to all kinds of new games. Patsy was a great student and somewhat pursued by the North guys, but she liked taking chances. She asked me to teach her to shimmy up the ally when nobody was around. After some brief pre-Olympic trials, every athlete went home. Patsy saw that I was alone and asked if she could try. "Of course, Patsy, but it is dangerous. Albert makes it look easy, but it's not," I cautioned. "It doesn't look dangerous or difficult to me. Let me try it" she said as if not to let the boys know what she was doing.

Patsy held her arms against each wall in the alley and jumped a little to get started. She set her feet on the bricks in the proper manner. But she couldn't get the hang of it. She tried at least ten times, each time showing some progress, but not enough. She agreed to play Baby in the Air and Swimming. I tried to convince her to play Halfball or Stickball. She declined because she would never get the balls from the sewers and she would get killed if she got caught stealing brooms. "Nobody steals brooms Patsy," I said in my philosophical manner, "We noticed that a broom is in the trash and we beat the trash men to it. We all know our brooms; we can detect a counterproductive broom, so we just put it in the trash for our busy neighbors".

The front steps and wall of the George's house were the bases for step ball and Buck-buck Come In. One time Renaldo saw Alicia scrubbing her front steps while Sonia was sweeping the sidewalk. The next day there were two cans of cleanser, Bon-Ami and Old Dutch, on the George's front steps. Someone in Sonia and Alicia's house owned a car. It was parked in front of their house and it was gray with four doors, a black running board and four black walled tires. I never saw anyone but Sonia drive it but it was gone For long periods at a time. Sonia might have driven Alicia to school before she took herself to her unknown school. Sonia never carried books when she came home from school. She wore sunglasses all year round. She warned us to stay away from her car when we played Wireball or Baby-in-the-air. She pretended that she didn't hear Katie Quinn when Katie said hello or how are you or where do you go to school? When Patsy invited Sonia to go swimming, Sonia said that she couldn't swim.

I wish that Violet could meet Sonia. She could advise her to meet people, even if they're uglier than she is or poorer than her family seems to be. Our husband killing former actress could advise them both on acting like you like people.

"Do you want fake white walls for your car Sonia?" was the next dictation I got from Renaldo. He said that Pep Boys was located near his school and they sell fake white walls for any car. "Sometimes I shop there when my friend hands me some TastyKake pies from their bakery next to Pep Boys. Signed: Renaldo the guy who brings you candy and cleanser."

Sonia once asked me how far Shibe Park was and where North plays their games. I told her and gave specific directions to her. I was excited because I thought we broke the ice with her and Alicia would follow suit.

"Just asking; nothing more than that," Sonia quickly let me know after she detected that she loosened up a little.

"Can Alicia swim with us?" "Alicia gets plenty of swimming in my parents' friend's pool".

Why does Renaldo shop for auto supplies? He can't drive a car; I don't care what he says. Where does he get the money to shop at all? He's always shopping for something he can sell or give away. Alicia and Sonia must be members of a religious sect that doesn't allow girls to wear bathing suits in public. I bet they'd love to go swimming with us at the fire plug. Deafy would give Sonia a ride on his cycle. Maybe I'll invite Violet and the St.

Joe guys to go swimming. Apollo Jupiter is telling everybody that Sonia agreed to swim at the fireplug on Labor Day weekend; he's nuts if he thinks she'll do that. Everybody is talking about it.

Sonia, Renaldo, and Apollo weren't even friends. That was a shame really.

Mom wanted to know if I knew anything about the robbery at the American store on Clearfield Street. "Somebody climbed the roof and somehow made a hole in it, then went in the store and took cigarettes and Davy Crockett ties."

Renaldo wanted to shimmy up the roofs so he could see the neighborhood. He went over to the American store's roof. Uncle Matt, Otto the Outrageous, Zeke the Mad Barber, and Doc the Clock all had brand new Davy Crockett ties.

19

Maria's

"She sold artificial flowers, artificial flowers" as the Bobby Darin song goes. Her name was Maria and her shop, which was named for St. Maria, was called Maria's. Maria was Maria's parent's favorite name because it was the Blessed Mother's name. Maria, the proprietor, wanted people to call her Tootsie because she was eating a Tootsie roll when she met an angel in South Philly, near 12th and Patterson. The angel appeared to be a regular guy, lanky and sandy-haired, with a crush on Maria, according to Maria. I was in the sixth or seventh grade and usually not interested in anything any adult said, but I was totally spell bound when Maria – Tootsie was just too hard for me to accept – told her story.

Maria is very pretty, even now and she's at least forty. Any angel worth his wings could have a crush on Maria. Big John said that she was a trophy for her husband. The name Maria came up so many times in our discussion; yet she wants to be called Tootsie. The Horse Head Lady, Violet, and Maria are all young and pretty. Maria's smart; the Horse Head Lady can draw, so she's smart too. Violet has musical talent and she reads Dickens, she told me that. They must have been at many proms. Do ugly boys, with odd shaped heads and different size ears like me ever get a date with the prettiest girls?

The story in Maria's own words (as I recall) goes like this: (These are Maria's words, except, of course, the words in bold letters).

A man goes to me, Hi! I don't mind him saying Hi but then he gets closer and looks at me like we've been sitting on a train for a long time. Then he asks me if I go to St. Maria's or Herald Angels. I laughed a little because Herald Angels is a boy's school. St. Maria's, but we have off today because our section, sophomore nine, sold the most chances for our annual bazaar, which we have every year since I came here last year. My name is Maria but the school was built before I was born, so it wasn't named for me; it was named for St. Maria Goretti. I think she was Italian and South Philadelphia is Italian; it makes sense if you ask me. I couldn't go to Herald Angels mister.

Herald Angels is all boys, but my boyfriend goes to college. I am a cheerleader for the Harps though, but that doesn't mean I go there. What's your name? This guy smiles and replies humbly, Raphael, like the painter. Do you live around here Raphael or do you live someplace else? I don't have just one home; I'm on duty all the time and I go wherever my boss sends me. I travel all the time and all over Earth and its surrounding solar system or the world as you know it. Do you fly to these places? You could say that. Do you always wear that white hat? Most of the time, do you like it? I like the gold lettering on the front.

Maria could star in a play about this encounter because she had her lines memorized. Her honest, cute way of relating the story couldn't be duplicated by even Katherine Hepburn. He knew that the school wasn't named for her. Maria was touched by this experience; she memorized every line and that was at least twenty years ago.

Raphael is an angel's name. I think he's the angel who asked Mary to be Jesus' mother. He doesn't live anywhere. I bet his boss is a Seraphim angel. Maria never has any customers in her shop. Sister said that angels probably looked like us when they're down here. I wish I was there with Maria/Tootsie. Angels must be all over the place. I have a Guardian Angel. I might have seen him and talked to him for all I know. I have to listen to everybody. I need to hear his name. If the name is Gabriel, Michael, Raphael or Angel Something or Other comes up, I will know he is my Guardian Angel. I hope that Renaldo's Guardian Angel is sharp and can keep him out of trouble. Albert's angel probably has given up trying to make sure that he lands on his feet or doesn't slip on the porch roofs. Why does Raphael go all over the place? He might not be Maria's Guardian Angel. His mission might be to make Maria a Saint or to convince her to be a Sister.

Maria continued her story. I asked him if he wanted a Tootsie Roll; I had two extras. No thanks, I can't eat candy. The American store was selling Tootsie rolls three for a nickel. I like Three Musketeers better, but they're a nickel each. Maria, we're all very aware of your kindness and concern for anyone who needs help. Never lose your humility and truthfulness. I have to get back to work now. Stay away from your boyfriend's fraternity parties. I know that you're in good hands now. Your pastor, Father Genoa is a friendly type and he is ready to answer any questions you have. You'll make good decisions for a while. But things change and you are very caring. Don't listen to anyone who tells you that God or the Devil don't exist. You kept your Catechisms from the first grade on. Look them over from time to time. The first two or three questions say it all. I'll say hello to Maria; she comes to our harp concerts every Easter. The guy, Raphael, walks away and – I knew it was him - goes toward Broad Street, doesn't turn either way on Thirteenth and doesn't go straight either. He just becomes invisible. I watched Raphael and when he was a block away, he was gone, poof. I wasn't imagining things and I knew it.

Her boyfriend went to Temple. He wouldn't listen to Tootsie's – she changed her name when Raphael disappeared – story and, in fact refused to call her Tootsie. Danny, Tootsie's boyfriend, was on Herald Angels football team a year ago and was an All Catholic All Star player. He got into the athlete's fraternity at Temple and played "some position or other on the team, maybe pitcher," according to Maria, on Temple's football team. Dan could carry an icebox on his back and walk a hundred yards.

Tootsie was a great cheerleader, I'm sure, but I hope that she doesn't cheer for a strike out when it was third down and one yard to go for a first down. I know many people who can carry an icebox up and down a three-story apartment complex. Can a half Catholic – maybe one parent is Protestant or Jewish – be an All Catholic, I wondered. Sounds like I better make All Catholic.

Maria had our attention. "My boyfriend, Dan Dolores, was a big shot on the campus. He was just a freshman and a 'fourth or fifth stringer' according to his friends at Angels. He always laughed at my St. Anthony and St. Francis of Assisi statues. I knew that I was being laughed at but I was dating Dan from the time I was in ninth grade. It was cool to be dating a junior and a star football player to beat (sic).

My girl friends were envious and happy when my parents wouldn't let me go to his junior prom. I went to his senior prom but refused to go to Atlantic City for a quick breakfast".

Dan's parents liked me and his mother wanted to teach me how to cook his favorite meals. Dan's father, whose name was Dante and whose nickname was Neck, told me about his arrival at Ellis Island and his decision to come to Philadelphia when most of the others on his boat went to New York.

Neck knew that he was tough and that Philly had a good Little Italy section. He wanted to be a lawyer or a butcher, but became an inspector on the docks. The rookie inspectors had to pass a grueling test to be hired. To pass the test, they had to pick up sacks of wet sand weighing at least seventy-five pounds and throw them into the Delaware River at least twenty yards out. Five sacks must reach the goal in two minutes. Mr. Dolores, Neck, practiced for weeks by working on the docks as a receiver of cotton bales and other materials, which he couldn't remember. He remembered that the other materials were marked 'Hazardous Materials, do not smoke closer than fifty yards from the materials'. Neck walked off fifty steps and ended up off the pier and next to the sandwich truck. It would be easy to remember. He stopped drinking during this training period and he used his massive hands to push down on his head while he pushed his head up from his back. This is how he got such a thick neck and a strong back, he said, as if throwing bales of cotton and carrying 'other materials' didn't count.

Mr. Dolores went through the apprentice program for inspectors after he set the record of ten sacks in two minutes and nine of the ten broke existing records for distance. Mr. Dolores, who took the name from Our Lady's Seven Dolors, inspected for many years until he got a white collar job – he jokes that the inspector's job was a black collar job – and started to get around parts of South Philly that most people never see. At this time he moved his family to a house that was at the end of a row, therefore more expensive and bigger inside. He got most of his furniture from the docks. He brought whatever "fell off the pier". Usually it landed on mattresses and pillows. Neck often wondered how a chair or a clock could be in such great condition after it fell off the pier.

The Dolores' house was colorful though nothing matched. It didn't have to match because only the guys who drove the big cars had furniture that matched. The Dolores had one of those radios that stood about five feet high and was made of wood and the carvings were beautiful. It was a regular radio and a shortwave radio as well. Operas were on all the time but Dan hated opera and he changed the station to Frankie Laine, Frankie Sinatra, Ella, and Peggy Lee. Neck was always angry when he had to find his opera on the radio. I think that Texaco sponsored the operas. Mrs. Dolores didn't care about radios. She preferred to read love stories from magazines and books. She read an occasional biography of some saint who underwent difficult family relationships.

Mrs. Dolores went to Goretti and almost finished. She had to find work and landed a good job with the government at 6th and Chestnut Streets. She started out as a file clerk and moved up to office manager in charge of hiring. Her first name was Mary but she preferred to be called Magdalene because she felt that only Jesus' mother should be called Mary and Magdalene made her feel humble. Mrs. Dolores made daily mass whenever she could. She tried to convince Neck to join her on Sundays at the seven or eight but he had a difficult job and required twelve hours sleep on Sundays. He also had to have steak or pork every day, including Fridays, so that he could maintain his strength. He got sick on fish as a kid in Italy. It was impossible for Neck not to eat or drink after midnight if 'your (sic) going to Communion' because of an unusual disease he had which required moisture in the throat at all times. Neck sometimes answered the door on Sundays when I was going to meet Dan at his house so we could both go to church, usually the eleven to accommodate Dan, a late sleeper and an undecided attendee until the last Mass.

Neck always looked at his watch (whether he was wearing one or not) and said 'That god d--- alarm, it never works when you want it to'. "D--- thing; I hate to miss Mass and disappoint my dear mother, God rest her soul, I think'. He promised that he would not miss Mass during Lent on behalf of his mother in Italy, who doesn't know where he went when he came to the U.S. To him, in truth, and later to Dan as well, Lent was just another season, except for Easter Saturday, when everyone went to church and to the Sodality Hall for breakfast. Neck couldn't see the advantage of giving up something for Lent. 'I lived in Italy and I'll tell you that I saw priests eating meat on Fridays. The Catholic fishermen even ate meat on Fridays, I saw them. They'd sell the fish and buy meat'. 'God can't have it both ways; what's good for the gander should be good for the ducks or something like that'.

Every party I went to I was with Dan and every dance I danced I danced with Dan. The guy that I really liked was a senior at South Catholic and a football player, who, too, was an All Star, All Catholic player who wore the number ten on his jersey and school sweater. I saw him at Mass and in line for Confession. He didn't pay attention to me, but I tried to meet him. Once I asked him if this was the line for Confession. He politely said that it was and that I could go before him. He didn't give the stock answer, something like, 'No lady, it's the line to the Toys department'. Another time I asked him for a match though I didn't smoke. The guy 'wouldn't budge'. He had no matches and he said so. He didn't say the old "good girls don't smoke, drink or curse". Again, he was polite. When I was cheering for the Pirates, I once yelled, 'go ten'. Number ten fumbled the ball for the first and last time in his high school career on the very next play. Nothing worked. I considered breaking off with Dan and spending the rest of my life studying scripture and praying for the souls in purgatory. If anybody dared to compliment me, I'd take it as pity for the way I turned out at seventeen. I knew I wasn't going to be a Sister because I liked different clothes for different seasons and, I guess that I started to remember how much fun it is to flirt with the boys, high school boys.

Dan asked about the frat party and I said 'no'. He was hurt, I think, but he recovered quickly for a guy who was just turned down by a girl he'd been dating for two years. Instead of pouting he was hustling a girl in his Economics class. He talked about her and mentioned that she liked football and had purple eyes and black hair like Elizabeth Taylor. She brought Puerto Rico orange soda to the practices and promised to someday bring enough hoagies for all the freshmen players. 'Can't beat that', I thought. Dan and I were finished and we both knew it. I'm not sure who was more relieved. He was; I knew it.

Dan and I didn't date or even talk to each other for years. Magdalene saw me in church at times and she wished me luck. She said that she missed me and that I was welcome at her house when Dan and Neck went to a wrestling match or to the Roller Derby. Dan became a hauler for the club. He moved to the Northeast to be near his wife's family. But that's off the subject.

I debated with myself about asking number ten to my junior prom. I made a novena, prayed several rosaries, made a Spiritual Bouquet consisting of two thousand short prayers fifty Hail Marys, ten Our Fathers, and countless 'My Jesus Mercies' then called him when I returned from Mass and Communion at daily Mass, which I offered up to St. Maria and St. Thomas. His name was Tommy and being in the best Spiritual position in my life, I called and asked for Tommy.

Hello. This is Tommy.

Hi Tommy, this is Maria De Antonia, you know, the cheerleader with black hair.

Hi Maria, I think I know you, but all the cheerleaders have black hair.

I'm the one who wears the Silver and Gold sweater.

He said that he could place me because the other four cheerleaders wore white sweaters with Angel's mascot, the Harps, sewn on the front. The orange and black caught his eye, he said, because he forgot the school colors and this reminded him. He didn't comment on my style or grace or athleticism or my hair, though black like the others, was much longer than the others. I didn't ask him if he heard me screaming for ten.

Would you like to go to the prom with me in April? I know that it's early – it was November – but I see you all the time and I'm afraid that another girl will ask you.

Another girl has and I said yes. Thanks for the generous offer Maria.

I felt that this just wasn't meant to be. The phone rang immediately after Tommy turned me down.

Maria, where are you? Where's Dan?

Who's this? Teddy, Dan's friend from Yonkers and I'm going to Temple now. I'm waiting for you and Dan."

He went to a frat party

There's no frat party tonight or for a long time until someone owns up to spray painting the president's front door. That's a long story, but there's no party. We were all supposed to drive up to New York where you can drink at eighteen. Didn't he tell you?

No. I just told him that I couldn't go to the frat party.

There is no frat party I said. I'm home tonight, all night, and if Dan calls I'll tell him that you called.

No, just tell him that the Beast and his girl friend, the Beauty, are headed up to Greenwich Village like we talked about.

I didn't have a chance to think about the frat party or New York - I was shaken up pretty bad - when the phone rings.

Is this you Dan? Dan who? I asked.

Maria, this is Tommy. I'm a little embarrassed, but will you go to my prom in May?

Yea, of course, I will.

Should we get together before the prom, like next Saturday night, to get to know each other?

Good idea Tommy.

Let's take the trolley to the C bus to center city and walk around, then go to Horn and Hardart's for supper. The C bus is better than the subway because you can see Broad Street, Tommy offered.

We call it H&H and I love their automat where you put a nickel or a dime in and open the door to get something, I said as I felt like dancing right on the spot.

H&H was fun. The best fun was the C bus because the driver wore a white hat with gold lettering on the front. He entertained the passengers by driving with no hands and singing songs in some strange language.

Do you want to go to the Temple stop? he asked assuming that Tommy and I went there.

No. I didn't think so. Have a good evening, said the driver who wasn't Raphael. I was sure of that.

What a story. Raphael took care of her. The new angel, the bus driver, is her guardian angel, I'll bet on it. Some girl thought they saw the Blessed Mother in Fairmount Park. Hardly anyone would believe her and Sister said that we'd have to wait to hear from the diocese what we can believe. I believe her. I hope that the Cardinal believes her. Why do we have to wait for the Cardinal to tell us what we can believe? I'll believe her with or without the Cardinal's directions, except if I get excommunicated. Maria never told a soul this story; not even her mother. She wanted Pop to hear it because he was a good customer. He didn't have to spend a dime, which he didn't, to be a favorite.

You never knew what you could buy at Maria's except artificial flowers, which Maria, not the St. Maria as she frequently reminded customers, made. She said that they were fresh, but Pop said she meant that she made them every day. Maria whispered in Pop's ear that she just received some beautiful wooden hand carved statues directly from the floods in Florence, Italy. She semi-genuflected, made a quick sign of the cross, made a fist and kissed the thumb of her fisted hand, and opened the curtain. The statues were beautiful and wooden and hand carved. Pop went nuts. He could see right through the statues to uncover every carving, every color – the Blessed Mother Holding the Baby Jesus had some bluish tint. Pop saw all kinds of things in the Blessed Mother's statue; things I'd never see. He was just imagining what went into the statue and how he could paint it on canvas if he owned it. The perfect model, it wouldn't move and ask if it was time for the donuts every ten minutes like I do at Pop's school. St. Joseph's statue was equally well-done, but it had little coloring on Baby Jesus' statue which depicted the Baby with outstretched arms and almost no color.

"What'll you say, Pop; 'ya interested for five dollars each?"

"Maria, I don't have five dollars right now, but can you hold the Blessed Mother statue for me?"

"I want you to have this Pop because I met your kids and they are strict Catholics, I can tell. I'll hold both of them until you can afford them".

"Look at these other statues from the same city, Florence".

Maria showed Pop statues of the Nativity scene with the Magi and the Shepherds. Pop looked. He was looking at them as he would look at a painting by one of the Grand Masters in a museum.

Pop, I'll buy you the three statues and the Nativity scene, I promise. I'll be the Yankees' centerfielder and I'll be rich!

20

Zeke

On Westmoreland between Broad Street and Ruth's diner is a dirty old store rented by the strangest real life barber to ever cut hair and shave a stubby face. His name was Zeke Jones, but he said that we could call him Zeke because he made up the Jones part. People who went to school with Zeke said that his name wasn't Zeke but the Jones part sounded familiar. They said that Zeke would brag about his latest accomplishments. He once yodeled for fifteen minutes. He wore a sign around his neck that hung on his front and back that said Bob's Pizza. Bob's Pizza restaurant got its license to sell food back after two years of trying to convince the Board of Health that the black little pellets on their kitchen floor were bb's, not what the inspector thought they were. The sign thing was Zeke's idea and it worked. Zeke suggested that Bob personally give all his customers a free whistle in either blue or white. I don't know what the customers, kids and adults, were supposed to do with the whistles, but they all loved them and everyone in the neighborhood had to have a Bob's whistle, blue was preferred.

Every crowd had at least three groups of guys: the sport's nuts, the academic nuts, the car nuts. Zeke was just plain nuts. He ate cranberry sauce sandwiches for lunch almost every day. During Lent, he sometimes ate seafood sandwiches, which smelled like cranberry sauce. His friends never saw the seafood because he claimed to be using Skippy peanut butter's recipes. Since you asked yourself, I'll tell you why he used Skippy and not Star-Kist. Because silly, Starkist makes tuna fish only and Skippy uses many seafoods in its recipe. Make sense? It shouldn't. He drank nothing but his special drink, once used by the early settlers of our land, the Pigeons, when they feasted with the Indians. In fact, it was Ovaltine in a canteen with a squirt of sweetened olive oil "for the complexion".

When Zeke was of high school age, a junior or senior, he went to church one day, probably by mistake. He found a red beret on the Lost and Found table at the rear of the church. He tried it on and it was excessively small. He kinda laid it on his head; it was flat as if he was carrying a floppy plate on his head. He planned to cut the beret so he could wear it all around school. He cut it and pulled it down as far as it would go.

"Hey guys, do you like my new beret?" Zeke asked.

"That's not a beret; it's a first grader's hat. First graders wear red. My sister wears red and she's a first grader. Did you go to the school and steal the beret?" said a friend of Zeke's of sorts.

"Zeke, it doesn't fit," commented a kind guy who didn't want Zeke to look foolish.

"Where'd jah get it Pierre?" razed a normally whimpish senior with big ears and red Ked high tops.

"Your clothes look great Emperor," added another wimp but this guy wore Chuck Taylor white high tops and smelled like the stable he cleans out five days a week.

"I won this beret because the French loved my rhymes. When the famous French poet awarded me this hat and I put it on, I decided at that moment to become a barber. Yep, that's it, I'm going to become 'Pedro, the French Tonsorial Master'. My mind's made up; the beret did it". Now that Zeke had finally committed to a career, high school would be in the way. Many people wanted Zeke to go to barber school. They insisted that he go now instead of high school. He didn't go to barber school then and, in fact, he never went to barber school. Zeke wanted to be active in school so he could make contacts for his soon to be business. He joined the track team and actually was fast. He'd be in first place right up to the finish line. His big problem was that he never crossed the finish line. He had this thing about "fine-knee-al-it-e" and he simply couldn't complete a race, even if he was ahead. The track coach thanked Zeke for his participation but asked him to leave the team. The coach suggested that Zeke join the Cross Country team – which had finish lines incidentally – because he looked like a cross-country runner. Zeke was a tall Robert Q. Lewis with a twist of insanity. He had black hair with streaks of white in high school.

At his first cross country race, Zeke took an early lead only to make a wrong turn. He was lost for two hours. He had to leave the

Cross-country team. Debating was really his forte, the Cross-country coach said to the Debating coach convincingly. "Good challenges and no finish lines".

Northeast was debating Central, considered the best debating team in Philadelphia.

As a Central guy was speaking his piece, Zeke stood up and screamed, "You're nuts you egg headed big shot".

His coach took him aside and told him he was out of order and quite rude. Zeke agreed he was rude. The next Central kid got up and really made his point. The kid was smiling as was his coach and two adults, obviously the kid's parents. Pride filled the room. Zeke couldn't help himself. He didn't want to be rude.

In a not too loud and certainly not too soft tune, Zeke said, "That's a lot a baloney".

It was time for Zeke to open his barbershop or try the Chess team, which, by the way, was also his forte. He always played board games, even during a fire in the house next door to his. He kept playing Chess with his opponent, King me de Francis, who excelled in Chess and Checkers.

The Chess coach laughed when the Debating coach suggested that Zeke join his team. The whole idea caused an otherwise split faculty to mockingly try to convince the Chess coach to pursue Zeke. The coaches had a ball at Zeke's expense. Zeke left the school and the school lost probably the best high school aged Chess player in the city.

Zeke started to play Checkers because no one could beat him in Chess, even the Russian Chess champion who lived near the Sun Ray. Boris, the champion, wanted Zeke to study the game and get into some of the best tournaments in the world. Zeke declined all such suggestions after he put on the red beret. He told Boris and others around him that it was at that moment – when he put on the red beret – that he knew he wanted to be a barber. He told that story to his first hundred or so customers.

The handwritten sign in the window of Zeke's shop said, "Salvador's (he forgot about Pedro)European and French Stile (sic) Haircuts and Shays (sic) for one price, twenty-five cents". Passers-by thought they'd get a stylish haircut and shave for a quarter. They seemed impressed by the name of the shop. If passers-by thought that, then they would be a good choice to buy yesterday's daily paper for next Sunday's price.

Zeke meant twenty-five cents for a haircut and twenty-five cents for a shave, not twenty-five cents for both, which is what most people thought. It would not be to anyone's advantage to argue about this confusion when Zeke had him lathered up and ready for a close shave. The sign in the window was a sign for intelligent people to stay away, which loyal customers would never do. They usually wanted a haircut and a game of Checkers. No one got a haircut until Zeke finished his Checkers' games.

Some anthropologists and their students from Penn and Princeton actually came to the shop to observe one of the rituals of the "tribes" of different people in North Philly. They saw us as unusually different from their fellow Ivy Leaguers. We were different, thank God. Zeke refused to let them in to observe unless they promised to be quiet while he was playing Checkers. One of the anthropologists actually had the nerve to let Zeke give him a Cary Grant haircut. Zeke agreed to the Cary Grant look and proceeded to give the professor the same haircut as he gave everybody for as long as he was a barber- short on the sides with a razor and a little longer on top. Zeke never let the customer look at the mirror until the job, and I do mean job, was done, and I do mean done. Our Prof was beside himself. The other Prof and the students put their quarters away and started to write more notes.

I'd love to see the report that the profs and students wrote. Who wouldn't?

21

Zeke's Shop

Zeke set up a Checkerboard on two wooden sawhorses. There were two chairs next to the board and competitors could choose which one they wanted to use. They could choose the heavy-duty chair, which Zeke got from one of the regular players. The chair looked comfortable and probably was so if you were able to sit still and not move the seat, unattached to the chair. The rips on the seat's cover were no problem; Zeke had a piece of linoleum tied to the seat. They could choose the sturdy wooden one, which a disgruntled Linton's Restaurant's former employee took home with him on the day he got fired. He gave it to Zeke for a shave. The chair was a bit wobbly but a pack of matches properly placed under the front left leg minimized the wobble. Of course you must disregard the "This chair is the property of Linton's Restaurant; do not remove under penalty of the law" sign if you wanted to be comfortable. If the shop got to be too busy, Zeke would go in the kitchen in the back and bring in two more chairs. There was no kitchen in the back. There were instead piles of odd things that people gave Zeke throughout the years. When I went over to look at the pinup poster, Zeke was coming out of the "kitchen". For a brief second I saw some of the odd things. There was a tricycle and a Mortimer Snerd doll. I saw something on the ceiling; like a fisherman's net. The room looked full.

Zeke plays checkers for money or things. His back room is loaded with things he won. I can't wait to see these new chairs. Yesterday was "Leave it All Out" day for the Department of Sanitation. Zeke looks forward to this day and even closes his shop for two hours early in the morning so he can beat the trash truck to the piles of junk on the sidewalks.

Zeke came out of the room, which had a shower curtain for a door, carrying two mean looking chairs. "Just got 'em yesterday and

I'm using them today. Glad I got 'em," our proud tonsorial master exclaimed.

I knew he got them yesterday because the trash pickup was the day before and trash pickup day is the day that Zeke gets furniture and miscellaneous items for the shop. Both chairs had some damage; one chair had a missing armrest and a split on one of the legs. The second chair had "Jesus Saves" on the back part of the chair, right about where the head would be if someone was leaning back. It had two broken armrests and wobbly legs. The seats on both chairs were covered with oilcloth with "Gimbel's White Sale" all over it.

Looks like Zeke went to the sale and was waiting for one of the tables to empty so he could get some chair covering. He's something. He's nuts!

If Zeke was in the process of playing Checkers, customers had to wait to get a haircut. Most customers stood behind Zeke and watched him set up his competitor. Some stood behind Zeke's customers and talked away to Zeke as he cut the customer's hair. Zeke would choose colors first and he would always choose red. He chose colors first because the other guy went first to choose the chair. If Zeke was in a best out of five series, he would start a deciding game BEFORE giving a haircut. Sometimes customers waited twenty to thirty minutes to get a haircut. No one seemed to mind for four reasons.

First, Zeke had an archive of old Sport magazines as well as old copies of Saturday Evening Post magazines with Norman Rockwell covers. If you were twenty-one and willing to pay ten cents, Zeke let you roam through his special magazines, which were kept on a table made of two old orange crates, one on top of the other. There was a cover on top of the magazines because Zeke didn't want them to get dirty since they "came from Asia and were very rare". If you were under twenty-one and had fifteen cents, Zeke would give dispensations from the minimum age requirement. If Zeke couldn't find the cover that was used to protect customers from getting hair all over them, he used the cover that covered the special magazines. Boys from the fifth grade to the twelfth grade hid Zeke's cover from time to time to save themselves fifteen cents. He was right most of the time; they were from Asia, so I'm told. Many customers wouldn't look at an Asian magazine for fear of getting caught by a neighbor or a son so Zeke put Sport or Wild Life magazine covers on top of the

Asian covers. This pile was not available to anyone under twenty-one and was labeled "Special Editions of Sport and Wild Life magazines. Must be 21 and(sic) older".

The second reason for the customers' patience was the fact that Zeke's reputation with a straight razor was sketchy at best. You wouldn't want to rush him. If he sensed your impatience, he might very well make you his next customer and give you a shave.

The third reason for customers' patience was that one could take the time to observe Zeke's customers, who were from all lifestyles and many different countries. Rodney, for example, claimed to be a former RAF pilot in WWII. He wore the shirt of an English officer, which was identical to the shirts that were on sale at the Army and Navy store near South Street. He spoke with an English accent that sounded like the accent of a native Philadelphian trying to imitate Eliza Doolittle's father. For example, he asked Zeke if there was a ward-der fountain in the shop. He asked me to go to Ruth's and get him a cup of caw-fee or a touch of tea. The English accent didn't cover too well. Eliza wouldn't be fooled.

Another regular Checkers' player preferred the name "The Inventor". He worked with "Alvin" Einstein to invent the electric light. This statement and others like it left one to question his integrity. This customer's real last name was Watts, like the measurement of brightness. A former Senator played golf with FDR and Ike many times. He beat Ike 95 to 90; he had the 95, go figure. He did wear an "I like Ike" button, which Ike himself presented to him in Gettysburg at the same spot that FDR (?) gave his famous address. His first wife didn't want to move to Washington, so he passed up the chance to be the Secretary of Stake (sic). He did get to several Steak (he meant state, I'm sure) Dinners in the White House where he gave advice to the big shots in many foreign countries.

A retired brain surgeon played Checkers on weekends. He graduated from Penn's medical school to become a surgeon. It took him three years to get his "doctor's diploma" then he went to LaSalle to get his diploma in the "nature stuff" that you needed to operate on "sick brain patients". The brain surgeon, Doctor Smith, retreaded bald tires when the surgery business was slow. He never beat Zeke in Checkers. He had the nervous habit of grabbing his foot and bringing it up toward his nose when he thought he was going to win. Zeke, whose background was quite interesting itself, smiled when the doctor grabbed his foot because he knew that he, Zeke, was going to win.

Zeke was the underground assistant Admiral who told Truman that it was ok to bomb Hiroshima and Nagasaki. Zeke worked with above ground Generals and Admirals to reach the conclusion that bombing was "just what we needed to win and nobody gets hurt". He spoke fluent Japanese but was under strict orders not to tell anyone. He asked us not to say anything. Actually, the place was crazy. Nevertheless, it was cheap entertainment.

The fourth reason for customers to stay and be patient was that they knew exactly what they would look like and there was never a doubt.

"Cut my hair like Peter Gunn's".

"Cut mine short on top and clean on the sides".

"Can you just trim the sides and take a little off the top?"

"I'd like a crew cut like I got in the Army".

"I want a DA so don't take anything off the sides".

Zeke would shake his head in agreement to all these and other requests. He didn't have to listen to his customers because he gave everyone the same haircut - everything off the sides and short on the top, if you had hair on the top. If Zeke went too far on the top, you'd get a baldy on the sides to keep the same look. Every man, including Zeke, looked the same when they left Zeke's. It was amazing. Whether he had curly hair, straight hair, long hair, short or very little hair, the result was the same. Zeke cut his own hair. Don't ask me how. Bif with one F, the toughest of the big guys, said Zeke sat on a chair, bent over as far as he could and cut away, just like a customer. Some customers treated themselves to a shave since they assumed it was part of the price. Nobody asked for the shave after the first time. Nobody relaxed as Zeke went to work with the razor and, when he rolled up his sleeves and snorted, like a mad scientist.

"Maybe I'll pass on the shave this time, it's getting late," was a frequent comment.

"Don't worry, I go fast," responded the Rasputin-like barber, who thought the customer was in a rush.

I watched Zeke sharpen a straight razor with his cowhide strap. He seemed to be thinking about his last Checkers' game or if he gave Truman good advice or not. He went on and on with the sharpening until someone coughed aloud to get him out of his trance. While Zeke was strapping up, first-time customers whose turns were coming up checked out of the shop. They never looked back or came back.

Zeke furnished his shop with things his friends gave him and things he picked up during his travels and what he picked up on trash pickup day. There was a complete set of fireplace tools against the wall, next to the totem pole made of five or six Quaker Oats cylindrical boxes stacked up, painted and glued together. A poster of some James Cagney movie hung next to the door with the hand-written sign that was at least three years old, "Men's Toilet – out of order – don't go in here". The sign was on the reverse side of a Ringling Brothers Barnum and Bailey circus poster. Some of the guys turned the sign around and kids read it as if it was current, asking their parents if they could go. A mirror hung on the wall in front of the barber chair so customers could watch what was happening to them. Most customers refused to look. A pinup of Betty Grable was to the right of the mirror. Someone drew a mustache and beard on Betty. Someone else drew an arrow going through Betty's head. On a small table near the front door were three handwritten signs, "Open," "Closed" and "Out to lunch or out to the post office". The "Open" sign never was posted on the door, neither was the "Closed" sign. The post office was at least an hour away and Zeke didn't drive. I suspect that Zeke found these signs when he occupied the building. They never moved from their spots on the table.

Some day I'm going to write a book about Zeke. About how, after each customer, he wiped the scissors against his dirty old white coat with the Temple Hospital Geriatrics Ward name printed on the bottom rear. Pop doesn't notice what's happening here or he wouldn't come here. I guess he really has to come here, Zeke's competitor is seventy-five cents and not much better with the scissors.

Zeke never gave up trying to become more European and classy. He planned changes to the shop so it would look like the pictures of French barber shops in Snip Magazine, the bible for all barbers. But the progress he made is for another time and another book.

22

Slash

Slash, the cool dancer with the neat car, which he hits people with from time to time, pulled up right next to the fireplug.

"Please don't stay there Slash; we're going to get the wrench soon and it's illegal to park so close to a fireplug," Patsy said in a very nice way.

Slash looked like he was shocked at her friendly mannerisms. He is used to hearing screams of foul language when he almost hits someone with his car or when his father sees his report card. Slash and his friends roamed Germantown Avenue, near school looking for girls. It was a good thing that Slash drove; otherwise, he would be the one hanging out the window trying to get the girls to go for a ride. The convincers had the same lines as the South Street clothes sales clerk and they wouldn't be believed if Slash said them. Slash received his DNAs when God when out to lunch and His replacement pushed the wrong buttons.

He had an egg-shaped head and a pencil thin neck, which made it look like his head could spin on his neck. It was rumored that Slash couldn't find a hat that fit when he and his crowd went to South Street to buy Ivy League paperboy-like hats. Cornelius Conman, AKA Cornelius the Convict, AKA Crooked Corny, Slash's best friend, said that the storeowner said loudly, "Sorry Son, we only go up to size nine and a half. Sidney across the street can make you one. He's not a hat maker by trade but he makes hats for Halloween costumes and circus performers".

Slash had buckteeth like nobody ever had. His mouth looked like a bottle opener. You could open a bottle by putting the bottle in Slash's mouth and pulling it down against the inside of his teeth. Slash was thin, maybe skinny, and his shoes would fit a seven-footer.

He wore a white glove on his left hand. Nobody knew why. At Mass, he wore blue rosaries around his neck and always carried a bible in his gloved hand, which he could sell as "like new, never opened" because he never opened it. He didn't have to; he was really the perfect gentleman. He was an usher for the early Mass and he took up the collection in the middle aisle. Girls mocked his looks but always ended their mocking with a complement to his kindness and "gentlemenlikeness". He was clearly the best dresser in his crowd though and the best dancer. He danced with girls who just wanted to dance with him, not date him.

Slash went to the Carmen movie to see what was playing and because there were supposed to be pretty girls there. Bif with one F said the girls at the Carmen were prettier and more "sew-fist-ticket" than the girls where Bif with two Fs lived. At times, the big guys chipped in and bought the gas for the night. The big guys knew the risks of riding with Slash. A car is a car and a driver is a driver according to the great philosopher, Renaldo the Purloiner. Renaldo promised Slash that he (Slash) would have a new car of his dreams someday, but he'd have to wait until he (Renaldo) learned how to drive from him (Slash).

One year, girls from Royal Roses College, who wanted to get into a sorority, had to dance with Slash at least three times and have him bring her home after Boulevard Ballroom Sunday night dance as an initiation. One of the high-level, already in sorority sisters met Slash at Zeke's barbershop. She was doing research at the time, as many students did, into the life of a typical inner city kid. The inner city part fit ok but the typical part was up for debate. This sorority big-wigess (big wigs for girls) devised this initiation as a trick on Slash as well as an initiation for new members. She laughed at Slash's Adam's apple, which went up and down like the lines on a defective television. The more she mocked Slash to herself, the more ornery the initiation. She had another mocking type initiation: the candidate would have to get a haircut from Zeke the Mad Barber at Zeke's barbershop, which had all male customers. The sorority girls voted Zeke as their favorite businessman for 1955. They were mocking him, of course. They didn't tell him because they didn't want to hurt his feelings. What they didn't know was that Zeke's feelings have been attacked so many times by so many people that he only considered his own feelings about himself, which were good.

Some people even envied Zeke. They would love to wear Phillies sweatshirts and pink striped pants along with bedroom slippers to work like Zeke did. His car was the envy of the neighborhood. It was an old black Olds with bullet holes in the driver's side front door. Zeke's neighbors claim to have seen him fire bullets at the car and then claim it was the Godfather's car.

During that same sorority meeting, which must have been a riot, the gorgeous women of Royal Roses voted Slash as their Man of the Year. During the research of the typical inner city, one of the sorority sisters took pictures of Slash and Zeke. In fact, they took several pictures of Zeke, his customers (including Bif with one F) and his shop. Bif with one F said that everybody cooperated and posed the way the girls wanted them to. The Colonel was at Zeke's wearing his Army & Navy store hat and shirt. The waiting customers read their X-rated magazines as if they were alone. The two kids who were there at the time wanted their pictures with the girls. Zeke changed his Phillies shirt to the "Millie's Five and Dime Beer Store" one, his second favorite. His favorite had pictures of Dagwood Bumstead and Mr. Bluster.

Bif with one F was there when one of the Royal Roses sorority candidates came in Zeke's shop. He said that she looked around the shop with wide opened eyes of amazement. The posters with glamour girls with mustaches and arrows through their heads and the broken mirror with "Kilroy was here" written on it with red lipstick held her attention for a while while Zeke finished a checkers game. She eyed the X-rated magazines but thought it better to leave them alone. She got up to straighten out Zeke's copied copy of the Mona Lisa – with glasses and goatee – hanging on the wall in a very crooked way. She made the mistake that everybody makes straightening out this painting: She moved the bottom of the painting to the left only to see the following on the wall that just became visible: "tomorrow's number is 53889. Don't tell Romeo, he'll kill me".

"Just a little off as a trim, please," asked our naïve victim.

"I'll cut your hair like Betty Davis, the Country singer if you want," replied the good barber, who didn't give the young woman any options.

Zeke never cut girls' hair before and he had no idea what Betty Davis looked like. No barber cut girl's hair; it would be a first for Zeke. Zeke, who kept his combs and scissors in a glass of Alka-

Seltzer normally, went to his checkerboard to get the scissors, which he was using to cut out coupons and pictures of dogs and cats. He, like Uncle Matt, hated dogs. He hated cats; Uncle Matt didn't. When all the coupons and pictures were all cut out, Zeke threw the cat pictures away. He didn't want to influence his customers to buy dogs or cats. He had to get the cat pictures out of the magazines so nobody would say how cute they were. He wiped the scissors against his jacket when he began to use them. Of course, he had to spit on the scissors before he could properly clean them. The girl saw this and started to move her body as if she had itches all over. Zeke dropped an Alka-Seltzer tablet in the glass so the woman could see the sizzle that sanitized his instruments.

Zeke didn't even shake out the semi-white, grossly soiled sheet he used as a cover for the previous customer. He started to put it on the girl when she got up and ran out of the shop. She was actually shaking and crying. Her fully pledged sorority sisters were waiting outside. She asked her sisters to take her to the nearest place where she could wash her hands and face. She vowed to burn the clothes she was wearing. Bif with one F said Zeke called the next customer as if nothing happened. Bob Can-of-Baloney was the next customer. Zeke took Bob's wig off and placed it on his lap to hold until he (Zeke) was finished. The pledged girls from Royal Roses came in the store to see what they just heard. They used the excuse that they thought one of them left her sweater there. Zeke told them to look around for it. They had a ball looking around acting serious. They opened the door at the rear of the shop as if someone would leave a sweater where they've never been. They saw all kinds of junk. Zeke made rounds on trash pickup mornings to pick up certain items for his shop. What Zeke picked up and didn't use right away was put in the back room. Bob Can-of-Baloney was adjusting his wig. Bif with one F said that Bob couldn't get the wig on properly in time to impress the girls so it was all over the place with the part parallel to the shoulders, not front to back. Zeke was telling his waiting customers that he had a best of five series Checker game. They could wait and read the magazines or come back. He said that he expected to win three straight games but there was no guarantee. As usual, nobody left. Slash went to the Sunday night Boulevard Ballroom Dance on Saturday nights. Only the best dancers could get in on Saturdays. He went on Sunday nights too. The scared stiff sorority candidate had to accept the option to Zeke's haircut. She had no other choice. She didn't want to look out of place so she stopped off at the Salvation Army and bought a used (really nice) dress for the initiation.

"Ladies choice, can I have this dance Slash?" the candidate asked.

"Do you want the next slow dance or jitterbug?" Slash wanted to know. He was the best either way. "I like to slow dance myself," he continued assuming that the girl didn't know how to jitterbug.

"Yeah, that's better for me too Slash".

"Do you like the Four Aces?"

"Yeah Slash, I do".

"Ok, let's dance".

"Three Coins in the Fountain," great, it's my favorite".

"I thought so; most girls like that one. Do you like mummer music?"

"I'm afraid Slash that I never heard mummer music; at least I don't think so".

"You'd like it".

"I'll find some and try it".

"Your dress is very beautiful. I'll bet you went to a Salvation Army store in a rich neighborhood".

"Well, not too rich".

Slash danced with his patented trademark "Ted"Astaire/Gene Kelly style. The co-ed immediately commented on Slash's dancing. She said he was the lightest on his feet than anybody she danced with before. I think Slash saw that as a compliment. He heard that before and was never quite sure it was a good thing. Slash was always as neat as a pin. Slash could walk ten miles through a hurricane and never get wet or messy. The Crisco in his hair kept it in place under any circumstance. His size thirteen triple x's were always polished. Slash was the only man his age, maybe fifteen or sixteen, who wore a handkerchief in his lapel pocket. He could do that and look good; Gatemouth and I couldn't.

"How'd jah get the name Slash?" the girl inquired.

"How'd jah know my name?"

"I asked around".

"I got the name on mischief night a few years ago when my tires got slashed while I was in a neighbor's house. The guy who did the slashing thought I was messing around with his friend's wife".

"Were you?"

"No, no, not that. I was selling raffle tickets for St. Christopher's hospital fair. His friend bought tickets that night while his wife went upstairs for something. What's your name?"

"Candy II. My mother is Candy I and my sister is Candy II too". This was all part of the mocking.

"Is your father Cake I?"

"No, he's Canal I and my brother is Canal I too. He's a twin with my other brother Suez I".

"Great names! I might change mine to So-harra desert. Is it confusing having two of the same name?"

"Not really. When we miss a payment, we tell the creditor that the bill went to the wrong II. Can we dance the next Cha-cha?"

"Yes. I'll find you Slash".

"Who's she Slash?" asked Cong-few-shush (Confucius).

"Candy II, this here is Cong-few-shush, like the Chinese sayings maker. He likes fast cars and he holds a lot of world records in speed and bike riding with kids hanging on".

"Candy II, are you Slash's girl friend? You're the third best 'look in' one but you have the best looking dress," Cong naively asked.

"No, we just danced".

"Good, will you dance with me Candy II? Call me Cong".

"Not this dance Cong; maybe later".

"What time Candy II? I mean I can remind you. Thank you for coming here tonight Candy II. I hope that you come back," responded an excited Cong.

"Cha-cha, Slash?"

"Next one Candy II, for sure".

"See you then Slash. Chow and Cha-cha".

Slash commented to Cong, "Monroe. That's Marleen(sic) Monroe for looks. But she can't dance at all; she can't follow too well".

"Maybe Slash, Candy II is too sweet to dance, get it? She's like Kim Novak or Marlene, the husband killer on Toronto," Cong tried to be funny.

"She said she can Cha-cha; we'll see," Slash wondered. In all fairness to Candy II, only a few girls could stay with Slash when he was dancing.

Candy II found Slash and they danced the Cha-cha to Louie Prima and Keely Smith. Actually, Candy II, like all the other girls, loved dancing with Slash. His pencil-like neck and his huge buckteeth didn't seem to bother Candy II; they never bothered Slash. Somehow, Slash saw himself as the Casanova type. I always thought of him as the Mortimer Snerd or Icabod Crane type.

"Can I have the last dance Slash?," Candy II asked almost begging.

"No, I have a richrule (ritual) that I dance with the girl who is the most wall-flower of them all".

"That's nice. How do you find her?"

"It's easy Candy II. The wallflowers come near me and decide not to take the chance of asking me to dance. Believe me, I would never reject them but they don't know that. The last song is always 'Good Night Sweetheart' by the Uptown string band. It's mummer's music but you don't do the Mummer's Strut".

This is an unreal story. Cong doesn't lie. Slash will get his teeth fixed or taken out; then he'll look better. He needs to put his elbows on a table and push his forehead real hard against his hands, keeping his elbows on the table. The pressure builds up the neck. It's what all the Irish do as part of their exercises. Bif with one F does this exercise. His neck goes straight down from his ears to his shoulder. He needs to throw away that suicide knob; it scares everybody.

Slash and Candy II danced to the next to last song, "How Do You Speak to An Angel" by Eddie Fisher. After the last dance, which Candy II danced with Cong, Candy II asked Slash if he could drive her home. Cong was listening because he still held Candy II's hand.

"Where do you live Candy II?" Cong asked.

"In Swarthmore, on the Main Line".

"The Maine line is near New Hampshire isn't it?" Cong wondered.

"Oh no, Confucius, it's about an hour and a half away. Do you know the Main Line outside Philadelphia?"

"I know it Candy II. My uncle once took me to Malvern for a retreat and he told me the Main Line is beautiful but expensive".

"OK, that's great Slash. Let's go," Cong said as he pictured himself on the Main line pretending to be a college student in an Ivory (Ivy) league school.

"Are you going with us Confucius?" Candy II wanted to find out.

"He's going to St. Boniface's parish. Renaldo will drive us in my car. Renaldo, this is Candy II," Slash said.

"Maybe I should go all the way to Swarthmore with use (you)".

"Renaldo, I'd like to get to know Slash a little better. Do you mind not going," Candy II asked in a kind way.

"No, let's go now though because I got some shopping to do," Renaldo said as Candy II looked on as if she or Renaldo was a nut.

Renaldo sat with Confucius in the front seat and, naturally, Candy II sat with Slash in the back. Renaldo couldn't start the car. He never started Slash's car. He never used the choke knob. He was way too young to drive but he took over driving for his customers. He finally started it but didn't do too well with the clutch and had the car bucking its way down the Boulevard. Slash let Candy II know that he was teaching Renaldo how to drive in exchange for a different car, which Renaldo will get for him.

"Shouldn't you be up front with Renaldo Slash?"

"Nah Candy II, he learns as he goes along and this is only his second day driving and already he's on the Boulevard". Candy II wondered if the jokes on her.

"Slash, why doesn't he use the steering wheel?"

"Renaldo, you're not ready for the suicide knob yet. Grab the wheel at ten-twenty. Don't worry Candy II; we'll be up front when we drop Renaldo off. Renaldo, where yah gone (going) tonight?"

"Just drop me off with Cong; I'll be alright Slash".

"Are you ok back there Candy II?" asked Cong, who took a liking to Candy II.

"Yes, I'm fine Cong. Are we almost at St. Boniface's?"

"Almost Candy II, fifteen more minutes," assured Renaldo, who drove like an experienced driver except for the few minutes he was on the wrong side of the boulevard.

"Don't worry Candy II; we'll have a lot of time together alone. Renaldo, does this gas station owner know you?" Slash was talking.

"Yeah, he does. I'll stop for gas," volunteered Renaldo.

"Renaldo knows everybody and everybody owes Renaldo something. Cong will pump the gas while Renaldo talks to the attendant," Slash reassured Candy II.

"Is it full yet Confucius?"

"Yes and a bit over the mark to boot Slash".

"Did it go ok Renaldo?"

"Of course Cong, but now I have to get a Penn football jersey; the one with the red, white and blue striped arms".

"Here Candy II is a beautiful glass with Tennessee on it. You can collect all forty-eight if you buy gas from Texaco".

"It's beautiful Renaldo".

"I'll get the whole set for you by next Friday if you want me to".

"That's alright; I'll get them in time". I felt relieved when Cong told me that she refused the set of glasses.

When they got to St. Boniface's parish, Confucius, and Renaldo got out. Slash got into the driver's seat and Candy II reluctantly got in the front passenger's seat. Slash liked her dress like the other guys and told her so. It was Scotch Plaid with a green shoulder wrap and ruffled neckline. Slash wanted to know if Candy II was comfortable before he took off. The radio came on for no reason. Slash said that that is normal. If you hit a bump sometimes, it'll come on. If you hit another bump sometimes, it'll go off. The Four Aces were singing, "Tell Me Why" followed by Perry Como's "Don't Let the Stars Get in Your Eyes". Candy II was feeling something she rarely if ever felt before: calm, comfortable and excited.

"The moon is full tonight Slash," Candy II said as if hinting something like a goodnight kiss.

"I know; it gets to that level every so often," answered Slash picking up the hint but not quite believing it.

"Your friends are very nice guys. They are so polite and courteous."

"They are I know that. I'm glad you like them Candy II."

"Is Bif with one F a nice guy too?"

"He's the best and he'll knock out anybody who bothers you or any woman".

"That's good to know. Your car is well kept on the inside".

"Thanks, but the outside has been hit a few times. I won't use the suicide knob if you're scared of it".

"Do whatever you want, it's your car".

"Yes it is but I want you to feel safe".

Candy II remained quiet throughout most of the trip. She paid no attention to where they were or how long the trip was taking. She was in a semi-trance. She left the trance when something came from under the seat. It was a trophy with the name Joe "Slash" O'Meara. He won the All Catholic track meet in 1955, this year. He didn't want to discuss the trophy or the meet. He said that it was over and it was great while it lasted. He didn't say that he dropped out of North and dropped out of Northeast public high three weeks after he started there.

Candy II told Cong what was going through her mind on the drive back to her college. Candy II was thinking:

Why is that moon full tonight of all nights? I'll ask Daddy to send me to Rome so I can throw a coin in the Trevi Fountain. Slash's suit is very cool. His hair is so thick and flat; like a red headed Gable. That's nice. He's only a high school kid. Actually, it's cute the way his collar is at least three inches from touching his neck. Zeke is a bit nuts but I'm going back to let him cut my hair. Renaldo is one to avoid even though he is a nice guy. He's bound to get caught someday. I'm gonna watch Confucius pitch. He said they'll play Episcopal Academy. I hope he pitches that game. Ted's brother plays for Episcopal. I hope it's Confucius against Zachary. I'll miss these guys, including Zeke. Maybe, especially Zeke; he is a piece of work. Renaldo promised to get me a girl's Scottish hat, a tam maybe, if I come back and a 45 recording machine if I swim there. I'm getting Eddie Fisher singing about speaking to an angel.

I'm keeping this dress; I love it. I thought it was all part of the initiation. I won't buy new clothes until I check out Salvation Army stores.

"Here we are, Royal Roses College. Is this the place? It's big. Do you have many brothers and sisters? I'll walk you to the door to make sure you're safe," said Slash.

"Thanks Slash".

"Your sisters are looking out the second floor window, see em? Who's Sarah?"

"Oh Sarah! You meant the welcome home sign to Sarah. She's a sister who was away last semester".

"The sign says 'Welcome home Sister Sarah. You passed the test. I saw Slash; Colleen took the bar exam in England".

Slash caught on but was too much of a gentleman to let Candy II (now Sarah) know that he did.

Slash walked Candy II to her door, bowed slightly and quietly said good-bye. The sisters on the second floor are mimicking Slash and mimicking "kiss him" using their lips to spell out the words and pretend to be kissing. Candy II didn't kiss him because she was afraid the sisters would never let up mocking her. She felt a little yucky about being too close to Slash. Slash wouldn't let her anyway; he knew his place. He knew that he was out of his element and he wished that he had a normally shaped head at least.

"He was a good dancer with a car to drive her home in. He liked his neck and teeth but he knew others found humor in them. He can join the Army or heaven forbid drive a jeep or a truck," Sarah thought.

Flash got in his car, didn't look back and drove away the same way he came. He didn't look hurt or angry that he was a victim of some kind of game. The sisters ran out the door, laughing as if the Three Stooges just left, to get all the dirt. One of the sisters held up an orange with a pencil in it. The orange had eyes, ears, a mouth and a nose, presumably this was Slash.

"It was the best night of my life. Slash should teach dancing; he's terrific. I met Bif with one F, Renaldo the Purloiner, and Cong-few-shush. I heard all about Otto the Outrageous, Horse Head Lady, Marlene the Mass Murderer and Violet and Doc the Clock and Gatemouth. Renaldo and Confucius liked my dress. I'll get a 45 player and a Scottish dress beret from Renaldo if I go back and bring him a donut from our cafeteria".

"You'd go back there for a beret?"

"No, but I'll go back to see everybody. They told me that I didn't hurt Zeke's feelings. Nobody hurts Zeke's feelings they said," Sarah rambled on.

"Well, you're in the sorority, congratulations," said the head sister, the one with the long sleeping gown and black eye shades sitting on top of her head.

"No, not me, it's not me to be a sister. I'll move out by Friday and go to the dorms. I'm changing my major to Anthropology so I can meet more exciting people like I met tonight," responded the new transformed Sarah.

"Sarah, be careful, don't get too emotional about one night," advised a sister.

"Yeah Sarah, you could end up marrying one," cautioned another sister.

"One what?," Sarah asked knowing the answer.

"You know what I mean Sarah".

"Did any of the Haverford guys tell you that your dress was beautiful? Did any Penn or Princeton guy promise to get you a Scottish beret? Can you swim under a fireplug? Name one guy who walked you to our door and left without trying to con you into letting him come in. Did you ever wear a Salvation Army used dress? I had more life changing events tonight than I had in eighteen years. I'm buying mummer's music; it's great and it's a tradition in Philadelphia. Eddie Fisher can sing, believe me".

"What will your parents say?" asked the brown shaded sister.

"I hope that they'll want to have the guys out to our house for a Bar-b-que. Did I mention the Tioga Ts? Gatemouth will make me a free hoagie or cheese steak. Can you believe that? Marlene is an old fashioned actress, who killed five husbands at least with another one ready to go at any minute. Their pretzels are hot when they get them out of the oven and Albert, one of the little kids, can shimmy up an alley to a roof, fall off, and land on his feet just in time".

"Sarah, don't quit school," a few sisters begged.

"You gotta be kiddin; I'll get a Ph.D. in this field. Anthropology. I'll write my dissertation about the guys on Carlisle Street. Good night sisters. I'll see you around campus".

Sarah changed her major as she said she would. It made no difference because you can't declare a major until junior year earliest. She had to have at least a 2.8 GPA to get her favored major at that time. She drove up to the Carlisle Street she heard so much about and got right into the scene. She met Horse Head Lady and watched Marlene go to the American store with her long black coat, huge red hat, extra large sunglasses, and black high top sneakers. She met Bif with one F at the Carmen and asked him out to dinner. He accepted with "a humble and contrite heart". She had a blast with Bif with one F and planned to do dinner with him repeatedly if she could. She appreciated his poetry and convinced him to keep writing poems. She went to Bif with one F's fight at the Cambria and went bananas when he won. Bif with one F was a total gentleman; that's all he knew how to be.

I'm glad that Candy II told Bif with one F everything, including how much she enjoyed the dance and the ride home. I wish Candy II, Sarah, could meet Bif with one F's mother and see

how well he treats her. She would like him even more than she does now. His poor grammar, Philadelphia accent, and boxing or bowling shoes would certainly turn her parents off; that's sad. If her parents would pay for Bif with one F's GED and college, he would be a brilliant poet and writer. They probably wouldn't want to pay tuition to a state school and Bif with one F couldn't be accepted into an Ivy League school.

Candy II went with the St. Stephen's boys, including me, to the Strand. She snuck in with the rest of us. She crawled through the open door at the front of the theater. She was so frightened that her family would lose their membership to the country club if she was caught that we let her go last so she could tell the police that she was trying to stop us. She got in all right and enjoyed the movie, "High Noon," a classic western. She passed up on the thirty cartoons and second movie, an Esther Williams' swimming one. We all passed on them too. She knew she had to be cool as she left with us; she was cool. Bob Can-of-Baloney looked at her in a strange way when she was leaving but Bob would never embarrass her by asking how she got in. She smiled at Bob and Bob smiled back; not the same smile as when he's handing out candy to little kids.

Candy II said that her South Street clothes really become handy at times like sneaking in movies. She couldn't sit with us for too long. She had to go to the ladies' room to wash her hands and knees. The rugs were filthy and a person's hands and knees got pretty dirty when they snuck in. We came back to Carlisle Street and Candy II's day was "a day of fulfillment". She met Otto the Outrageous and Switch; two more goals completed. She hoped that she could meet Gatemouth but she didn't have time to go to his store.

Otto the Outrageous greeted her with a bow with his right hand on his stomach and his left hand on his back.

"How may I serve you Miss Monroe?" was his first encounter. "Welcome to my Princedom. Do you like it?"

Renaldo gave Otto a real sword by now and he was more frightening than ever. Switch, the always intoxicated, was in a rush. He had a client and he couldn't find his hat, which he was wearing. He drank Listerine to "clean my breath from germs and the 'onion stink' ".

She came when Albert, the climbing fool, was around and he had new sneakers, black, high top Keds, which he got from a

Milkman who saw him roof running. Albert was outfitted for just one thing: an Olympic meet on Carlisle Street and his inevitable gold medal in Roof Running.

"Oh goody, the Olympics. Is Albert here?" Candy II (Sarah) asked hoping that he was and she could fulfill another goal.

"I'm here up on the roof," Albert screamed from the roof.

"How'd you get up there?" Candy II asked. It was a dumb question for anyone who knew Albert.

"I'll show you madams". Joan from next door came over. She's the one who jumps out of windows and thinks she's Edith Piaf.

"See, it's easy getting down". Albert just hung by his feet from the roof of the three-story house and let go to flip over and land on his feet. "Going up is easy too. Just put your right foot here and pull with your hands until you can get the left foot going. Then you just keep doing it until you make the top. Wanna see me run across the porch roofs?"

"Maybe later Albert, I'm stunned at what I just saw you do," Candy II said as she bowed her head and made the face of someone who just ate a rotten egg.

"Watch, it's easy to run across".

"Oh my God Albert; you make me crazy".

"You make me crazy too because I like you and your rich car. I'll run the roofs blindfolded if that will make you go to the movies with me".

"Albert, I'd never let you watch a movie if I went with you".

"I know; it's ok".

23

Otto the Outrageous

I was walking home from school feeling rushed though I had the usual amount of time. Things got a little rough because I hadn't received forgiveness for telling a huge lie to Sr. Helen. I told her that Forest Forester and I served four masses when we served only one, then played football for a couple hours.

"Stop and clearly identify yourself, young man. Did you wait for the light to turn green before you proceeded?"

It was the outlandish Otto the Outrageous. Otto's real name is Raymond, but he decided that he was a king in a past life, not "this Raymond fellow". I guess that he preferred being a king than a high school graduate. He dropped out of high school to reclaim his kingdom. His kingdom stretched from Broad and Spring Garden to Broad and Westmoreland and from Broad Street's east side to the river. He has never forgiven his great, great grandfather's Court Jester for losing the king's territory over a dispute over who was his great, great grandfather's favorite. Otto said that the Jester bet the stableman and, after consulting the Wizard, the stableman won. I didn't need this nonsense now. I kept walking at a brisk pace.

"Can't you see that I am wearing a new royal garment?"

"No Otto, I can't," I said under my breath, "It looks like the same robe you always wear and the turban is as soiled as it was when it was a large towel hanging on the Flynn's clothes' line".

I promised myself that I would buy Otto a Carmen Miranda hat with bananas and pineapples on it. He steals towels and sheets off clothes' lines. The sheets became robes and woe-be-tied the poor naïve person who hung out a colored sheet. Otto loved to be in living color. He would never part with his sword. He made it himself by taking wood off the ash pile after the firemen left the storage building's fire. He nailed an eight-inch piece of plywood close to the top of another piece of plywood, maybe three feet in length. I knew Otto when he was Raymond Doyle, a prolific comic book reader and a good scooter maker. Raymond helped us to get old milk crates and spare pieces of wood. We used these materials to make a scooter. We nailed the crate to a two-by-four and attached a skate part to the front and the other part to the back of the two-by-four. Otto was tall and strong.

He played JV football for North and he started all the games. He would have been on the varsity but he refused to wear the varsity uniform because he hated the shade of red of the helmets and jerseys. The coach told Otto that he would play in only those games when North wore their white jerseys. Otto wanted a white helmet. The coach couldn't coax Otto into the red helmets so Otto quit the team. What a shame it was too. Otto could catch anything thrown at him. The big guys chose him first for every sport because he was the best athlete in their crowd. Once, in a JV football game, Otto tackled the wrong guy, got up and chased the right guy and tackled him too. In another JV game, Otto played fullback – he was usually an end – and ran for three touchdowns in the first half. This was against La Salle, a team that is highly respected for toughness.

"I'm now in garnet and gold, can't you see?" firmly stated the Outrageous one, who gave the first and second graders one Mary Jane or waxed root beers for pulling him down the street in a wooden wagon.

He sat in the Radio Flyer until he reached an audience when he stood up and started in on the problems of being an unappreciated and unrecognized king. He wielded the sword as he proclaimed his right to royalty.

"Your Highness, I'm late for school. I will get a closer look when I come home," I humbly told the Outrageous one.

"Better yet, meet me at the paper branch at 3:30 this afternoon so you can show all the paperboys your new royal garments."

"I'll be there if Renaldo the Purloiner gives me the real sword he promised me. I'll have to wait til Sunday when Renaldo does most of his shopping," committed our Prince.

I didn't want to talk to anyone, ever again after I lied to Sister Helen that Andrew and I served four masses and couldn't help being late.

I have to get to Confession. I'll put off the apology for lying to Sister for a while. Father Martin won't ask me to apologize before he gives me absolution. Father Curran might make me unless I mumble and he doesn't understand me. Maybe I'll put what I did in between some serious sins that I didn't commit. It's easy to confess sins you didn't commit.

Father, I stole a hundred dollars, hit my sisters, cursed, lied to Sister, robbed a bank, set off the fire alarm, and teased Uncle Matt, the dog hater. How can I ask for a special Confession? Grandmom always said that, "It's a long lane that has no turning". She said that it means you won't get away with lying to or cheating other people. Things always work their way out. It means that things change and bad days turn into good ones. Oh no, there's Uncle Matt the Dog Hater.

Uncle Matt was about a hundred years old. He was small and bent over. He wore a black hat and a full-length black overcoat all year round. He carried a cane, which never hit the ground, like a baton. He had dark rimmed glasses and looked at you over them. His shoes were black and well-worn. They needed heals for sure and probably soles. When he talked to someone, he would grab the middle of his cane and pump it up and down like a drum major. He whispered. His occasional attempt to stand straight exposed his sometimes white, sometimes off white shirt and his new Davy Crockett tie and coonskin cap. Renaldo the Purloiner gave the tie to Uncle Matt. Renaldo gave Davy Crockett ties to Doc the Clock and anybody who would tell Sophia, our gorgeous neighbor that he wanted to take her to a dinner and movie and that he would pay. Renaldo added that he would drive and he wanted to know what color car Sophia liked. Renaldo was about thirteen and Sophia about eighteen. Sophia was sought after by all the guys; Renaldo was sought after by all the police. Uncle Matt liked Renaldo because all he had to do was ask Renaldo for something and he got it.

Uncle Matt's old tie was black with a tiepin shaped like an arrow. The new tie didn't have a tiepin to go with it. Uncle Matt walked around the neighborhood all day long, every day, rain or shine. Dogs attacked him on numerous occasions and felt that he had to take action. He wore an old black bowler sometimes, but not today. A hundred year old man with a Davy Crockett hat and tie would have been a riot to see except for Otto the Outrageous and his nonsensical wardrobe. Uncle Matt's had to wear his long, black coat because, even though he was on the witness protection list, he didn't want the Communists to see his medals for fear that they'd notice his *"Honor Medal for Being of Courage,"* which is the only one given since the "France and Greeks War of Third Century after that night in Bethlehem". They'd know it was he if they saw that medal. He couldn't take the risk.

He carried doggie crackers in his coat pocket. He put the crackers on electoral wires that fell to the ground during storms and hurricanes. The junk yard dogs that hung around the abandoned railroad spur in packs would eat anything and they were very hungry after a storm. Uncle Matt must have been a veterinarian and an electrician to recognize this. Well, he really wasn't either. We all knew Uncle Matt's background. His friend, Flanagan, who was a onetime secret service agent from Switzerland, who uses an assumed name, told it to our crowd many times. Flanagan wears a straw hat so people will assume "he isn't as intelligent as he is".

Uncle Matt was in the German army and captured by the Allies in England. He became a spy for the Allies and reported to Eisenhower and Patten every month with new information. He went to the United States after the war to live incognito with the assumed name of Matthew Jones. He lost his house and all his money in a game of Chinese checkers to the local dry cleaner. We used to joke that he "was taken by the cleaners".

"Seen any dogs on the way Billy?" asked Uncle Matt as he pulled a couple doggie crackers from his pocket. His black tie came out with the crackers.

"No Uncle Matt, you're ok to walk to Lehigh. Stay away from the railroad lot and you'll be fine," I assured my friend.

I couldn't help but wonder how a well decorated war hero could be so concerned about dogs, but he was. I do remember that he wore an old army shirt and hat with his long black coat at times. He also hung around Uncle Sam's Army and Navy store.

"I gotta run Uncle Matt. Have a nice walk. You're ok to Lehigh or even Dauphin," is all that I had time to say.

That's enough. No more interruptions. I have to figure out what to say in Confession. Oh God, this can't be true, there's Father Jimmy Higgins. He's home from the Missions, I bet. I served his first mass and he knew me. This Confession will be too

easy. I hope Pete the Cop didn't see me sneak down Butler Street. Wouldn't it be great if he broke his leg and Pop wouldn't catch me lying. Did Uncle Matt buy that Davy Crockett hat from Renaldo with his new tie?

"Good morning Father Higgins, welcome home," I said

"Thanks William; how's school?"

"It's fine Father and do you hear Confessions?"

"Yes, of course, do you need to go?" Father looked at me as if I had to get a murder off my mind. This was worse.

How can I not destroy Forest Forester's reputation? It wouldn't be fair. The good thief is going to heaven. He's the only one in history that we're sure of. He asked for forgiveness in his own way. I'll just say a prayer for the conversion of Russia. That will cover me until I get Extreme Unction. Blessed Lady dressed in light Notre Dame blue, I will never get into this type of mess again if you help me get out of it. I'll tell Father Higgins that I forced Forest into everything. Sister should have known that I was lying to her. She's the one being deceitful, not me.

"Not now, Father, but maybe on Saturday, if you're still around."

"I'll be around. God bless you. How's Fran?"

"He's on North's football team and he goes to St. Joachim's annex."

Bishop Sheen said he hoped that, when he died and saw Jesus, Jesus would have a smile on his face. I've got no chance for that. Bishop Sheen also said that the saddest words ever said were, "they received their rewards". I got my reward for being such a big deal to the Tioga Ts to be able to join their gang; eternal damnation.

24

Fortitude Farrell

Before I introduce you to Fortitude Farrell, I'll remind you about Bif with one F. He's the toughest guy in this area. He's about twenty years old and he won a big heavy weight fight at the Cambria against a pro fighter. He hangs around here (the Carmen movie) to make sure the bigger kids aren't bullying the little kids. He wears bowling shoes. The main reason for that is money. He gets bowling shoes free from the owner of the Strike it Rich bowling alley. Bif with one F sometimes wears boxing shoes that some of the trainers at the Cambria give him. Sister St. Catherine at St. Stephen's, Bif with one F's seventh grade teacher, won't give his poems back to him. She cherishes them and claims that a genius wrote them. Bif with one F sings in St. Stephen's choir during regular High Masses, not Christmas or Easter High Masses. Bif with one F combs his jet-black, tar-like hair like Tony Curtis. All the boys do until they get a haircut from Zeke the Mad Barber. Fortitude Farrell, who knows many movie stars, threatened to tell Janet Leigh, Tony Curtis' wife, about the hairstyles. Fortitude said that Tony never plays on his looks and that he would laugh it off anyway.

Fortitude wanted to go to a movie with me to see what it was like. I warned her that most kids from the fourth grade on sneak in at anytime during the movie.

"Hey Bif with one F, come over here, there's someone I'd like you to meet," I called.

"Bif with one F, this is Fortitude Farrell," I introduced him.

"Nice to meet you Madam. May I say this to you? Your car is the best car I ever seen. Is it a convertible?" Bif with one F opened up. The top was down but Bif with one F wanted to have a conversation.

"Yes, it's a convertible and I'm happy to meet you too Bif with one F," Fortitude said as only a lady could.

"Oh, he told you my full name. There's a Biff with two F's who lives at K&A and I'm not him," Bif with one F clarified.

"Where's everybody Bif with one F; it's usually more crowded by now?" I wondered aloud.

"I know Bill but I don't know where they all are. The movies, 'Rear Window' and 'On the Waterfront' are famous for being great and the prices are still a dime for one person. Mr. Cunningham is losing money and he can't keep up the movie theater. On good days, he brings in less than his salaries," Bif with one F said with a sad, sad voice.

"I agree Bif with one F that the movies are great; I saw them in New York," confirmed Farrell.

"Here's some little kids. The bigger kids are around back, sneaking in. Mr. Cunningham doesn't ask to see the report cards before he hires an usher anymore so the ushers aren't the caring type," mentioned Bif with one F.

"Does the owner pay you to watch over the little kids?" Fortitude inquired as I noticed that she was developing a real liking for Bif with one F.

"No Miss Fortune, but I don't pertechnically (sic) care. I make enough money at my accounts payable jobs at the pier and bouncing at Romano's place. I get $5.00 for most cases for being the collector and $10.00 if the case requires a nightstick or specially made knuckles. I get free food at Romano's and money for each removal," was Bif with one F at his finest.

"You better go in. Sit in the left middle and on the end of the row," Bif with one F recommended.

"I know Bif with one F, I come here all the time. The kids that sneak in come up the right side and never stop talking and throwing popcorn," I told Bif with one F.

"How much for two tickets Bif with one F?" Fortitude wanted to know.

"Twenty cents Madam; that's two nickels or one dime each" Bif with one F told her though he mentioned this before. His answer made no sense. He meant two nickels each or one dime each.

"Bill, do you want me to hold your ticket or put it in the box?" Lester, the ticket taker, wore a maroon uniform and white shirt, which needed some work. His sneaks didn't fit too well with the maroon bow tie. If he held my ticket, he and the cashier could make money or he could give it to a friend.

"Put it in the box Lester, but give us the stubs," I told Lester because I wanted a souvenir. Fortitude was special and I didn't want to forget her.

"Lester thinks I might want to use the ticket next week," I told Fortitude, who was getting a good education.

The movies were good and Fortitude liked them again. The ushers kept putting their flashlights on us saying, "No smoking or keep your feet off the seats". The owner's son, Dickie Sickie, who snuck in the theater for the fun of it, asked if everything was all right at least five times. He asked Fortitude, not me. The movies ended and we walked to her car. Fortitude wanted to get me some ice cream or hot dogs. I mentioned how much I liked H&H's little chocolate cakes. We went to Hornies (H&H). Fortitude liked the automat. She spent a lot of money to get chocolate cakes for me. Her apple pie looked good. I had chocolate milk. Fortitude asked for a special drink, milk with a raw egg and a sprinkle of ginger. We got everything from the automat except Fortitude's drink. Fortitude settled for cinnamon, not ginger.

"It's not First Friday and you're too late for pancakes anyway," the friendly waitress commented. She's everybody's "Irish Mother". Her name was Clara and her brogue was unmistakably county Leitrim.

"Do you remember me?" I asked knowing that all the waitresses knew all the St. Stephen's kids from First Friday pancakes.

"Yes, you have the map of my home country written all over your face and a freckle for every good Catholic," answered Clara with the heaviest brogue I ever heard and white dress with a green apron and a green flower pinned to her dress.

All the waitresses at H&H had white dresses, green aprons, and green flowers. They were all about five-foot-four with gray hair and a bit more than average builds. They were mostly old and caring. The occasional young waitresses were uncaring to us seventh and eighth graders. They perked up suddenly when a North guy with a big neck and a friendly smile came in. The North guys were famous for big necks – at least the football players were. Their friendly smiles came and went depending on the age and looks of the nearby girls. Pretty girls got smiles, not so pretty girls got frowns.

"You must be Irish," Fortitude brilliantly concluded.

"I am that. And you must be the famous model from Nicetown, Miss Farrell," Clara surprised Fortitude and me. "I'm as Irish as Paddy's Taproom pig on Paddy's Day, Miss Farrell and so are you. It's easy to see that with your beauty and pleasant smile".

"I'm from Nicetown, I model, and I found out recently that I am famous but only in Nicetown. You should see my smile when I get up in the morning," answered my humble date.

I hope that Edie the Seedy and Flo from Kokomo see me with Fortitude. They're using my favorite First Friday table and they know it. Pop really got mad when I said Edie the Seedy. Girls can like older boys but boys aren't supposed to like older girls. That's ok, they are terrific to all the St. Stephen's kids.

"Well, I'm Clara MacGuire from Leitrim in Ireland. The county seat that is, Carrick-on-the-Shannon. That is Roland behind the counter. He is a native Philadelphian. The girl with the green corsage is, believe it or not, Molly Malone from Belfast. Could we get a group picture with you Miss Farrell?" Miss O'Hannolyn asked as the others awaited Fortitude's answer.

"Sure; just show me where you want me to go," Fortitude volunteered.

"That's a nice camera," I suggested.

"Tis that lad and a pretty penny to get for sure," Miss MacGuire assured me.

The waitresses straightened out their dresses and adjusted the flowers pinned on their front pockets so they (the flowers) were in full view. A few more H&H people got in the picture. The cooks and the servers from behind the counter joined in as they all ran their tongues over their teeth and straightened their hair. The manager, Mr. Malachy – we call him malarkey – stood in the back. I sat this one out. The customers had to wait and they didn't seem to mind. In fact, the customers took their own pictures. The picture circulated around North Broad Street and ended up hanging on the walls of several bars and diners. Fortitude autographed Gatemouth's copy and didn't know how to make it personal. She knew she couldn't sign "To Gatemouth" and I didn't know his real name. Fortitude, who now wanted me to call her Miss Fortune, started to talk about the challenges she faces as she moves up in the world of fashion.

"My friends fear that they aren't loved. When they are in a relationship that's about to break up, they, me included, get this hollow-like feeling like there is nothing left in life. They feel that their careers are going to end because some director or designer will drop them like the relationship dropped. They usually blame themselves for the breakup and they hope and pray that everything will be as it was. They try to get comfort from friends and family but that doesn't work after a short time. Loneliness and sadness take over their lives. They feel ugly, fat, and unattractive to the audience and directors. They get around to their old selves after weeks, months or years of insaneness. Worst of all, they settle for some real creeps and allow themselves to be disappointed repeatedly. Do you know what I mean Bill?"

"No Miss Fortune, I don't," and I didn't.

"That's great. Does Bif with one F get that way?" asked Miss Fortune.

"No, not Bif with one F or even Biff with two Fs, they're too tough. None of the big guys get bad hurts from girls. The big guys like girls like Sophia across the street but never approach her because she's too beautiful I think. Their families hurt them more than girls did. Big guys never get lonely or sad; they're so tough that they punch each other as hard as they can and nobody cries. Only girls and ladies cry," I proudly told her.

Fortitude wanted to drive around a little and then go home. We drove all around Hunting Park and then I suggested that she might like Lehigh and Germantown. She did and made me promise to show her the ropes around the area, especially selecting chickens and buying horseradish and orange marmalade. We passed Our Lady of Mercy and I told the story of our basketball game. She knows Ramar and O'Donnell and wants to meet Mousy and Fitterman. I didn't mention Buzzard, whose story is too sad to mention. We drove by the North Philly train station and I told her the Mickey Mantle's autograph story. She met Willie Mays and did an advertisement in a magazine with Whitey Carr. She meant Whitey Ford. She was close enough with the name so that I knew whom she meant. We came to the corner of Broad and Clearfield and Fortitude let me out.

"Hubba-hubba, the girl is a beauty queen," interjected Otto the Outrageous.

"Hi Otto. Fortitude, this is Otto the Outrageous, a Prince. The government confiscated his Princedom and he's been on a personal

Crusade to get it back," I educated Fortitude. I couldn't call her Miss Fortune or misfortune.

"Nice to meet you Prince Otto the Outrageous, I'm Fortitude Farrell," was her simple reply.

"Shush and be quiet. I know who you are. Your Look magazine picture hangs in my gardener's house and mine as well. There must be silence until the coast is clear," Otto whispered.

"What's this all about Otto?" I really didn't care but I asked anyway.

"It's not Otto and then again it is. I can't be seen here for very long. Please excuse me madam and Bill. I'll be right back," Otto confused us with his nonsense.

"Fortitude, you can go home if you'd like; this is gonna be nutty, believe me," I warned Fortitude.

"I would pay my salary for doing the Look picture to see this. I am in love with all the people I've met and I haven't met Doc the Clock or Renaldo the Purloiner or Uncle Matt or Cee Gar or Uncle Dan or Buggy," Fortitude exclaimed.

"You'll meet them and Deafy and all girls and women on my paper route," I promised.

"Don't forget Celeste," Fortitude wanted to see her old friend, the Horse Head Lady.

"I can't, I see her almost every day," I said.

I couldn't believe what I saw coming out of the small tool-shed the workers use at the Gulf station being built. Fortitude was aghast and thrilled at the same time; I was aghast and I live here. Otto the Outrageous took off his toga (a bed sheet from somebody's wash hanging outside to dry) and put away his real sword, which he got from Renaldo, before he went into the shed. The sword was a genuine antique and very valuable. Renaldo the Purloiner took good care of his friends.

The person coming out was somebody else and I wondered who it, he or she was. The creature was Otto's height and build but even Otto wouldn't go this far to attract attention. He wanted to remain invisible to the world. The person/thing wasn't scary, but it, he or she could have been from another planet. The Thing-person came close enough so we could tell who it was; it was Otto the Outrageous in disguise.

"Can you hear me? Otto whispered as he moved his head back and forth, I don't want anyone to notice me. They're after me because

I'm getting close to proving that this territory is mine. My new name is Chester Field and you can call me Smoky. Is anybody staring at us?" Smoky asked.

Nobody was staring at that time but Smoky had better get used to stares. Fortitude did not understand Smoky. How could she, she was sane. No other neighborhood had an Otto the Outrageous.

"Smoky, I wonder if you would describe your outfit and where you got the components of it. I want to go there and get some real clothes," said Fortitude in a serious, professional way.

Smoky replied, "I will do just that, I will describe my outfit and tell you where I got each item. I normally go to the Louvre in Europe or the very, very famous men's shop in Galway Bay also in Europe but not in the real Europe like Poland and Malta. Bill, is the coast clear? I can't be noticed. The city and the FBI are plotting a plot to send me back to wherever my father, the King, is from. I can't remember. There is so much evidence to show that I own this land around here to the river that they have to exile me to keep me quiet. Fortitude, would you notice me if you weren't looking for me?"

"Yes, I would because your outfit is so unusual, you stand out".

"Maybe I'll remove a few things. My outfit, you want to know where did I get it from; let's see".

He kept going, to Fortitude's delight, "My Carman Miranda hat came from Carman Miranda who was performing at a club nearby. I don't know the name of the club but Renaldo knows her very well and he traded her a Cherry Red convertible for the hat. She threw in these earrings and high length shoes, which don't fit. The hat is at least ten inches high and I'm over six feet tall. The buckteeth were a gift from the dental students at Temple (the buckteeth looked like the wax kind that some kids eat after wearing them to scare people). I got this horrible sports coat from Dick Crean's or Robert Hall's, I forget which. I hate the colors but Renaldo got such a great deal for it that I couldn't say no to him. I think he gave the sales clerk five tickets to see the Yankees play the As. Renaldo, this very kind man, threw in some luggage and a sports coat he got from Gimbel's".

The sports coat is an old Mummer's coat from when one of the fancy divisions had a Batman theme. I remember these outfits well. Several characters from Batman comics were in the parade. The coat is purple with white question marks and yellow

exclamation signs all over it. Renaldo the Purloiner could get into any place he wanted to "buy" things.

Back to Otto, "Renaldo got these pants for me. In exchange for the pants, he will give its owner two Schwinn bikes for his kids, one red, one blue. These pants are worth a lot of money, I'm told. Al Jolson and Eddie Cantor both wore these at different times in Vaudeville shows. The owner of the pants said that Al Jolson sang Mammy for the ninth time during a trip to the Steel Pier then gave his pants to the first person who could name the Three Stooges and the Marx Brothers".

"I had these shoes from when I was Otto. I painted them the gold you see for the Mummers' parade. The Uptown string band needed more musicians so I signed up. I didn't play any instruments so my cousin went for the audition in my name. He plays the accordion. I got an accordion at the pier at Market Street and faked playing it during practices and in the parade. When we passed the judges stand, a judge looked right at me as if he caught me faking. I was nervous until I saw him smile and move his head to the cadence of our music. Is there anything else? Oh yes, my makeup, it's whatever color was on the shelf of Strawbridge and Clothier's ladies' room. I paid a girl two Irish potatoes to go find some perfume and makeup. I don't normally wear makeup or perfume but I can't be caught, I must be *in con spit chew is* (the way Otto said it)," rattled on Smoky.

"Thanks Otto, I mean Chester, Smoky. I plan to return many times to this neighborhood because so far I am crazy about everyone I met," Fortitude laughed and said in all seriousness.

"I'm happy for that Fortitude. I like you too. What can I call you for short, Fortitude?" Smoky asked.

"You and only you and Bill may call me Mary Anne. Would you let me take your picture as Smoky with Bill at your side? I have an idea about a layout for casual clothes and your outfit fits my idea to a T," Fortitude requested.

"I will do that for you with the finest of pleasures and intensions (sic) with or without Bill. People take my picture all the time with my Otto robes and crown," Otto accepted the request.

"Say cheese; perfect! ya wanna see?" Fortitude asked hoping that we'd love the picture. Her Polaroid was the latest and the greatest.

"No. I was thinking about carrying a shillelagh with this outfit, what do you think? I think that would be perfect, a bit of the old sod. Renaldo is going to the Irish and Polish flea market and he will get me one if I ask him I'm sure," Smoky never quit talking.

"See you later Smoky, you look great," said Fortitude who was a different person than Miss Fortune.

"See you later too Bill," said a sad looking Smoky.

"Mary Anne, those pictures stay with you and only you until the queue (he meant coup) goes away," cautioned Smoky.

Fortitude took several pictures of Smoky. He posed as if it was an ordinary thing to do. Fortitude asked me if I knew certain philosophers.

"Do you study philosophers, like Kierkegaard and Aquinas and Augustine?" was her very tough question.

"No. I thought that the first guy played for the Steelers or the Rams. He played end and kicked the extra points and field goals. The other two are Catholic saints and Augustine was the one who saw a Child on the beach trying to clear out all the water or something like that. The Child was Jesus himself and He told Augustine that he (Augustine) had a better chance of emptying the ocean than he (Augustine) had of understanding the Trinity. Aquinas was also a saint and his first name was Thomas. That's all I knew about him," I tried to be honest.

"That's good, especially Augustine," Fortitude said as I wondered why she was asking these questions.

Fortitude went on, "Have you heard of any philosophers Bill?"

"I heard of Plato, Confucius, Bishop Sheen and Harry Chong, a Chinese cleaner's owner, I know; why?" I wondered.

"Have you read anything they wrote?" Fortitude asked.

"No but Pasqual the shoemaker tells us about right and wrong in his country, Italy. He watches our games and calls time out so he can give us direction. Pop said to be polite and listen. Mr. Chong has a thousand Chinese sayings and they are good. Are philosophers like prophets?" I went on.

"Yeah, I suppose they are," Fortitude said with a crazy face, like ducking her head down and looking up at me.

"Then I heard of Isaiah and John the Baptist".

"Bill, as you get older study the philosophers and prophets you just mentioned. Bye Bill," Fortitude got into her convertible.

"Bye Mary Anne".

"I'm coming back just as soon as I can".

Fortitude is getting enough information today that she could write a book or a trilogy. I saw Sonia and Alicia looking at Fortitude through their front window. Sonia could learn a lot from Fortitude; so could Violet. Renaldo took a big risk getting that sword for Otto. It's worth a lot and Otto tells people where he got it. I want to introduce Fortitude to my family. I wonder if Fortitude could be my girlfriend until I finish North. Dr. Ida had an older girlfriend for two months last summer. When I'm at Notre Dame she'll be about thirty two. Judy and Mary are more my age and they are pretty and smart. Sister said to be nice to the sixth grade girls because you'll marry one someday, I don't think so Sister, not a sixth grader.

Celeste Boyer, the Horse Head Lady, wasn't home to greet Fortitude. Fortitude agreed to go swimming with us if her manager said it's ok by her contract. Sonia was still watching everything going on. I saw her looking down from upstairs. Celeste Boyer, Mrs. Boyer, I mean, came out of the alley and made sure Fortitude was gone. She asked me if she could meet Mom. Of course, she could but she'd have to wait until Mom came home from work at Pep Boys. I never asked Mom what they talked about, but Mom and Mrs. Boyer took the subway to 2nd and Market Streets on the next Saturday morning.

Celeste told me a great story, "Your Mother is a Saint, Bill, you're so lucky. She took me to South Street and introduced me to Sal the Owl, who is a Temple fan, and Ishmael 'the Italian Clothes Magnet' Steinberg (steen-burg, not stine-burg). I saw all kinds of dresses and shoes and other things. I met Marie and Rodney Sinclair and Amigo. I feel like a model again. Ishmael and Sal bartered with your Mother and me. We promised to tell everybody about their stores when they ask where did I get the clothes (sic) they were going to give me. I agreed to model Sal's latest offerings at the Philadelphia Flower Show and the Army/Navy game".

Mrs. Boyer continued, "I'm having a dress altered at Sal's. He usually has a tailor make alterations on the spot, but the tailor said that he was tired of being *needled* all the time and he's taking a day off."

"Mrs. Boyer, you didn't get Sal's pun; needling tailor Ishmael said".

"'Oh, now I get it,'" she said in reply. Ishmael gave me a dress and a coat, all for helping to cater his son's Bar Mitzvah later this year. Later I will barter with the Clothes Magnet for sweaters and blouses. I will model on television on Sunday nights at commercials' time during the Boston Blackie movies. When can you get Fortitude back so I can see her and she can see me?"

"You call her Mrs. Boyer; she'll be thrilled to hear your voice," I suggested.

"I will; I really will. I will swim under your fireplug if she does too. I love this neighborhood now," gushed a new person with an old name, Mrs. Boyer.

Mrs. Boyer, Horse Head Lady, and Fortitude met somewhere. It had to be a positive meeting for Mrs. Boyer because when Fortitude came back to Carlisle Street, she was part of a team of models, photographers, and reporters, who were doing a full advertising spread for women's fashions. Fortitude made it a point to come over to me and thank me for getting her together with Celeste Boyer. The idea of the photo shoot was to show women's clothes with the inner city in the background.

Actors played our parts playing Halfball and Roof Running. None of the adults made the filming though I saw Marlene, the husband killer who was an actress at one time, watching the goings-on. Fortitude asked me if I wanted to be cleaned up and dressed and be in an advertisement in the background.

"No thanks Fortitude, I'm always dressed this way and I feel clean," I answered.

"That's ok Bill," was the only answer I got.

Mrs. Boyer posed with an actor acting as Luigi the Lamp Lighter. Her broken down fence looked repaired and painted, probably for the photo shot. I didn't hear her dogs. Smokey, Bif with one F and Doc the Clock weren't around. Actresses played the roles of Mr. Z and Violet. Violet was much prettier than the actress who played her. Mrs. Z was more realistic. Pop said that actors and actresses had to play the parts they did because of some union contracts.

"Bye Bill, good luck in school," Fortitude bid me.

"See 'ya Fortitude," I bid her.

"Stay in touch and go to Notre Dame and get on those Yankees," she urged.

I didn't watch all of the filming, but none of the kid actors shimmied or played Buck-Buck Come In. The cops opened the fireplug so the actors could do what we do better. Fortitude wanted to see Johnson's Wax and I was trying to decide to tell her where it was or to let her find it herself.

"Toronto and 15th," I yelled.

"Thanks Bill. You are my hero again," yelled Fortitude in return.

I went in the house. The actors and crew finished up and went to Johnson's Wax. I had papers to deliver, thank God.

25

Grace Kelly

The sun was shining and our Wire Ball game was in the sixth inning of a seven-inning game, when Candy II pulled up in her car, a fifty-some Packard with the coolest hood ornament and headlights. She was not alone but it looked like her passenger was her clone. The car pulled up to the area where Candy II always parked, near Toronto Street away from the Wire Ball "field" a three story building with two sides on Carlisle Street. Two movie star-like women got out of the car and walked toward the field. They both wore sunglasses, both of them had blonde hair, and both of them had blue and green clothes. One had the green at the top and the other had the green at the bottom. Candy II (I knew her right away) had Our Lady's blue. The other woman had a darker blue. They looked alike.

"Is Bif with one F around? How about Slash?" Candy II asked excitedly.

"No," somebody answered.

"Is Confucius nearby?" Candy II struck out.

"He's at practice and he usually goes home after practice I think," Bobby said.

"Do you remember what movie we saw when we snuck into the Strand?" Candy II was having fun.

"High Noon," the four of us answered.

"That's right and do you remember the star of the movie, the woman star?"

"Grace Kelly," yelled everyone, even the kids who didn't go to the movie. Candy II's clone smiled broader than Candy II did.

"Right again. Boys, meet Grace Kelly. She's visiting her family in East Falls and I told her all about Carlisle Street".

"Are you the real Grace Kelly or just a standby (he meant standin)?" Richie wanted to know.

"I'm really Grace, not *just* a standby. But the stand ins or standbys are talented people and I was in High Noon. I'll get along I supposed even though you didn't pay to get in," Grace graciously smiled and commented.

"Do you know Kim Novak and Gina Lolabridgida?" I asked for my sake and my friend Jim's sake.

"Is the Duke your favorite actor or Spencer Tracy?" somebody snuck in a question before Grace could answer.

"Who's your favorite actor?" Grace asked in return.

"Fess Parker, James Cagney, Barry FitzGerald, Duke Wayne, and Bob Steele"

"Who's your favorite actress?" Candy II asked.

"Grace Kelly," was the unanimous answer.

"Is Albert here?"

"No Candy II, why?" I asked knowing that she wanted Grace Kelly to see Albert in action shimming the alley and dropping off the garage roof headfirst.

"I want to show Grace how he shimmies up the alley to the roof".

"I can show her," I bravely volunteered.

"Ok Bill, she'd like to see how it's done".

I did it but not at all like Albert could do it. Candy II looked disappointed but thanked me anyway.

"You were wonderful in *Rear Window*," said a woman I never saw before.

"Thanks, I enjoyed making that movie," a gracious Grace said.

"I knew your father when my husband worked in construction. Did the nuns teach you? Why did you become a movie star? You are more beautiful in person. The woman on the corner is an actress. Can I get an autographed picture of you? I hope that you never get married, you're too beautiful for one man to marry all your life (as stated)." These were some of the comments and questions posed to Grace.

"Candy II, how did you get to know Grace?" asked the woman who knew Grace's father.

"We met in New York when I was right out of high school and thinking that I'd like to go there instead of college," Candy II answered though nobody was listening.

"Will you and Jimmy Stewart make another movie? Where 'didjah' make *High Noon*?" the questions kept coming from all over the crowd that built up to more than I ever saw, except maybe when the big guys thought that Sonia would be swimming at the fireplug.

"Candy II, you are just as pretty as Grace. You should have been an actress too," said a little second grader who nobody knew.

"Grace, I hope you marry Cary Grant or John Wayne".

"We'll see if they're interested, but thanks for two good choices," Grace continued being gracious.

Grace Kelly and Candy II were very polite and tried to answer all the questions. Grace commented on the pavements and street. She said that they were beautiful and so clean. She also walked around the block with Candy II and a bunch of us. We showed her the fireplug where we swam in the summer. She agreed to swim with us when it got hotter. I wanted her to see Johnson Wax's lot and the Day Rider's hideout, which Welchsko and I made near the North Philly station. Neither Grace nor Candy II had the time to see these places. I wanted to take them to meet Gatemouth and get his famous cheese steaks or hoagies. They shuttered when I mentioned these foods. I don't blame 'em, they can't get out of shape, especially Grace.

Candy II interviewed some of the women who came out to see Grace Kelly. They filled her with tons of information about our neighborhood, its people, its stores, its churches, its uniqueness and the overriding attitude of hard work and integrity. Candy II wanted to go to Zeke the Mad Barber's shop but she cautioned Grace that she might not be recognized in Zeke's and not to be hurt by it. Candy II promised Grace and the rest of us that she would finally get a haircut from Zeke. Somebody gave them directions as I started to run to Zeke's so I could watch the haircut. All the goodbyes, good lucks and God bless you(s), all the autographs signed, and all that was left to do was to go to Zeke's and watch Candy II carry out her promise. I heard the voice I'd know anywhere and came back for a moment.

"Not so fast ladies. Let me take your picture. Renaldo just gave me this camera for a map of inside of the Clearfield Bar and Grill's basement. My name is Doc the Clock cause I get all wound up and run 'til I need to be set again. Grace, does this sound like Jimmy Stewart. "Well lah, well lah, what do we have here?" Doc the Clock wanted to hear that it did.

Doc the Clock's Jimmy Stewart sounded more like Duke Wayne and his John Wayne sounded more like Yul Brenner.

"Exactly like him, he'd enjoy listening to you imitate him," Grace told a little white lie to protect Doc's ego.

"Stand in front of the store and behind the hydrant. I usually get money for my imitations. Say hello to Zeke. Tell him that Doc the Clock will pay for your haircut later".

The first and second graders gave Grace and Candy II coins from the small steel press factory on the thirty-one hundred block. These were coin shaped pieces of the steel that fell to the ground when the steelworkers made something that needed lots of coin-shaped spaces. Some gave the women pieces of tile that was in the back of the tile store on Allegheny Avenue. There were tons and tons of tile pieces in boxes in the back of the tile store. The two women graciously accepted the gifts as from the heart. Grace made a fuss with the little kids.

They will never forget that moment. Neither will I. Grace is perfect in every way, pleasant, humble, and famous. Rich too.

Mrs. Boyer, the Horse Head Lady, came from the furthest person away from Grace to the closest one to her.

"Remember me Grace? It was in New York. I was modeling for a living and you were studying acting. We worked out together. You played volleyball and hockey with the men. I played once or twice but you played all the time and you were very good," Horse Head Lady told Grace.

"Celeste, are you Celeste? Now I know. You got married and moved to Philadelphia," Grace remembered.

"I'm back to being Celeste Carroll again. I was Boyer. The kids call me Horse Head Lady because I draw horses in the street. Life was good raising horses but Edmond left and went back to Europe. *You* did well though," beamed the Horse Head Lady.

"Thanks Celeste. I've been lucky so far. This is Sarah, my friend, who is on her way to Zeke's to get a haircut".

"The kids call me Candy II. It's a long story why they do".

"Do you still model Celeste?"

"Actually yes, I model for two women's clothing stores on South Street. They don't pay me money but I get some very nice clothes. I'll watch for your next movie".

"Good and it's good to see you again Celeste".

"I guess the public won't let you alone if you go to South Street to shop. I'd introduce you to Sal and Mel, my terrific bosses".

I took off for Zeke's again.

"Ladies, it'll be twenty-five cents, not twenty-four or twenty-six". Zeke was as crazy as a loon. I never saw him cut women's hair; no barbers cut women's hair. No beautician cut men's hair either.

This will be hilarious. Zeke won't pretend that he's someone he's not. He won't let two beautiful women interfere with his checkers game. I hope he's having one when they arrive. The floor will look like a shaggy rug of hair. It always does at this time of the day. I hope that Zeke at least washed the cover he puts on you when he's cutting. Will the men stand up and give the ladies their seats? I bet they do. Fran doesn't go to Zeke's. I wish he did today. I wish Pop and Mom could be here too.

Candy II's car pulled up and in they came smiling to beat the band as they say.

"Hi Zeke, remember me? I felt a little dizzy so I left before you could cut my hair. I'm here now," asked a very sweet-talking Candy II.

"Just have a seat. Corporal, move the magazines so the ladies can sit down," Zeke ordered a war hero. Corporal played checkers every day, several times a day to prepare to beat Zeke. He never could.

"Ladies have our seats. We have a checkers game scheduled in two minutes, right after Zeke's done with his customer," said the Corporal. Zeke finished up with his customer and started a game of Checkers.

"Corporal, Lieutenant, let's begin".

"Ok Zeke".

"I'm red. You're black Lieutenant. You can't help him Corporal".

"I won't".

"Zeke, can I get my haircut, just a trim, before the game?" Candy II asked.

"No".

"This is Grace Kelly and she's on a busy schedule".

"Don't matter, a games a game. There's magazines on the table over there. Don't look under the sheet; they're men's for reading. Look around; there are plenty of interesting pictures to see. The Lieutenant is easy, I'll have more trouble with the Corporal. Then we can start your haircut".

As promised, the Lieutenant lost quickly. He looked dejected because he was wearing his lucky Army shirt. He wore it during two or three encounters with the Germans and Koreans. He wanted to win so he could be red next game. Red was his favorite color. The ladies did look around. They saw some interesting pictures all right. Zeke added pictures of his high school reunion even though he didn't graduate. There were some baby pictures of Zeke and his cousin from the coal country in upstate Pennsylvania. Zeke labeled the baby pictures "little Zeke at two" and "Zeke's first boo-boo". There were several "Zeke and Todd" pictures. Zeke was in so many reunion pictures smiling and holding his famous cranberry sauce sandwich on rye bread. He wore his favorite colored shirt, green and black. It said, "I toss for you, Boss". It was from Zeke's friend Romeo's pizza parlor. Zeke got the shirt free and two all-you-can-eat tickets for wearing the shirt at the reunion and at work at least twice a week for six months. He wanted to wear the red beret he stole from the church's lost and found table but he lost it. Zeke had another section of a wall, called the "Wall for Pictures," (WFP) which he recently completed. The wall was white, suspiciously white like the white paint used to paint lines on Broad Street.

The WFP had a picture of Zeke's parents holding their favorite baby wild turkey. Zeke wanted to show off his beautiful ex-girl friend, Gwendolyn, "the Bullhead," Mercier, from Marcus Hook and other places. One of the older guys, Switch maybe, named her Bullhead because she looked like an ugly bull. Zeke made sure that her picture was eye level for all to see. Bullhead signed the eight by eleven photo, "To my favorite expert barbarian (I think she meant barber) and all his customers, Love, Gwen with all my heart and sole (sic) forever". There were photos of Philadelphia's landmarks. There was a photo of the 39th district police station. There was a photo of "classical cah-lone-nickel" (colonial) art, the outdoor rest room at Valley Forge, near the tower. Then there was the rare photo of the Uptown string band as they were taking off their costumes when the New Year's Day Parade was over. He had several autographed photos of the Phillies and Eagles players. The women must have noticed that all the players used the same pen and all their signatures were alike. If they missed that, they were probably concentrating on the misspelled names. Steef Dan Buren (Steve Van Buren) comes to mind.

Of special interest to Grace, I'm sure, was the picture of Marilyn Monroe with a goatee and an arrow going through her head. Jane Russell, a new entry to the WFP, was spared the arrow but she had the goatee and horned rim glasses. Finally, along the WFP, there were two photos of scantily clad shapely women advertising oil changes and spark plugs. Candy II didn't think anybody was watching but I saw her take Bullhead's picture down and stuff it in her clothes. Grace was gracious the whole time. She walked through the shop as if it was the Louvre museum.

This is better than I thought. Candy II can hardly hold her composure and the movie star acts like she is impressed by the shop and its incredible gallery of art. Grace noticed the Alka-Seltzer sizzling glass with the scissors, clippers, and the combs half way in it. Zeke sanitized his tools in Alka-Seltzer. to sterilize them. She acted as if she didn't notice them. The crowds outside are getting the dirty windows dirtier by peeking in as they breathe heavily on the pane. Some people write notes to Grace using their fingers on the fogged up windows. I bet some will come in with an excuse to be there. I wish Mom and Pop were that famous. I know that I'll be well-known after my first full game with the Yankees or Notre Dame. Candy II is as pretty as Grace is but she isn't as nice to everybody. Buggy should marry Grace and Bif with one F should marry Candy II. That leaves Violet, Fortitude and Sophia for Otto and Gatemouth.

The Corporal was easier than the Lieutenant was today and Zeke went back to work. He honed his razor on the leather strap and wiped the scissors and comb off against his shirt with the RCA dog listening to the phonograph and the words, "Dogs love music. People love Gil's hoagies". The saying on the back of the shirt was slightly ironic. It said, "Eat 'til your heart's content". Candy II got up to get on the chair. She purposely did not look at the Alka-Seltzer glass where Zeke sanitizes his combs and razors or Zeke or the "white" sheet that will be around her neck in a few minutes. She just wanted to say she was the first woman to get a haircut at Zeke's from Zeke himself.

"Next, Mike's son," Zeke pointed to me.

"Oh no, not me Zeke; I'm waiting for someone to bring me a quarter or two dimes and a nickel. I'll finish this article about zebras in the National Geographic".

"Get the cut now and pay when they come."

"I'd rather wait, Zeke".

"Ladies, who's first?" Zeke didn't miss a beat. He probably had another checkers game scheduled.

"I'll go first if you don't mind Sarah".

"Grace, you'll never live this down".

"I just want about a half inch taken off the bottom; it won't mean a thing".

"Ok Grace, you'll be the first woman," Zeke called out totally unconcerned about Grace's fame and fortune.

How can I tell Grace that Zeke cuts everybody's hair the same way? Look at all the people with cameras. They're coming in with fake reasons to be there. How much for a massage? Do you mind if I see your pictures? Can I help you clean up the floor? Every excuse possible; this is nuts!

It was nuts. Ten to fifteen people came in the shop to take pictures of Candy II and Grace. A picture of Grace Kelly getting a haircut from Zeke the Mad Barber would be priceless. One woman had wax paper to catch Grace's hair. The Lieutenant and the Corporal asked people to leave but Zeke insisted they stay and look at his photos and posters. Grace was as cool as shaved ice as she pointed to the places on her hair to trim, ever so slightly. Zeke broke out the hand clippers, which chop up the hair and pull it until it hurts. Flash bulbs kept flashing with promises to give Zeke copies.

Grace started to sweat. The clippers and the razor got to her.

"Just a half inch at this spot please Zeke, no more than that. Do you really need those clippers? Can't you use a scissors?" Grace panicked a little.

Zeke didn't respond. Instead, he walked around the chair sizing up the job as he always does before he gives everyone the *same style* haircut. Fifteen Kodak Brownies lined up, fixed on Grace's hair.

"Do you want your ears to show up?"

"Yes Zeke, just a half inch from the back bottom please".

"I'll have to clean my glasses to see your ears. Should the neck show up?"

"No, just a half inch. It's very long right now. Do you really need the clippers?"

"It'll be a quarter or twenty-five cents in change. These scissors are dull because of Acme's coupons and the Green Stamps I cut out".

"Maybe I should come back next week Zeke," Grace suggested with her hands set as if she was praying.

"No need for that Madam. The clippers work most of the time".

Zeke clipped about a half inch off the back bottom of Grace's hair and stopped. Grace was thrilled. Terry Fitzgibbon's mother got the hair and acted as I did to get Mickey Mantle's autograph. Terry will surely die when she thinks about this incident. Grace thanked Zeke repeatedly and tried to give him a five-dollar bill. He didn't have $4.75 change so he couldn't accept. Grace then told Zeke to keep a quarter for Sarah's hair cut and keep the change as a tip. Zeke wouldn't take a $4.50 tip for anything. He'd sooner let it go.

"Ok Zeke, I won't pay this time but the next time I'll pay double. If we ever do the *Philadelphia Story* movie, you'll have a small part. You are the most honest businessman I've seen in years," Grace exclaimed with great joy.

"Next time just give me a quarter or twenty-five cents and a grape water ice," Zeke told Grace.

"Zeke, I'm late and I'll come back tomorrow," Candy II said.

"Oh Sarah, we have time. Zeke doesn't take long," Grace urged Candy II.

"Hurry lady, I got customers waiting".

"Ok Zeke, but I want the same as you gave her".

"It takes two minutes. It takes more time to put on the sheet than it takes to cut your hair. Ok, let's go".

Candy II wasn't concerned about the clippers. She knew Zeke knew what she wanted. The Corporal broke out in a rage, screaming at the soldier who stole his Army boots in Fort Dix right after the war. He screamed louder and louder. The Lieutenant tried to calm him down until he remembered when he lost his commission due to a revolt among his charges in the Philippines. They revolted because he wouldn't give the guys a leave yet he took several leaves to clear his mind and heart. He, the Lieutenant, started to scream at Bowen, Hamilton and Temple for leading the revolt. Zeke didn't flinch. He began to cut Candy II's hair.

This time it took much longer and Candy II tried to believe that everything would be all right until she felt the cold clippers on her neck.

"Just a half inch like Grace's; right Zeke? I see more hair on this sheet than I saw on Grace's".

"I'm almost done. I just have to trim around the ears".

"The ears! Why the ears?"

"So it looks connected with the back and top".

"Can I see what you're doing?"

"Only when I'm finished."

"There, like it?"

"Oh my God Zeke, you took it all off and I asked for a half inch. I gotta leave; I can't be seen ever. Will it grow in?"

"I think so. It usually does".

"Grace, we have to leave. Will you buy a hat for me?"

"I have hats, baseball caps. Do you want one?" I offered Candy II.

"Yes, of course I do".

"Sarah, your hair looks great! It is the best style I've seen in years. This guy charges a quarter for what I get for $40.00. And he is better. Sarah, I want a picture of you so I can show Mr. Magic in Hollywood what I want. The studio bosses will love it. Trust me, it's beautiful," encouraged Grace.

"Actually, I agree Grace, it's different and exciting for me. Thanks Zeke. See you in a month". Candy II loved her new style, quite different hairstyle.

"Want the cap?"

"Are you kidding? No one could see my haircut if I wore a hat".

Bif with one F came in the shop to escort the women to their car. Candy II asked him to be there just in case there was a mob scene. Candy II introduced Bif with one F to Grace. He bowed slightly and told Grace that he was honored and 'impressive' to meet and greet her. Candy II told Bif with one F everything, the mocking of Zeke and Slash; the sorority initiation; lying about her name, which is Sarah; the downgraded clothes "just to fit in" and, of course, her complete turn of heart. She didn't join the sorority and she lives much more comfortably as a college student with a new major, a new attitude and a new set of friends. She wanted to see Slash but no one had seen him for a long time. Rumor had it that he joined the French Foreign Legion. That rumor went away when we realized that you had to be able to read English at a fifth grade level to join that group. They would teach you all the French you needed. Other rumors had Slash joining the Army or moving to Ireland with a rich, homely Irish girl named Nell. Renaldo the Purloiner tried to give Slash a newer car in exchange for his old one and teaching him (Renaldo) how to drive. But Slash didn't show up at Sonny's Used Car lot at their appointment time, 2am on Sunday morning.

Sonny's had high priced cars, like Hudsons, Packards, Cadillacs and Studebakers. When Slash chose his car, Renaldo would "work out a deal" even though there was no one at Sonny's at the time, and be back to him in fifteen minutes or so with the keys and a case of oil. Slash expressed a real interest in doing this but the interest faded a lot during the past week.

Slash's best friend was either Cong-few-shush (Confucius) or Eddie the Idiot, who recited Poe, Longfellow and Shakespeare but couldn't find 3rd Street if he was on 2nd Street and there was no obstacle between the two streets. He read Chaucer, Dickens, Twain, and Homer, but failed three subjects in the seventh grade. Eddie memorized whole chapters from both the Old and New Testament and he could tell you what the authors meant but he failed the driver's test twice and finally passed when he recited Poe's Raven to the state trooper. Confucius was the last person to see Slash when Slash met him on Johnsons Wax's lot where Slash hid money under some of the rocks. He, Confucius, had no idea where Slash could have gone. He had no family that anyone knew of and he lived "in private" as long as anyone knew him.

Candy II said, "Tell Slash that he's the best dancer and he should be in movies. After all, Fred Astaire is ugly and he made it big".

"I won't tell him the Fred Astaire part," I said.

"Goodbye Sarah. Goodbye Grace".

"See you around Confucius. Stay in touch," Candy II said as she sped off.

That's it? What about Horse Head Lady? Will you be back?" I can't wait to see *The Philadelphia Story.*

26

Gatemouth

Going north on Broad Street were several beautiful row houses. These were not like the row houses on Reese Street and Carlisle Street. These houses were three or four stories high and brown stones provided the foundation to them. Inside their first floors were offices and a large parlor. I think some dentists and lawyers had their offices in these houses. At the end of the street, the 3100 block of Carlisle Street. was a drug store. I went there once or twice if Intimes was closed or didn't have what Mom or Pop wanted. Bobby Gillespie's father liked rock candy so he brought some for his Dad when we went to Hunting Park or Confession. Very few unusual people frequented the drug store, but one of the most unusual was nearby, Gatemouth. One other thing, Intimes had great malts and hot dogs. Renaldo the Purloiner drank many "ah" malt and "purchased" many boxes of Whitman's chocolates at Intimes. Renaldo the Purloiner *purchased* everything that Intimes sold at one time or another for somebody or other.

Gatemouth worked at a small restaurant, called Gulliver's Alley, near Allegheny Avenue after you cross Allegheny Avenue going north. He took orders, especially "to go" orders. He got the name Gatemouth because, in the opinion of the big guys, his mouth looked like a gate with openings at every other tooth. He had to smile because the boss told him to be friendly to the customers. When he smiled, the gate was open for full view. Gatemouth had a strange body or Gatemouth had a problem with posture; either way, Gatemouth appeared to bend to the left and the right at the same time, kinda like an S. If he looked in a carnival mirror, he'd look normal. He was very tall. He wore Ked's high top sneakers. He was skinny and he wore tee shirts all the time, even at church. The tee shirts revealed his skinny arms. He rolled up the sleeves of the tee shirts to impress the girls, I guessed. It worked; they were impressed. He never had a date or a girl who seemed to like him. Too bad, he was a terrific fellow.

Gatemouth wore a long white apron and always had a pencil on his right ear. His hair was jet black and parted in the middle, like Alfalfa's of the Our Gang show. Come to think about it, Doc the Clock, the phony cripple who sang songs and limped for money, sounded and reminded me of Alfalfa. Gatemouth never tied his sneaks. His Bermuda shorts gave one the chance to see the world's skinniest legs.

"What can I get for you, sir?" uttered Gatemouth, the insecure Gatemouth.

"Two vanilla malts with extra malt and a ham and cheese sandwich," the Big Deal replied, looking like he was the affluent executive, which he will never be.

The phony buyer knew very well that he wasn't going to pay for the malts and sandwich. Gatemouth got stuck with two malts and a sandwich. This happened many times, mainly on the afternoon of a Phillies or A's game. Those Big Deal losers had to have something to eat on the way to the game.

The big guys on our side of the street wouldn't do that to Gatemouth and they'd call him by his real name. I noticed that Perry walked away. He's a good person and he plays football for North, which means he's tough. I think you have to go through a Marine obstacle course to make North's team. That's what Tommy Pitts told me when I told him I'm going to Notre Dame on a football scholarship. Gatemouth told Mr. Sheehan that he had a black belt in Judo when he was hired. His black belt was used to hold up his pants, that's all. If Gatemouth could act, he could play Icabod Crane in *The Legend of Sleepy Hallow* or the Scare Crow in the *Wizard of Oz*. If the big guys messed with Gatemouth after work, he'd massacre them with Judo chops. No, he wouldn't. Someday the red car will pull up and the Big Shots will have to get in and go for a ride to police headquarters.

I hope the medical students or the dental students from Temple are in Gulliver's Alley when the guys con Gatemouth. They'll do something. They have to do something because they have to help others in distress, it's in their oath, I think. They carry around needles with poison for protection.

Gatemouth's parents would cry if they saw their son so mistreated. I got to watch it because I almost cry watching it happen. Blessed Mother, why do I want to cry like this? Let me use St. Michael the Archangel as my way to Jesus. Lattner, Lujack, and Warden never cry. I don't cry either so why do I pray to Mary Our Blessed Mother? Guaranteed they pray to Archangels and a saint like Saint George, the dragon slayer.

27

Paris France France

There was a short note taped to Paris Singleton's door. I saw it when I threw her paper at the door of her nice row home on 16th Street. "Young man, please knock on the door when you are here". I knocked on the door and Paris answered.

"Thanks for knocking Bill. I was told your name is William, but I'm sure that you prefer Bill. Bill, I want you to change my last name to France, I'm Paris France as of this Friday. I won't miss being Paris France Singleton. Most anybody can be Paris France Singleton, anyone named Singleton, I mean. What do I have to do to make the change?"

"I'll do what we do when a woman gets married and changes her name"

"What's that?"

"Nothing at all really; I just send in a card with your new last name. You don't have to sign anything".

"Nothing at all, are you kidding?"

"Yes, I'm not kidding. I'll make the change for you. Did you get married?"

" No, not yet, my ideal man has been waiting for me to become Paris France France, so we can get married".

"Want to know why I changed my last name? It's easy, my father wanted me to since I was born but never said anything to me. He was a wonderful father, who worked hard to raise me and my sister and two brothers. It is a gift to him for Father's Day, probably his last Father's Day. He's very sick and the doctors aren't optimistic".

"What's he have?"

"Many things; he was injured in the war and suffered chronic pain from infection caused by a bullet in his leg. He was exposed to chemicals that have harming effects when he was assigned to a lab in an Army research center somewhere in some unknown-to-us country. He was the lab's director and led several studies dealing with and defending against germ warfare. Our family wasn't told where the lab was located or the nature of his assignment. We were still living in Paris. The Cathedral of Notre Dame was our parish. It was wonderful. However, we rarely saw our Dad for about two years. He came home in November for Christmas. It was the best Christmas because we saw Dad and Mom and they were so happy to see each other. Did you get gifts? Not then, but on December 25th we each got a jig saw puzzle of different parts of the USA. I got New England and that's probably why I went to college there.

"What college was that?"

"Dartmouth, in New Hampshire, and I loved the cold weather, the unbelievable fall colors, the birds in the air in the spring, and most of all, the people. I loved the New England accent, you know 'cah' for car and 'pack' for park, 'pack' the cah. I retained my French accent and my classmates insisted that I do all the talking and ordering everywhere we went. I sang *I Love Paris* in Dartmouth's spring musical. I sang it in English and French. I got to meet many boys by singing in that musical".

"When boyfriends asked me for a date, I suggested that we go to a French restaurant. The servers didn't speak French, but the owners did. Desserts were free most of the time once the owner found out that I spoke French. I made my Holy Communion in Paris at the Cathedral of Notre Dame. We lined up to receive at the spot where Maureen O'Hara stood with the Hunchback, Charles Laughton. Did you know that every architect who worked on Notre Dame remained anonymous? A French priest, Fr. Soran, founded your favorite university; did you know that?"

"No. I guess the Fighting Frenchmen would never go. What university are you talking about?"

"Wait'll I see Mary".

"Mary who? That's worse than not knowing the name of Mary's university. Our Blessed Mother, crazy, who doesn't want you to feel bad because you feel closer to her than you do to *manly* saints and protective archangels, like Michael. She says all the time that St. Michael is such a devout angel and he writes heavenly poems; they show his true emotional strengths and vulnerabilities. Mary constantly reminds us how much she craves hearing the rosary and other prayers prayed by men who trust her and feel assured that she will tell her Son about their requests. Generals, admirals, soldiers, sailors, business executives, boxers, athletes, priests, bishops, cardinals, and popes come to her in prayer, especially the rosary. Whole armies knelt as one group before a critical battle and recited the rosary. Yes, even Leahy, Lattner, Hart, their quarterback, number 3, I can't say his name, it's Italian like Goog-lee-oh-mo, come to her in time of need and at others times as well".

"Mary understands your question; why are Notre Dame's school colors gold and blue and not green for the Fighting Irish? She has told me during football seasons about your description of her in light blue, like the sky on a bright, sunny, clear day and the shade of gold of the chasuble Bishop McCormack wears at Midnight Mass on Christmas and the High Mass on Easter. She liked the fact that you liked her light blue colors. She prefers light blue. It's her, she says!"

"Like you, she loves the beautiful background to the clouds that are light blue – you call it Our Lady's blue and she loves that the canvas we call the sky presents to artists, dreamers, lovers, optimists, saints and anyone else who takes the time to look and reflect".

"But, Paris, I also saw a light blue sky and sparkling gold clouds, I'm sure that I saw them but then again I'm not sure".

"You saw them Bill and so did many other people, including me. Even Mary was impressed a bit more than usual. She thanked her Son for His precious gift of golden clouds".

"This is insane, Paris France France. Are you real?"

"Of course I'm real; shake hands. Isn't Our Lovely Lady dressed in gold and blue beautiful?"

"I guess she is".

"You know she is".

"Paris, I dream of going to Notre Dame. I'll take going to Notre Dame more than I'll take anymore presents for Christmas or birthdays, including Pop's hard boiled eggs. I'd sell my Yankee autographs for just one semester under the Golden Dome. I can picture the Golden Dome and Rockne's stadium and the band playing the Victory March when we all come running out of the tunnel".

"Your Pop's hard boiled eggs; that's saying something. He makes the eggs look just like the people with birthdays. When you were waiting to bat for the first time in your life and were lowest in the lineup, ninth, did you look at the sky when the seventh and eighth batters were up at the plate?"

"I think so, because I was scared I'd make a fool of myself and my Pop, that's why".

"Your Pop wasn't there".

"I just wanted to be sure to make him happy because he liked baseball and he believes in me and has sacrificed so much for me. Mom is the same, but I want her (make that Mom.) I can't refer to my mother as she or her) to be proud of my school work".

"Did you make a fool of yourself Bill?"

"A little bit when I couldn't find second base. But I thought of Pop smiling and shaking his head when I ran toward center field, thinking second base was there".

"Bill, you said a decade of the rosary, the third Glorious mystery, the Descent of the Holy Ghost upon the apostles before you batted. Do you remember that? Mary didn't want you to walk or try to get hit with a pitch like your coach wanted you to. She knew that her Son would let you see the ball and smash it to the heavens. Everybody watching the game was concerned that you wouldn't see the ball or you'd see the ball and let it go by. Mary wanted to convey to you that either Jesus or the Holy Ghost would have the pitcher serve you a beautiful fastball to hit. Somehow the message got through although you still were the one who had to swing or walk or get hit by a pitch".

"I was so surprised that I could see the ball so well because I never played real baseball – most of the balls we used were old baseballs with no covers or covers of electric tape. I faced slow pitchers on Johnson Wax's lot. I saw baseballs come unraveled on the way to home after the pitcher threw it. I watched baseballs unravel as they went through the air and rolled to the outfield. Sometimes we had to call the game because all we had for a ball was an orange colored spongy-like little ball, the core of the baseball. The ball that we were playing with on that day reminded me of the ball I caught when Granny Hamner hit a foul ball in batting practice".

"I saw beautiful women, like Mom, Violet, Horse Head Lady, Sophia, Maureen, Theresa. I saw Marlene, Mrs. Z, the woman at the library, the women who cut the chickens' heads off on Germantown Avenue, Alicia, and the Irish ladies at H&H's. There was Mary L., Joni L., Maggie, Violet, Maria, Patsy, the FBI woman next door, Mrs.

Kleinmeister and Joan of Arc Piaf, her sister. I saw Mrs. Z, Velvet Blue, you and even the Crazy Lady from my paper route with the broom".

"You saw me Bill?"

"Yes and I saw the Sisters wearing their habits and looking beautiful and holy. Their bibs and triangles on their veils were so white that I thought they weren't white but were a color made in heaven just for this event. I heard St. Stephen's choir, my favorite choir, singing Hosanna, Hosanna, Hosanna and Ave Maria in Latin. They sang something about Lourdes and Bernadette in French or maybe it was Greek. I said all the Latin responses I ever knew to myself. I thanked the Bishop and all the priests in our parish for hearing my confession so many times saying the same things like stealing cars, faking Sr. Helen out, pretending I didn't see Doc the Clock or Otto the Outrageous, not helping Uncle Matt when the big guys threw the basketball at him. I wondered if I ran out of forgivenesses with God. I multiplied seven times seventy and got four hundred and forty=nine. I saw all these things when I was getting ready to bat. I guess you can say that I saw a lot in about five minutes; I did".

"Time didn't matter, Bill. Why didn't you mention Sierra from Our Lady of Mercy when you mentioned beautiful women?"

"I saw her but I always see her, all the time".

"Think hard, who else did you see?"

"I saw the most beautiful lady ever seen by anyone on earth. She had a habit like the Sisters but hers was in Our Lady blue. She had sparkling gold trim on her habit. Gold like our Bishop wears on special occasions. She had black eyebrows and very white teeth. Her skin was shiny and I forget if it was white, like Mom's or brown, like Mrs. Brown's or yellow, like Mrs. Lu's. She was looking at me as if to say, 'Swing if the pitch is over the plate'".

"She likes sports as long as the players play by the rules. Mary likes your Olympics, except that she thinks you and the rest of the Olympians should get the proper agreements from the neighbors. Mary, Our Mother, loves Deafy. She sees him as a wonderful man, who enjoys making people happy. You can't imagine how much she loves the Fighting Irish playing for her school. She loves Bif with one F and Otto the Outrageous as well as Renaldo the Purloiner and Doc the Clock. She loves all the people around here."

"When I tell my Dad that I changed my name to Paris France France, I will be free to marry my boyfriend. I'll leave the neighborhood shortly after that and I'll cancel the paper with at least two weeks' notice. I lived here because my Dad lived here at one time many years ago. I studied languages at Dartmouth and I hoped to teach French at Little Flower or North. Little Flower had too many French teachers already and while North's disciplinarian, Fr. Walsh, (Knobby to the boys), interviewed me for the job, three boys were brought in for fighting, smoking in class and slamming their books closed with chalk remnants inside. This was supposed to make the teacher think that the smoke he sees is only chalk remnants, not Camels or Old Golds".

"Knobby told me about a classroom where the boys locked the teacher out and were laughing so hard they couldn't open the door. He yelled, 'This is Knobby, open this door NOW'. The class stopped laughing and someone opened the door. Knobby went into the room and saw five or six out of the fifty students who he knew from Jug, the punishment for messing around. He couldn't assume that they locked the door. He couldn't blame some of the students for not opening the door because it looked like the entire football line was in that class and they presented a threat to anyone who wanted to do the right thing".

"He asked me what I would have done with this class. Of course, I didn't have an answer. Of course, then, I didn't get the job. Knobby told the class that everyone was expelled, not suspended, expelled unless the students who did this own up to it. He left the room to get the necessary paperwork. When he came back, his five suspects owned up. Knobby made them apologize to the teacher and their fellow students. He said that none of the five could participate in spring football practice and they not only got ten days in Jug, they had to mop Jug up for ten days. He also reminded the class that priests hear confessions at 7:30 am every school day".

"Where is your boyfriend now?"

"On his way to New York I hope. He's moving from Albany, New York to New York City where he has a better job".

"What-z he do?"

"He plays baseball for the Yankees now. He's a third baseman and he is moving up to the big leagues. He played baseball for North then went to college for four years. Add two years in the Army, playing for the Army baseball team all over the world. All that plus just one year in the minors and he's a Pin stripper, playing next to Phil Rizzuto and ninety feet from his favorite player, Yogi Berra".

"Where'd he go to college?"

"Guess".

"Temple".

"No, but he lived on 16th Street, now on your paper route.

"Michigan? I met a Jesuit who went to Michigan".

"No. I'll tell you. Notre Dame. Graduated in '52".

I couldn't decide if Paris was an angel or a saint. She probably was a woman, who had special powers from above or down below. Maybe her fiancée had special powers to hit a fast curveball, or start a double play or steal bases. I saw no new names in the Yankee lineup. He might have been a substitute. I never saw Paris France France again and I'm sure she remarried her beau as planned. I hope she did anyway. She moved away less than a week after we had our discussion. She cancelled her subscription and paid me three weeks when she wasn't a customer.

Shortly after meeting with Paris, I was thinking about what I saw (or maybe didn't see) that day sitting on the bench. I was convinced that the whole thing was a dreammer, a pleasant dream but a dream nevertheless. I dreamed about the Yankees and the As a lot and I dreamed about Notre Dame at least ten times a month. I was a dreamer and easily mesmerized if my thoughts were about pin stripes, the Golden Dome and beautiful churches and being lifted up to God with beautiful Catholic, Latin ancient music. Just a day or two after this reverie I was in the altar boy's room for the six going through the cassocks, looking for my lucky one, the one with Jimmy Mullin's initials on the inside collar, The black JM cassock wasn't hanging in my lucky spot, fourth in from the left. I began to think that somebody took it home or Jimmy came back to get it for old time's sake. I was about to settle on another black cassock, when I heard a woman's voice – no woman was ever in this room before while I was preparing for Mass – saying with the softest voice imaginable, "Isn't she beautiful Bill? The most beautiful woman God ever made. Do you agree; your earthly mother doesn't count; I know she's your most beautiful right now!"

I didn't know who was talking to me. I saw no one in the room let alone a woman. I let it pass as part of the dreams I had a few days before. The sacristan and the other altar boy didn't show up. I had to hustle to get the cruets and the dish for cleaning father's hands before the Consecration.

As I approached the sacristy, I saw a woman carrying a new or just washed bundle of white cloths, probably sanctifiers. She was dressed in a long, light blue coat, a South Street special for sure. It had the South Street look, a collar that folded perfectly, a length that wasn't sold anywhere else, between long and short, between the knee and the hip, a belt in the back with two buttons and an American flag patch sewn on the front side where the heart is. South Street clothes looked like 5th Avenue clothes without the fancy labels. Her skimpy hat, not South Street, showed me she had black hair. I was about to ask her if she saw a woman in the altar boy's room but she was looking at the Crucifix on the altar and I let it go.

"Do you remember Sister Prophetess from last year?" spoke this mysterious woman who was dressed for January- and it was June - and spoke with the softest voice imaginable.

"She met her Maker the day after she was in your classroom after years of teaching young men and woman about the evils surrounding them at this time and the fortitude they must have in the future, especially the boys. Sister's name was Sister Bernadette of Lourdes, S.S.J. and she spent her life giving up everything she owned to follow her marvelous ministry. She studied aberrations related to Mary, Our Blessed Mother".

The woman turned around after talking to me and looking the other way, said, "It's almost six and Father will have to hurry to be on time. The woman looked like she was happy doing the terrible job of cleaning altar cloths - like Mom looked when she came home from her crummy, dangerous, factory job. Mom was tired and not too anxious to start dinner for six or seven, but she sort of smiled and asked us to call whoever was still outside playing.

"I hope you stay for the 6 (six am Mass)," I asked because I felt she wanted me to.

"Of course I'll stay. I've seen you boys serve the six many times and I love the six," returned the mysterious, holy, and Catholic, very warm – physically and lovingly - woman.

At two minutes to six or so, Father Visitor arrived and quickly got ready for Mass, which was on time. I got in front of our Celebrant and he followed me as we approached the altar. He was carrying the chalice, paten, burse and the keys to the tabernacle. His vestments and the veil covering the chalice were red, signifying that it was a feast day of a martyr. The Sisters were there in the front three rows on St. Joseph's side of the church as they always did at the six. Father Visitor introduced himself to the congregation – about fifty strong including the twenty-two good Sisters - before he made the sign of the cross.

"I'm Father McDevitt, a missionary priest of the Maryknoll order. I will not leave right after Mass this morning so I'll be happy to hear confessions if you'd like. You are true Catholics to come here this morning in the hot humid weather that is Philadelphia in July. I'd like to begin as we begin every Catholic service with the Sign of the Cross".

This priest is spending more time introducing himself than most priests spend to get to the Gloria. Maybe he's buying time or something like that. I can tell that this Mass will be long and I'll have to run part of the way home to get breakfast and leave quickly. Father doesn't know I live a mile away. He'd take his time even if he did. I hope that Doc the Clock and the other Broad Street gang are home in bed when I leave. I couldn't take Doc and his nonsense today.

I was planning my trip home during Mass – day- dreaming again - when I noticed Father McDevitt looking around for me. It was time to take the book to the other side of the altar. I picked up the book and started down the five steps, I saw the mystery lady who was in the sacristy with the altar cloths. She changed from her very warm coat to the habit of the Sisters of St. Joseph, of Chestnut Hill. She was a Sister and I never saw her before. I never saw a Sister out of her habit; I thought that the habit stayed on by the grace of God. She was right in the middle of the other Sisters. She was moving back and forth as if she was in a rocking chair. She stared at the Blessed Mother's altar when she came up to Communion. Father McDevitt kept my streak alive of predicting long Masses.

I should run after the Sisters to talk to the new, yet old, Sister. I can't do that; I'm late and I'm not an apple polisher. I'll see her in school and she'll want to talk. What a morning.

Sister Helen didn't know what sister I was talking about. Their convent hasn't had a visitor stay over for three years at least, she said. There was no Sister Bernadette of Lourdes in the order. Sisters never went out without their habits. Sister Helen said that Father Martin said the six and that I seemed normal.

"Bill, it sounds like you had a wonderful dream about two Sisters who don't exist anywhere but in your mind. Your imagination was in high gear. The Sisters go to Confession to their spiritual advisors but not after the six".

28

Brother

"Mom, at Tioga Street I hear loud religious music. The choir sounds joyful and the people yell out, 'Amen!' all the time. I looked in the Zion church this morning coming home from the 6 (6am Mass). It had to be a Sunday religious service because everyone was perfectly dressed up. The women wore huge hats; almost all were either purple or bright yellow. The little kids wore suits and dresses; all very colorful," I told Mom.

"What were they singing?" Mom asked.

"Songs about Jesus. I couldn't understand all the words but they were swaying and holding their hands up over their heads. They were joyful and smiling to each other," is how I described what I saw to Mom.

"Sounds like a Fr. Devine service. Were most of the people colored?" Mom asked.

"Yes. How did you know that?" I answered and asked Mom.

"That's a Fr. Devine service. He has a big following and the people dress like royal families at the races at their Sunday services. Their clothes are colorful and beautiful," Mom said with a look of mixed emotions.

There was a Chevy station wagon parked on Broad Street. The sides of the wagon looked like real wood but it was hard to imagine real wood on the sides of cars. "Brother's Auto Body Repair – SA-2-6723" was on a hand- painted sign attached to the car. The station wagon was old in years but brand new in appearance. Maybe the owner fixed it up and painted it. The wagon was more popular than the new cars for some adults; younger people couldn't keep their eyes off the new cars, which looked completely different from year to year. The tires on the wagon had white walls that covered at least 80% of the tire. The hood ornament was not the standard one for the wagon. It looked like a Packard or Hudson ornament. I had the 10 one Sunday so I walked past the Zion church later than normal; the congregation was letting out. The apparent owner of the wagon was pointing out its features to interested congregation members. The inside – I was an interested non-congregation member – was spectacular; green seats and a highly modified dashboard with gold trim around the gauges and speedometer. The radio's normal position on the dashboard housed a bright gold cover with the word "Savior" etched on it. The radio was on a stand attached to the floor between the driver and the shotgun seats. I heard someone refer to the apparent owner as Brother, a short to average height man, who was dressed to meet the Lord in person. Two little girls, like five or six years old, stood next to the car, their car to their friends, and waited their turn to meet and please the Lord if dressing properly for church had value.

"Pop, you wouldn't believe the station wagon I saw on Broad Street," I told Pop.

"Yeah, I know, Brother's Chevy station wagon. Did you get to see the insides?" was Pop's reply.

"I liked the green seat covers and the wooden gearshift," I told Pop and I did like these things.

"Brother's business is on Uncle Ted's beat and all the cops bring their bodywork to Brother. He's the best around at bodywork and he refuses to overcharge anybody in the Lord's name. Brother hums religious hymns, probably old Negro spirituals, as he works. This, he told Uncle Ted, keeps him working 'at the Lord's quality and speed'. He is not a member of Fr. Devine's congregation, but Mr. Joe Brown and his family are. I'll bet that Brother had well polished and well-heeled shoes on. All of us who are blue-collar workers wear polished dress shoes on Sundays and at weddings and funerals. Take notice to Mr. Brown next Sunday; I guarantee he has spiffy shoes on. I'll take you with me the next time I go to the Pink Sisters on Green Street. We can stop over to meet Brother. Why don't you introduce yourself to him after Mass next time? You can tell 'em you're Sergeant Teddy's nephew. Ask him if you can visit him to see his shop and to see his work area with the big oven for baking on the new paint," Pop went on.

Sister Helen didn't get many requests to serve the 10 and she wouldn't consider me for the 10 unless it was an emergency like last week. "Sister, I have to be near the church after the 10 is let out; do you want me to serve the 10 as well as the 6?" I asked hoping to have an excuse to talk to Brother. "No, the 10 is covered but God bless you for asking," replied Sister as I just picked up some good graces. I walked to the Zion church in time to be there when their service let out and waited near the station wagon until all the people left the church.

"Nice car! Is it a station wagon?" how dumb of me.

"It's a station wagon; an old station wagon," replied Brother without laughing at me.

"Do you know my uncle?" was my second dumb question.

"I don't know; who is your uncle?" asked Brother, still not laughing at me.

"Teddy, the police sergeant," I said thinking that further identification wouldn't be necessary.

"From the 39th? Yes. I know him; he's a good cop. He chases after the bad guys all the time," answered an appreciative Brother.

"He's my uncle," dumb comment number three for me.

"You said that," said a slightly smiling Brother.

"Does your car run well?" I asked as I stopped counting dumb comments.

"Yes," replied Brother with no signs of being annoyed.

"You fix dents and scratches?" I inquired as if I didn't read the ad on the station wagon which said, "we fix dents and scratches".

"Yep, I do. Does your Caddy need work?" Brother asked with a full smile.

"I'm still in grammar school and I can't drive. Can I visit your shop and watch you paint cars?" was a good question from me.

"You can visit but you can't watch. It's too dangerous," said a serious Brother.

"I want to do car bodywork after high school," I said and wondered where that idea came from.

"Well, there's room for you in our business," said Brother as he eyed some friends who probably wanted Brother to join them.

"I wish some of the big guys in our neighborhood would get into the business; they always cut school or classes and they waste time. When can I come to your shop?" I asked.

"That's up to you; I'm there six days a week, Monday through Saturday," replied Brother as our conversation ended.

I got to Brother's Shop and found it interesting. There were no bathing beauty posters like in Zeke the Mad Barber's shop. Instead, there were pictures of Jesus and some angels. The floor of the shop was clean; no paint or grease. Brother wore old beat up clothes as I expected. I saw a car with huge dents on it and a fender hanging down in the rear. Parts of the car were repaired and sanded but there were plenty more dents to bang out or replace. The repaired parts looked good though not yet painted. Brother could take a piece of metal and weld it onto a damaged car. Pop said when Brother sanded and painted the metal, you'd think it just came off the new car lot. Brother's wife, Sister, stopped by the shop at lunch and dinnertimes to give her husband and "favorite person" some good food. Brother worked 'til he couldn't work anymore; usually from 8a.m. until 7 or 8p.m. The day Pop took me to Brother's there were four cars scheduled for work before the close of business that day. Brother promised the owners that they would have their cars back in three or four working days, which included Saturdays. Brother occasionally purchased "totaled" cars from insurance companies. Brother had a picture of his station wagon on the wall. It looked like its only use was for scrap metal, if that even. The front end ended up where the driver's seat should be. The driver's seat ended up where the back seat should be and the back seat was crushed. Brother gave the insurance company what they asked for the wagon. He worked hard to make it a showcase wagon - one that Chevy could use as an ad on TV.

Brother told Pop and me about the graveyard of totaled cars. He, Brother, spent a lot of time at the graveyard picking up parts and pieces of metal and car windows and mufflers and scarcely worn tires. He also bought every interesting hood ornament he could find. Brother asked Pop what he was driving. "My two legs; I don't drive", said Pop. "Praise the Lord, here's a healthy man," prayed Brother, impressed by Pop's admission and humility and good health.

Brother knew we were from St. Stephen's because I told him so when I met him on Broad Street. He asked Pop all kinds of questions about the Catholic faith and Pop did a decent job responding, I think.

"Why don't you eat meat on Fridays and during Lent?" was question number one from Brother.

"As a sacrifice for the souls in Purgatory and to worship God on earth," Pop answered with a reasonable response.

"Do you worship them statues that are all over the place?" was question number two.

"No, we just keep them in our houses to think about the saints and Mary," answered Pop with the right answer, I thought.

"Who's your favorite saint?" asked Brother."

"St. Joseph and St. Christopher because one took care of his family and the other keeps drivers safe. I also like the Sacred Heart of Jesus," answered Pop with no delay.

"My church is full every Sunday; is yours?" bragged Brother.

"It is and we have six Masses each Sunday," Pop informed Brother.

"Why are you a Catholic?" asked Brother.

"Why do you go to the Zion church?" volleyed Pop.

"How many kids do you have?" asked Brother.

"Five. And you?" answered Pop.

"Two, both girls. If I see a car in the cemetery that I could fix up for a good price, do you want me to buy it for you?" asked Brother who hit it off well with Pop.

"No, not now, maybe in a year or two," responded a disappointed Pop.

"Were you in the war?" Brother continued the conversation.

"Yes. I was in the Navy in the Far East," Pop told him.

"I was in the Army. That's where I learned to fix cars. I'm glad you stopped by; come again," invited Brother.

"We will," Pop and I both said, and we planned to return.

We went home and Pop and I talked about Brother's skills on the way. I liked the idea of humming spiritual hymns when I'm working to make my work high quality and fast. I made up my mind to try it out at school. I got the opportunity to prove Brother's theory about hymns and quality right after dinner. I had tons of homework, which was unusual because Sister Rose didn't usually load us up. I started to read about the Wright brothers and Kitty Hawk, North Carolina. It was in the springtime but I selected "O Holy Night" as the internal ambience while I read and wrote a short story about the people from Brother's church and the body shop. It worked for a while until the doorbell rang. It was Eddie the Idiot.

"I made Mom mad. Some girl needed a date to the prom and Mom told me to call her and go to the prom," Eddie the Idiot told me.

"Did you call the girl? No, Mom did. She gave me the phone. I recited Romeo and Juliet to her. She was happy and told her mother what I was doing. She said she saw me going into Bingo at the Polish club. I let her know how I win all the time," Eddie the Idiot, who can memorize poems, numbers, and other information but can't hold a job, told me.

"I play fifty cards in my head. I put them on the table in five rows. I have the cards memorized and I can yell, 'Bingo', when my number is called. She asked me to go to the prom".

"What did you say?

"I said no because I was a duck. Then I did my Donald Duck imitation. She was crying now and she hung up after saying thanks to me," bragged the idiot.

"Eddie, why do you talk like a duck?" I inquired.

"Wanna hear my Willie the Worm imitation?" Eddie the Idiot asked me.

"No thanks," I politely replied.

"Ok, I'll be Willie and you are Filbert the Flea. 'Fillll- bert, are you ready to show cartoons?" offered Eddie who didn't know what no meant.

"Eddie, I'm doing homework. I'll see you later," I said as I started to close the door.

"Ok Filbert. Did you see Mickey the Mouse?" Eddie doesn't know when to stop.

"Good-bye Willie," I did know when to stop

"See you soon Buckaroo," Eddie said as he saluted me.

Eddie broke my meditation and studying and went back to normal, trying to memorize the pages. I hope Sister doesn't make a big deal about this chapter. I scanned every car I saw going to school the next day. Brother could have almost every one of them as customers. I know Renaldo has taken some cars to Brother to get a paint job. He barters with all his vendors. He gave Brother an authentic totem pole carved by a tribe of Indians. I think Brother sanded, primed and painted Renaldo's car. Good thing for Renaldo that Brother didn't want to see an owner's card or the real license plates. Renaldo throws the real license plates away and puts cardboard plates on the cars he paints or has painted. Renaldo eventually gets real plates and puts them on or "sells" them to the new owner for a nominal additional price. Automobile seat covers, floor mats or five Three Musketeers' bars are some examples of what he'll accept for a car. I noticed that the value of what Renaldo is bargaining for has nothing to do with the value he asks from his fellow negotiator. Five Three Musketeers' bars could get you a bike, a car, or a black and white TV. The negotiator with Renaldo should never propose what he has to give up. It makes no difference with Renaldo as long as everybody is happy.

Pop and Mom should buy one of the big guys clunkers. Switch, the driving instructor who is never sober, leaves his old clunkers under the bridge for people to take. He handwrites notes on cardboard and puts them on the windshield. The notes simply say, "You can have this car. The keys are under the driver's seat. See Renaldo if you need plates". Switch doesn't end sentences. He writes a whole note in one sentence. Brother would have chemicals to get the smell of beer and cigarettes out of the cars. Maria asked Pop to buy an old beat up clunker that one of her husband's partners wants to dump in the Delaware River. He has ten days to decide. Pop won't take the car.

"Who's humming? Please stop it whoever you are," asked Sister Rose.

"Sister can I have your permission to hum hymns while I read or listen to you? It helps me be a quality student", I said thinking that Sister would be happy I was humming hymns.

"Learn to hum to yourself", Sister suggested.

"I can sing to myself but I can't hum to myself," I told Sister Rose hoping she'd reconsider.

"Then sing to yourself. Humming is for birds. Ask God to make you a bird," Sister let me know by her look she had enough.

"Sister, look at my story about Kitty Hawk; isn't it the best I have done so far? I was humming when I did it. Try it sister," I told Sister when the candy was put out to be sold.

"William, I have sixty-four seventh graders in front of me. The work will not get done if I hum or they hum. Read," Sister said as the class started to eat fudge and candy Irish potatoes.

"William, stay after school for five minutes",

"William, who told you about the humming while you work?" asked the good Sister.

"Brother, the best auto body man around showed me," I answered.

"Well, don't do it in class. Do it at home if it helps you," Sister graciously told me.

"But I'm humming hymns; that's the idea to make it holy and God will give you the speed and quality," I tried to convince her to let me hum in class.

"Your paper was far superior to any you have done so far. It was twice as long as any you have done too. Keep humming at home," Sister encouraged me.

"Try it Sister," I shot my last comment on the subject.

"I will," assured Sister Clare.

I got an earful from my walking "friends". Can you hum and eat? Do you plan to hum while you're playing tackle on the dentist's lot? The Fairhill guys will make a fool out of you. "Does this make you humm-ble?"

Brother continued to keep busy at his work. I'm sure that his reputation grew as he provided quality and speed that nobody believed possible. I knew his secret and I used it sometimes when I remembered. Pop and Mom bought clunkers, believe me. Only one of the clunkers clunked because of dents and scratches. The car couldn't pass inspection with some of the big dents. The cost of repair, even at Brother's, was more than the car was worth. We lived with the dents and scratches with our other clunkers. Actually, we loved our clunkers.

Pop recommended Brother to all his friends with cars. I told the cabbies but they told me that no outsider could get the right shade of yellow. The formula for the shade of yellow was a secret, known to a few body works people. The cops' red cars had the same thing. Anyway, the cops knew Brother already.

It would be a good excuse to meet the As and Yankees by telling them about Brother. Slash knows Renaldo well or I'd tell him myself. Sophia probably has friends of her own doing this work. Besides Sophia probably will never have an accident because she is such a lucky person. Uncle Arthur doesn't know about Brother. I'll tell him next time I see him. I want Brother to be wealthy as well as wise, healthy, and holy.

A voice came to me. *HE WILL BE All THESE THINGS. HIS WEALTH IS RICHER THAN MOST MILLIONAIRES. HIS WISDOM IS AT A HIGHER LEVEL THAN HYPOCRITES AND THE MISINFORMED "INFORMED" MEMBERS OF SOCIETY. HIS*

HEALTH IS MY GIFT TO HIM. HIS HOLINESS WILL ONLY GROW WITH TIME. THIS IS TRUE FOR YOUR PARENTS AND MANY LIKE THEM. BE LIKE THEM WHETHER YOU HAVE BARRELS OF MONEY OR NOT. LIVE THE LIFE OF A SAINT. ASK THE HOLY GHOST TO HELP YOU UNDERSTAND THIS. WISDOM IS A GIFT FROM THE HOLY GHOST, WHICH ALLOWS YOU TO THINK AS I THINK. UNDERSTANDING ALLOWS YOU TO SEE THE CROSS OF JESUS AND GET THE MEANING. KNOWLEDGE LETS YOU IN ON WHAT I AM CAPABLE OF DOING IN YOUR LIFE IF YOU JUST BELIEVE IN ME.

The voice was masculine yet soft. Here I go again like with Sister Raphael, expected to do the impossible. I should have asked the voice who he was and if he had the right boy. I need to steal broom handles sometimes, I'm too afraid to ask someone to give me their old brooms. I can't feel bad if I take two handfuls of bottle caps when I'm told to take a couple. The Holy Ghost is a ghost, not a magician. I want to be wealthy with money not with faith or happiness like Mom says. I see Mom and Pop with no money when Pop's out on strike and he gets so little delivering bread. Mom's health can't hold up with her working at lousy places. Pop and Mom and my friend's parents are like Brother. Pop's brother and sister died very young and it makes me a real sissy when Pop sings 'My Buddy, your buddy misses you' and I get emotional. Buddy was Pop's big brother and his favorite person. Helen loved her youngest brother and sister. She called them the little kids. Aunt Grace and Pop were the little kids.

God, why did you make Pop so heartbroken? Mom's brothers died in Scotland, they were little, and she will never see them again. My grandmothers are the people You should be preaching to; they are saints already for all they have been through. Can the Holy Ghost make people feel better when such tragedy and hardship hits them? I hate the rotten fathers who leave their kids and wife to try to live for themselves. Stupidity, selfishness, and laziness. I'm buying the house of Mom and Pop's dreams when I get rich. Rich with money and I'll still go to church and Communion. If I see any dogs making messes on our pavement, I'll scream. Dogs are animals, not humans. They should be in the fields with horses and deer and cows. They make such a rotten stinking mess all the time. I hate their owners.

I could punch my Pop's father. I don't care if Pop says he was dapper or brilliant. I think he is a sad sack of a father and husband. I'll ask the Yankees to split my pay 50/50 for Mom and Pop and for me. I'll sit still at Art school and I'll let Mom have my donut. I'll carry the ashes out because Fran is always working somewhere. If Horsehead Lady's dogs jump up the fence, I'll kick it in and throw the ashes on them. If the Crazy Lady chases me with her broom, I'll take it and swing it over my head to chase her away. I'll get all As and I'll be perfect for Mom and Pop. I gottah get to Confession to get started with my new lifestyle. I never felt this good because I know I can do what I want; it'll be easy. Oh Blessed Mother, don't let me chicken out of this. Holy Ghost, I trust you to make it all easy for me. Doc the Clock and Otto the Outrageous can expect me to be nicer to them starting now. Mom and Pop will never feel lonely without their brothers and sister again. I feel like I could play for Leahy right now. I'd beat out Lattner and Googahlahohme without practice. Life will be fun all the time from now on.

29

The Iceman

All of our neighbors had iceboxes at one time. When they could afford to buy Frigidaires, they did. Frigidaires did not require ice; iceboxes required ice. These iceboxes had a shelf on the bottom to hold a block of ice, which cooled the box and kept food and milk fresh for a few days. When the ice needed replacement and the people had the money, the Iceman came riding his horse drawn truck-like vehicle onto Carlisle Street. He stopped the horse in front of the customer's house and carefully placed the reins on his seat. As he looked at the order on his note pad, he counted the blocks he had left, and considered what he had yet to deliver that day. When he was satisfied, his artistic work began. He verified that the customer was home and capable of paying.

He grabbed his two-foot-by-two-foot piece of leather from the side compartment of the truck; looked at it as he was rolling up his sleeve as if to get a TB shot. Next, he put on his leather apron; painstakingly tying it around his waist and knotting it either in front or at the back, depending on the brand or the age of the apron strings – aged aprons lost several inches off the strap. The leather apron was the same length as the distance from the waist to the bottom of the pants. He took his dull looking tongs off the truck's secret compartment on the passenger's side, below the door. The horse was not moving at all, even when the bugs were surrounding him or her. Dogs came around to see what was going on and to study the horse. I saw dogs that I saw near Johnson's Wax. I know they get thirsty. And they would probably consider ice as nature's way to transport water to dogs. The horse didn't move; it was a statue. All street games stopped. No one would dare to run across the porch roofs at this time and no parent would ask their kids to go to the store while the work efforts of Iceman and his horse were in progress. It was noontime on Holy Thursday. The master was at work and it was something that simply couldn't be missed.

The Iceman clutched an ice block in his tongs and pulled it out and down to his knee level. He inhaled, then hoisted the block up, sighed, and exhaled. He put the ice block on his left shoulder, positioning it for the long walk to someone's kitchen. He walked into the house after kicking something off his right shoe. The Iceman knelt down on a towel that the customer placed in front of the icebox and cleverly put the ice block in the right place. He stood up, groaned, stretched his back and shoulders and accepted the payment. He was not young and this must have been tough on his back. If we were inside the house, we would clap in appreciation for the extraordinary effort. We were quiet outside the house but the Iceman felt the admiration of the crowd. I knew he did because I saw a smile from a man who never smiles.

I never saw a skinny Iceman and it is no wonder. Did you see how he power lifted the ice block from his knees to his shoulder? Our Iceman had the build of a five-foot-ten block of granite. He had to get the ice in the house quickly to make sure that it didn't melt too much. I guess that I don't understand why big shots, and movie stars make more money than Icemen, Ragmen, Lamplighters, and Moving Men. These men have harder and more dangerous jobs than movie stars and big shots. Big shots and athletes must have developed special skills that I couldn't see. Ice Men never have those skills. They just do the same thing day after day, year after year.

Why doesn't the Iceman bring a shovel with him so he can clean up after his horse? Some of the 15th Street people will be around to pick up the horse mess. They use it to fertilize their gardens, I think. The Iceman knows this and lets it stay until they pick it up. He's a good person.

Our regular Iceman wore an Ivy League cap as some of the Irish do; he was Irish; he had to be. His face was ruddy from heavy work and the sun, not from Schmidt's beer and Iron City beer as it was with some others. Richie Cione, my friend who gets balls out of the sewer sometimes, asked the Iceman some questions.

"What's your name Mister?" asked Richie.

"Iceman," answered the Iceman. I was glad that he liked his name.

"What's your horse's name," continued my friend.

"Finnegan," replied the Iceman.

"Does he eat sugar and carrots?" another kid asked.

"Both," the Iceman doesn't say a lot.

"Is the ice heavy?" the same kid asked.

"A little sometimes; depends on the size of the cube," the Iceman made our Q and A session enjoyable.

"Can we pet Finnegan?" we all kind of asked.

"You can feed him carrots. They're under the front seat," said Finnegan's owner.

"Is 'yat' real leather?" asked Bobbie, a good football player. He was referring to the piece of leather on the Iceman's left shoulder.

"Right off the cow's coat," was the funny answer.

"Where do you live?" Richie won't quit asking questions.

"Nearby. Ok, come on now, take your ice; I gotta go now," the Iceman had enough. He was busy and his profits could easily melt.

We grabbed all the ice we could off the back of the cart and broke it into small chips with our teeth and jaws. The Iceman packed up his cart and moved the reins slightly to the left. Finnegan started to walk away. The 15th Street people with flowers and grass cleaned up after Finnegan, who wore a hat with holes to let his ears move around. He also had a flower on his bridle. Finnegan and the Iceman left in a slow pace.

The Halfball game reconvened with two out in the seventh and bases loaded. The Iceman planned how to get to the next customer. Albert Ford, the kid who holds records in alley shimming, wanted to know who wanted to climb roofs with him. Doc the Clock walked by reminding us to change our clocks this weekend. Life on Carlisle Street was at peace and in a quiet stage. The stage was ripe for a disaster to occur. Disaster happened and our disaster Uncle made it happen.

Uncle Matt walked down our street for the first time, I believe. He had his cane and bag of doggie biscuits. Uncle Matt, an old man who walks with a cane, used to put doggie biscuits on downed telephone lines. The telephone and the electric company's lines were up so Uncle Matt couldn't put the biscuits on exposed wires. He wanted to talk to the police or FBI because he saw a violent killer on Broad Street. He might be suspicious to the FBI because he wore his famous long, black, heavy overcoat and it was quite warm. His pajamas were lower than his pant's cuffs; they always were in any weather. He wore his also famous derby, a black one. He didn't need a hat; his hair was brilliant white and thick.

242 It's a Long Lane That Has No Turning

What you could see of his white shirt wasn't white. His tie was plaid and nicely tied in a perfect Windsor. He was very old; in his late seventies I would guess. He was an emotional wreck; he saw someone, for sure. Maybe he did see a killer. His back hunched over with osteoporosis but it wasn't nearly as much as it usually was.

Some of us – Richie, Bobby "Wasteland" Wagner and me - rushed to Broad Street and saw a cop walking from the drugstore swinging his nightstick and whistling Peg of My Heart. His nametag told us that his name was Officer O'Malley and you'd swear he was Officer O'Malley if you didn't know him and we didn't. The Irish looking O'Malley stood perfectly straight as if listening to a Drill Instructor. His appearance was impeccable, even his tie was straight. His shoes glowed and they were not patent leather. He'd let his nightstick drop from his hand and when it dropped, he'd flick his wrist and the stick came back up; pretty good trick.

"Officer O'Malley, there's this old man on our block who claims he saw a killer around here," Bobby got it started.

"What block is that?" asked the obviously uninterested cop.

"Right there, Carlisle. We'll show you the man," we answered in unison.

"Officer, my name is Matt. I can't give you my last name at this time. I'm a Secret Service agent assigned to the FBI and Edgar would fire me if I gave you my last name," was how Uncle Matt met the good officer.

"I see. Tell me who you saw and where you saw him," asked O'Malley, whose shift was probably just about over.

"I saw him driving a wagon, a horse drawn wagon," offered the emotional old man.

"What did you see? asked O'Malley as if he was expecting Uncle Matt to say the Tooth Fairy.

"The brutal killer, Finnegan, Finnegan Mulholland I'm sure of that for sure," continued Uncle Matt, Everybody knows him".

"Where was he Mr. errr Matt?" was O'Malley's logical next question.

"On Toronto Street, near Broad", stated a very upset streetwalker, who just saw a ghost.

"Why would a known killer return to an area where everybody knows him?" O'Malley was making me mad with the way he asked his questions.

"I don't know but it was him, I'm sure of it. Nobody looks like that person," assured Uncle Matt.

"Did you see the killings?" was O'Malley's next logical question.

"No, but I heard about them from many people who were there," Uncle Matt said. I began to lose some faith in Uncle Matt.

"Where are the people who saw the murders?" was the officer's turn.

"I can't remember who they were but there was more than one," said Uncle Matt.

"Don't leave the area until we tell you it's ok", ordered O'Malley.

"But officer, I can't 'testifate (he meant testify)," sobbed the whistleblower.

"You mean testify and yes, you can testify. Just don't leave this area Uncle Matt", ordered an angry officer anxious to go home.

"I won't Officer," assured Uncle Matt.

"I'll call this in to the precinct. I want you to describe the murders you didn't see and you can't remember the names of who you did see to a homicide detective. I'll be ten minutes," demanded O'Malley.

Uncle Matt went into a long description of Mulholland as O'Malley started to leave. "Mulholland is a big drinker, a nasty big drinker who likes to fight when he's drunk. At least twice Mulholland went into a bar and got drunk. He grabbed the throat of the first man near him and pulled him outside. He threw the man on the ground and gave him a chance to run away. Men can't just run away, especially in front of their families and friends. Just imagine a man running away from a fight if his kids were watching him".

"I'd run, Uncle Matt, unless I had my revolver. Go on," said an unknown busybody bystander.

Uncle Matt continued, "When the man got up and made a move toward Mulholland, he put his life on the line. The two men I heard about looked like a train hit them. Mulholland, who has nine black belts, hit them harder than a train," claimed Uncle Matt.

"Why does Mulholland have nine black belts? Does he have nine pairs of blue pants? Go on," joked the same by-stander.

"Mulholland wouldn't let up on the man he pulled outside and nobody dared to help him or call the cops. The man died of injuries by Mulholland. The terrible murderer went back into the bar, and continued to drink as if nothing happened," Uncle Matt went on.

"And you saw none of this in person?" asked the disgusted officer.

"None, sir officer, sir. Mulholland went home and was at work delivering ice the following day. The cops did nothing about it," said Uncle Matt as he looked like a fool to everyone, including me.

"What happened to the body?" asked the officer who started to write things down.

"Cleary's funeral home picked him up and took the right steps to bury him after mass at the Catholic Church. Cleary's did the same thing with the other man I heard about," Uncle Matt kept it up.

"Ok, don't leave town, OK?", again ordered Officer O'Malley.

"I really won't. I promised you already," assured Matt as he looked down the street toward the subway station.

Officer O'Malley called into somebody by using the police call box on Broad Street. Uncle Matt left quickly to get out of town and wasn't seen or heard from again. He made a dreadful mistake and he realized it. All this sickened me. The Iceman was a friend in some ways, a very quiet friend. I told Mom and Pop and they appeared stunned by this incredible news. Mom said that the Iceman was in our house many times and that he was always the perfect gentleman, who hated to have to collect money from his customers. Pop was home once when the Iceman delivered ice and he gave the Iceman four or five bottles of Gruber's soda and sometimes a glass of, yep, ice water. If the Iceman got any tips at all, they were gifts, like a slice of pie or a piece of fruit. Mrs. Berg once gave him Hot Cross buns right out of the oven of her bakery, which is still the best bakery I've been in.

Finnegan wore jingle bells at Christmas time and had two shamrocks glued to his blinders around St. Paddy's day. He also had American flags on his harness all the time. I tried to think about these good things but it wasn't easy. I knew I was in for a difficult time because I didn't want anything to happen to Mr. Mulholland. He was family like the Moving Man, the Rag Man, the Pretzel Men, all the people at Paddy's Taproom, the Clearfield and all my mentally distorted, but kind friends and customers. The word spread faster than Uncle Matt could get out of town, which was faster than you could say Jackie Robinson.

Doc the Clock and Otto the Outrageous, looking his ridiculous best in a sheet wrapped around him and a cowboy hat two sizes too big led a swarm of locusts-like people who converged on Carlisle Street. Old Lady Leather Heel, the shoemaker's wife, took time out from her pocketbook and wallet repairs to check things out. Lady Leather Heel never leaves her position in the shop. Customers go to her if they have a leather product that needs repair. Incredibly, she made everything look brand new. Doc wanted to know if anybody knew what happened. He said that he made the rounds. He didn't miss a bar in a five-mile radius, which is believable because he'd typically sing a few songs (terribly) and do a couple imitations (nobody could guess who he was imitating), have a beer or two, pick up a couple dollars in tips and move on. Doc's imitation of Jimmy Stewart was a perfect John Wayne. Everyone thought that if anyone would know what happened it would be Deafy because he shined shoes and cars outside the bar called "Just a Small One Bob".

Most people knew where Deafy was but no one would tell where he was even if they knew. The locations of his hide-a-ways were super secret like the sins confessed to a priest. None of the fireplug swimmers knew where Deafy lived; he just kinda sort of was there. Deafy wasn't seen for weeks, which was not too unusual, especially if the weather wasn't too hot and humid. It was a good thing we got the Rosehill kid's fireplug wrench just in case Deafy was gone for a while. Renaldo the Purloiner was a friend of Uncle Matt's. He got Uncle Matt some clothes, money and occasionally a place to sleep. He was "shopping" at Kelly's Corner when all this was happening. The last person Renaldo wanted to talk to was Officer O'Malley.

O'Malley caught on to Renaldo but hasn't been able to catch him in the act of "transferring" goods from the store to his house. Renaldo enjoys being on the run from O'Malley. One time, around St. Pat's Day, Renaldo "purchased" a case of Harp from the backyard of the Clearfield Bar. He asked one of the bigger guys, maybe an eighteen or nineteen year old, to give it to O'Malley with best regards from Renaldo. It was the first and maybe the last time the bigger guys drank Harp. O'Malley never even saw the case.

It was difficult to sleep at night thinking that our Iceman might be a murderer. I kept thinking of the Cagney movie where he went to the electric chair for murder at the end. I couldn't sleep that night either. Of course, I felt sorrow for the people Cagney murdered and their families.

"Who will visit the Iceman in prison?" Richie wanted to know.

"I will Richie if he's in Holmesburg; Pop and Mom will take us," I answered.

"I haven't seen the Iceman for days, more days than normal," mentioned Albert, the world class "alley-shimmier".

"He is probably in Vegas or North Dakota by now Albert. Finnegan is alone and hungry I'll bet," said Richie.

"Finnegan is in the custody of the police, you can bet on it Richie," said Patsy, the senior at Little Flower who is the only girl who swims at the fireplug.

Mr. Mulholland could be right here in Philadelphia, in the Tioga Street haunted house. The people in Tioga will hide him. They once hid a well-known burglar," said one of the big guys.

"I think Officer O'Malley distrusts Uncle Matt. He didn't see the crimes or remember who did and that stinks bad for Mr. Mulholland," chimed in Renaldo the Purloiner.

"You're right Renaldo. Notice how he was quick to spot Mr. Mulholland, though. He remembered Mr. Mulholland," said Patsy.

Uncle Matt felt sorry he brought the subject up, I could tell. I wish that Otto would leave the sword that Renaldo gave him at home. He's crazy enough to go swinging it around and he could kill somebody. Mr. Mulholland has to be innocent. Mom said that even if he is found to be innocent, he will have to go somewhere else because people won't believe he's innocent. Why was Uncle Matt so scared with O'Malley? He's an FBI agent isn't he? Oh Blessed Mother, tell your Son to do something, anything to help our Iceman. If He needs assistance like the servants at Cana, I'll be one of them. Those servants obeyed Jesus and they're in heaven for sure. While you're at it Dear Lady of Fatima and Lourdes, help Renaldo, ask Jesus to forgive him. Believe me; he knows not what he does. His family life was sad. Bishop Sheen said that the only person we're sure went to Heaven was the Good Thief, who asked Jesus for forgiveness at the right time. I'll make a Spiritual Bouquet of ten thousand Hail Mary's and Five thousand Our Fathers. This is terrible; I hate everything about this crummy neighborhood. Nobody works harder than these people do and nobody anywhere has less money or things. All the

stupid cars break down all the time. **Pop and Mom have lousy jobs and they know it. God, where are You? I want to see Your Love and Kindness RIGHT NOW, not tomorrow, now.**

Jesus and God have to know what these people deal with; all work, no money and they are the best citizens because they defend America and pay their taxes. They pay their bills and are respectable like Grandmom always says. Decent people do that. They want a better life for their kids and they will do whatever it takes to get there.

Several weeks after all this happened, our parents received a letter from the Army asking them to come to a meeting at the Methodist church on 13th Street. A well decorated officer led the meeting. Right before he began to speak, Brother asked if he could say a few words. Nobody at the meeting knew Brother because he lived a few miles away, near Germantown and Lehigh. He had an auto body shop and he was the best body man there was in the opinion of his customers. Tonight Brother looked like he probably looks when he goes to Father Devine's church on Sundays. He was dressed in the best that South Street had to offer and that was good stuff. He wasn't tall, maybe five five and big, maybe one hundred and thirty pounds but he was impressive anyway.

"General, sir, I just heard about my friend, Finnegan Mulholland. First, he didn't kill anyone; he couldn't. His shoulders were too sore to make him do anything like punch real hard. He always wanted to carry the ice in the houses by holding it downwards in the tongs. He did that most of the time, but on Carlisle Street he used his shoulder and it hurt him bad, real bad, General. He knows the kids wait to see him lift the ice on his shoulders. Second place, sir, Finnegan never drank alcohol since the war. He drinked (sic) soda and coffee at H&H, sometimes with me. The bartenders at the SOB's knew what he drank and started to squirt it out when they saw him coming in. He drank 7Up, Gruber's, Puerto Rico, sometimes Hires, and Nihi root beer," Brother told the Army officer and the crowd.

"Thanks Sir, I will talk to the bartenders at SOB's myself. What's your name Sir?" asked the Army officer.

"I'm Brother to the people here and my customers and Jeremiah to my close friends, including Finnegan, who we, in my neighborhood, call Chief Don Eagle, or just plain Chief. Chief looked like a wrestler with his muscles and Mohawk-lookin' haircut," was Brother's lengthy response.

"Our kids loved him and he knew it by his smile, I could tell. Chief gave the kids some extra ice and let them feed Finnegan. He would put the babies on top of the horse and hold them for a few minutes. I don't think he got to a married life. He was pretty messed up in the war, I guess. If I knew he was in trouble I'd ove (sic) come earlier. He never hid himself here. Would a murderer do that? I'm here as a witness to the facts I just told you. Who saw him murder two men?" finished Brother.

"Thank you Brother. May I call you Brother?" asked the General.

"That's my name General," Brother replied.

"Thanks for the big promotion, Brother. My name is Major Tom Zigbee. I served with your Iceman when we fought together in France. I was his immediate officer and I thanked God everyday for him. Irish, our nickname for him, was as strong as an ox and a fierce hand-to-hand combat expert. I called role one morning and Irish noticed that almost all our platoon had Irish names. He was an expert on the Fighting 69th or the Irish Brigade in the Civil War. He saw a chance to resurrect the group under a different name, maybe the Feisty Shanty Irish of the 88th Brigade. The Irish and non-Irish loved the idea. At least we thought they did. Irish noticed a couple guys always standing in the rear and looking serious at the crazy meetings the Shanties had. They were trying to recruit more Shanties. The beer and blarney flowed all night long. Irish kept his eyes on the two, checking out their moves and actions during battles. He didn't like what he saw and he followed them one night to what appeared to be a drop-off point. They dropped things off every week and they started to miss the Shanties' meetings altogether. He told me about this and I asked him to keep at it," told the Major.

"A villager from a rich vineyard took a bag from the two and handed them American money, a huge stack to boot. Now before I continue, I think you should know that Irish led us as the point man for over a year. He was up front and a sitting duck for the enemy. He pulled many a wounded soldier into a safe area. He went out on solo paroles many times. He saved American lives by single handedly taking out the enemy. I recommended him for a Silver Star and a Bronze Star for bravery beyond the call of duty. He eventually received both. We both knew we had to do something about our two outsiders. Irish was a Sergeant, not an officer but we were not in the line of command business at that time and he was the best of the best".

"Hey Flood and Magee, when are you coming to the Shanties meeting? We meet tonight at eight near the mess hall. I'll come over to remind you at 7:30," said Irish. This is how Irish set them up.

"Make it nine and I'll go to the mess hall. Me too! replied Magee and Flood".

"That's it, Irish told me, we'll wait for them to leave there around 8 and ask them questions. These were all Irish's ideas. At eight on the button, Irish saw them leaving. Where you guys gone (sic)? Nowhere. What's in the bag? Nothing. You guys sound like kids. Give me the bag. He grabbed the bag and saw handwritten notes with copies of maps I presented to the platoon. Irish grabbed them both despite their opposition and brought them to me. We lost about eleven good men and I saw every one of them when I looked at Magee and Flood," said the Major rubbing under both eyes to push the tears away.

"I ordered some of the troops to put them in a building we built for these purposes. One morning when we were bringing them food, we found the building empty. Some body or bodies got them, and took them to a densely forested part of the woods near us and cut their throats. Naturally, everybody thought it was Irish who killed them because of his toughness and hatred for the enemy. I conducted an in-depth search for the killer or killers. No one even seemed suspicious. We buried the traitors and I let the army take it from there. I knew Irish didn't kill the two traitors; he'd use his wicked arm strength to strangle them, not slit their throats," continued the Major.

"Nobody said who did or did not do the deed. Nobody owned up to it and there was no evidence pointing to anyone. I have to say that I didn't sense sorrow or sadness in the camp. Our chaplain, Father Tom Foody, knew nothing and, if someone confessed the crime to him, he couldn't say *anything.* Irish didn't blink an eye or change his mood even though he knew that in the minds of the soldiers, he did the crimes. They thought of him as a hero. I started to think that the traitors' contacts might have had something to do with the crimes. I believe that they, the contacts, murdered the two of them. Anyway, a few days after the crimes were committed, we heard that people in this neighborhood were spreading false rumors about Irish, the more they spread, the more unbelievable the story became until what you all heard. The Army feared Irish's safety and moved him to some out of the way unknown place. We put him in the witness protection program for several years. He wanted to come home. He was homesick and his family missed him as much as he missed them".

"The Army felt that he was away long enough and the rumors would be forgotten and granted his request to return to his old neighborhood. He set up his ice delivery business and life was getting good. Oh, did I mention that Irish suffered severe wounds while leading us through French vine-yards. The bullets hit two places, his shoulder and his stomach. The medic shook his head as if Irish was dead. We got him to a MASH unit and he came out of there in flying colors. You know those tough Irishmen".

"In view of all the rumors flying and out-and-out lies, we asked Irish to leave again and go back to the witness protection program. Trust me; he didn't commit murders here or in France. He's my personal hero and I read about many heroes when I was at the Point. Thanks for coming here tonight. Say one or two prayers or more for the finest Iceman and man I know. Good night my friends," Major Zigbee finished.

"Good night Colonel Zigbee. He couldn't commit murder, Colonel," Brother said one more time.

"Brother, you promoted me twice tonight. Good night," said the Major, "don't worry about Irish, we'll take care of him. I'll him that you said hello".

"Thanks Colonel, I feel better now. Justice will be done."

30

The Movingman

If there was a common denominator for all the adults in our neighborhood who provided services to households, it was strength. The Iceman carried big blocks of ice with his tongs and strong back and shoulders. He sometimes had to go up two, three or more flights of stairs carrying enough ice to cool someone's icebox for a week. He had to move quickly because he wanted to give his customers as much of the block as he could. On hot days, the ice melted quickly. The Ragman was strong as well with his ability to toss a 25-pound stack of papers or rags to the top of his pile, at least ten feet high.

The Ragman could toss a large bundle of papers a good distance, sometimes even overhead. He tossed heavy bundles of rags also. He did this all day long, every day. These were amazingly strong men, but they weren't the strongest; that title belonged to the Movingman. This person was not real.

Gorgeous George can beat the Movingman in wrestling but I don't know how. Gorgeous looks like a woman but he is the best wrestler there is since Argentina Rocco retired. People want the golden bobby pins that Gorgeous throws into the crowd. Bif with one F could be a good Movingman. He's the strongest of the big guys. He might beat Gorgeous George. Pop could outrace the Movingman but probably couldn't beat him in *Punch As Hard As You Can*.

Whenever one of our friends came running out of their house to announce, "We're getting a new icebox today at 3 o'clock," we would all assemble at the house to watch the action. At 3 o'clock sharp, a truck or wagon drawn by a horse showed up and the Movingman got out carrying his heavy-duty straps. These straps were about four inches wide and several feet long. The man went to the back of his truck or wagon, usually a truck, and jumped onto it. A few seconds later, the new icebox or Frigidaire appeared on the back of the truck. The Movingman got it there with his unusual strength. The Movingman then jumped off the truck and put the strap around the icebox. He pushes the icebox to the edge of the back of the truck and takes off all the packing materials, which included cardboard and wood. The next move is unreal. The Movingman backs the truck onto the curb near the third base area that was for Stickball games. He chases all kids away from the truck. He makes strange contortions with his face. He tightens his belt and makes sure his pants are in his socks. He makes more of the same facial contortions. He swings his handkerchief's knot from his Adam's apple to the back of his neck. He verifies the style and color of the icebox or Frigidaire with the owner. Then he earns his pay and then some.

The Movingman wraps the straps around the icebox or Frigidaire and pulls them to secure these heavy objects. He holds the straps with his hands and wraps the ends around his fists. He pulls the straps together in front of his chest so they almost meet; he grunts; he puts his teeth in the position that a snorer would and lifts the icebox off the truck and onto his back. He bends down, almost sitting down, to put the icebox or Frigidaire on the street while he goes inside to remove the old icebox. I'm sure that he breathes a sigh of relief when he finds out that our neighbor lives on the first floor and not on the fifth floor, like so many of the customers on my paper route did. Soon the Movingman comes out of the house screaming "Watch out kid" to some little boy with curiosity, who is at the bottom of the front steps. He is carrying the old icebox to the back of the truck. He somehow maneuvers it onto the truck. Usually he backs up to the truck with the old icebox strapped to his back. He stands on his tippy-toes and jumps a little to get the icebox on the truck. Amazing! He prepares to take the new icebox or Frigidaire in the house and sets it up for the customer. He has to bend down as he did when he put it on the street minutes before. He picks up the new icebox or Frigidaire and immediately bends forward. He stands up straight and goes inside. The whole process took less than fifteen minutes.

"Sir, Mr. Mover Man, Sir, could you leave the wood when you're done? We build scooters and use some of the wood for our furnace," I asked despite being intimidated by his demeanor. Pop liked to burn wood in our coal furnace. I liked it to; the ashes were lighter.

"Get a wagon while I move the truck," replied the Movingman, who does this every time he comes to our block.

When the Movingman had his horse, we got a chance to pet it and feed it sugar cubes. His horse was big and strong, unlike Sweet Pea, the Horse-radish man's weak looking horse with a straw hat with his ears coming through and blinders. Sweet Pea wouldn't eat sugar; it had to be horseradish or carrots. I always thought that Sweet Pea used to be the Movingman's horse until it got old and tired. The Horse-radish man probably bought Sweet Pea for a cheap price. Actually, the Horse-radish man looked like Sweet Pea a lot.

"Take as much wood as you can fit on to the wagon. Watch the nails and be careful bringing it home. OK kids, that's it; I gotta go now," the Movingman told us.

"Thanks Sir. See you next time Mr. Mover," somebody said, probably Bobbie. Richie never got old wood. He had a real scooter and 15th Street people burned only coal. Carlisle Street people saved the coal as a last resort.

The Movingman cleaned up the street with a broom and dustpan. Rumor had it that most Movingmen delivered ten to fifteen iceboxes or sofas a day. I never saw a Movingman carry a sofa, but others did and they were amazed. Our Movingman owned his own business. "The Movingman" was the name of his business. Someone with white paint and a well-used paintbrush, probably the Man himself, painted "The Movingman" on the side of the truck. The lettering was so awful that it was a perfect advertisement. You couldn't overlook the truck because of it and you couldn't forget it either because of the lettering. The truck had two wooden gates on the back, which were pulled out of slots on the truck to use and put back to get going again. Rope and old neckties held the gates together. The gearshift was on the truck's floor. The knob on the gearshift was a Blatz beer handle used for pouring out Blatz beer. Being banged around and collecting dirt and bird droppings made the truck a truck, a worker's truck, not a silly flower truck like the one I saw in a parade. Customer satisfaction didn't include the truck's appearance; this was Carlisle Street and its residents would be more upset with a spic-and-span truck that looked new, which would be a sign that the owner was either lazy or wasteful – spending money on paint and wax and professional lettering made no sense to most of the residents. Customers wanted things moved, unbroken, on time, and at a low price.

Our Movingman moved furniture, appliances, and other heavy items for several stores and Philadelphia's Utility Company. A major problem with our Movingman's truck that I hesitated to mention was the floor between the driver and the shotgun was gone, rusted out completely. Now that I think about it, there were wires hanging down from the dashboard. Oh, and the dashboard; it had a few defects, nothing major. There was no speedometer; the radio didn't work; the lighter wouldn't go off while the truck was running and you couldn't remove it and by the way, the glove compartment door kept opening. That was all the major problems.

All the Moving Men looked like the rugged type; the kind of guys who would wrestle the bear at the circus and win. Unlike the Bartenders at Paddy's Taproom, the Moving Men did not look ready for a screen test at MGM studios. Rather, they looked like a combination of the Ragman and the Fish Man. Wallace Beery looked like a Movingman in some ways in The Champ. Our Movingman looked like a California redwood, tall, thick and red-haired. He'd be hard to fit for a suit on South Street. However, the tailors, like Sid and Abe, could make him a suit in a few hours. It would cost about $17.00, $2.00 more than the average suit because it would require more fabric. The alterations would be part of the price as usual. Even the Movingman couldn't outwear South Street's suits. I hoped that somebody told him about South Street.

Moving Men wore bandannas wrapped around their necks. They usually had a hanky tied around their heads and, sometimes, a towel stuffed in their shirt collar. Most Moving Men were short, stout, and somehow never fat or bald. They always had closely trimmed hair and Popeye-like forearms. One Movingman, who fits the description from the previous sentence, had an imposing tattoo on his arm. It read, "Liberty or Death & USMC".

There had to be a place where Moving men bought heavy-duty flannel shirts for a good price. They all wore them, all the time. At the end of the day, Moving men liked to stop at places like Paddy's Taproom or the Clearfield Bar and they should. I'm sure that the Moving men spent time in the service because they weren't 4F for physical reasons, I can assure you and that the draft was very active in their younger days. I bet that most of the Moving Men didn't wait for the draft, but signed up for duty, duty that put them in the most harm.

The Movingman at the Crazy Lady's house on my paper route has a tattoo that really means liberty or death. I don't think he meant his death.

It simply says Liberty or Death and there is a dagger under the words. I've seen him go into the Clearfield Bar once in a while. He encourages crazy Doc the Clock to do imitations. Doc does the imitations then asks the patron whom he imitated. They rarely guess correctly. The Clearfield Bar has an arm wrestling contest every Tuesday. Sometimes skinny men win these contests, Reds, the bar tender/bouncer told me. Nevertheless, no skinny man could beat this guy. Like Pop, his wrists are huge from polishing bearings with sandpaper eight to ten hours a day at least five days a week. One day Alicia, Sonia's younger sister told me that Sonia and she were getting a new Frigidaire, one with a motor that didn't require an Iceman. I told one or two people and the word spread like wild fire. About ten kids, ages 6 to 13 or so, came to Alicia and Sonia George's house with wagons. We bet baseball cards on whether the Movingman would have his horse or truck. I said horse because I hoped it would be the horse because I couldn't stop thinking about the floor and the dashboard on the truck. That truck was dangerous.

Coming down the street the wrong way was a truck, not the Movingman's truck. The truck stopped in front of the George's house and a Movingman got out. He wasn't our Movingman. His very sissified truck was painted blue and white and a sign painter painted the lettering. "The Strong Bros. Moving and Storing" took up both sides of the truck.

"What's with the wagons kids; is today wagon day?" laughed the new Movingman.

He easily took the new Frigidaire off the back of the truck because the back of the truck came down to the street level. He went in the house with a special thing called a dolly. In two minutes, he came out of the house with the Icebox strapped to the dolly. He rode the back of the truck up to the edge of the truck and unloaded the Icebox. He jumped off the truck, grabbed the dolly, and loaded the Frigidaire on the dolly and went inside to deliver and install it. He was done in five minutes. He unpacked the Frigidaire in the truck so there was no wood to take home.

Our Movingman carried a Frigidaire with a motor in it as if it was an Icebox. We'll never see Movingman again. I'll miss seeing his truck pull away with the piece of cardboard for a license plate. I'll never forget the license plate number: 836S229. I didn't notice the new guy's license plate.

31

Old One-eyed Connelly

At least once a year, sometimes twice, Pop took Fran, Vince and me to somewhere in Delaware or English Creek, in New Jersey, crabbing. I preferred English Creek because the owner, One-eyed Connelly, was always there ready to tow us to the "best place to get the big ones". "Yesterday, three 'fellas from upstate caught two bushels in two hours and they were big bushels too," old One-eyed coyly claimed as we were mouthing the same thing. We memorized this line, which we heard every time we went to English Creek. Pop always brought along two apple baskets just in case our luck changed. We never caught two bushels though we did fill one-and-a-half bushels one time, when it as just Pop, Fran, Vince and me. Pop insisted that we go to bed early on the eve of the trip. We used the parents' bedroom, which faced Carlisle Street.

Our friends were playing Buck-Buck Come In at the wall directly across the street from our house, at Sophia and Alicia's house. Sophia and Alicia didn't care if we played Buck-Buck against their house. Their parents forbid it. The game wasn't a distraction really, but we couldn't resist.

"Keep the noise down out there or we'll call the cops," we screamed to our friends, who looked up and laughed.

"Call the cops, I don't care. I know you won't anyhow," was the quick response from Terry McShay, an Irishman from the other side of Broad Street.

It was a joke and we all played into it very well. McShay boxed in Flynn's basement and he could punch hard. I felt his right hand the one time I fought him. He was older but a member of the Tioga Ts and I wanted to be a Tioga T, the gang Fran, my older brother by 11 months belonged to, the Ts. Flynn stopped our fight after Terry's right to my face because he (Flynn) made up an excuse to stop it.

Thank God, thank Terry.

This trip was going to be different from the others because Buddy Sam and his friend, Ace of Hearts, were coming with us.

I think I beat Mousy at Flynn's. Flynn's brother said I hit him when he was down. No I didn't. Beryl the Frog said I was lucky to get the homer against him. "The centerfielder was in too much," he said. Ole Le Roy said "it was the longest homer he. s seen at Hunting Park". The centerfielder didn't change his position when I came up to bat. Pride is the basis of sin says Bishop Sheen. I'm not a long ball hitter. Frog threw a sweetheart pitch. The guys are playing at Johnson's Wax today. Richie can't play third, he'll get slaughtered. Buddy Sam and Pop walk the picket lines, carrying signs. So will Big John but later. Pop will do whatever the union boss tells him to do during a strike including walk out. I heard Pop tell Mom that a long strike or two strikes close to each other would force him to find another job and lose his seniority and retirement. It kills Pop when Mom goes out to work on the presses in a lousy shop. I should charge for modeling at Pop's art school. They'd have to pay me a lot of money because they couldn't get a boy or girl with my odd-shaped head and different size ears.

Pop always used his car on these trips. He has to, even though it breaks down about half the time. Buddy Sam and his friend, Ace of Hearts, plan to crab in between Schaeffer's and Schmidt's beers; they tried to fit a little crabbing in if the beer needed to get cold. They should never crab and drive. We lost our brakes one time driving home. Pop didn't say a word, knowing that it would have shaken us up. Clutches went sometimes. The engine wouldn't kick over at times, but we knew how to fix that. The battery required a tap or two in the area next to the positive terminal. We knew the exact spot well. But brakes? Pop pulled the car over and got it to stop. Most trips went well.

When we got to Old One-eyed Connelly's, Pop pulled his car into the area next to One-eye's pier and listened to his canned speech about the two guys who caught a few bushel yesterday. One-eyed had two eyes, but he couldn't control his right eye. His right eye blinked all the time, even when One-eyed spit and cleared his throat every ten seconds. One-eyed was indescribable unless the listener or reader had seen someone on a two-year binge.

He apparently shaves infrequently and the blade must be red with rust when he does. He stands about five feet eight or ten. He looks like a middleweight fighter who lost a few rounds. His hair is totally unkempt and colorless. His smile has that "person who lived on a deserted island for fifty years look". His overall appearance matched his smile. Connelly might be his real name because he wears the same kind of plaid sports coat that the patrons at Paddy's Taproom and the Irish patrons at the Clearfield Bar wore. His shirt, which looked familiar for years, was red plaid. His yellowish t-shirt with the v-shape at his shirt's collar had to be his pajama top. He couldn't take that shirt off each night, it had to stay on throughout the night. Connelly's paperboy cap was unusual and ragged around the edge. The hat had some fishing hooks and lures pinned to it. He never took his hat off. If he did, he couldn't put it back on. It was very fragile looking: like faded colors and a few threads hanging down the front and back. Salt water, fish, fish scales, crabs, beer, whiskey and dog hairs did a number on his hat. An absentminded mechanic, who didn't know you're supposed to use rags to cleanup, not your pants, handed down his pants to One-eye. Connelly adds his personal touch to the hand me downs. He adds fish smells and a touch of stale beer odor to the pants. It must be like putting on a sandy, wet bathing suit for One-eyed every morning when he dresses for work.

One-eyed lived in a shack with his trusty, rusty dog, named, Feather. The shack was a combination of angler's cabin and an abandoned shed, "closed by sheriff's order," and an outhouse. Feather could use a bath but she looks happy and content to lie around all day.

The outside grounds of the shack was a large lot with sand, weeds, old rusted anchors, bones (don't ask), rocks, stones, transmissions, car passenger and driver seats, boat motors, boats, and oil barrels rusted out at the bottom, and a beat up old car which looks like a Chevy but it could be a Ford. It must be in working order because old One-eyed gets around. I never did get to see the back of the shack or the area around the out houses, his and hers, I assume. The pier was functional but squeaky and wobbly. The boats were somewhat safe as long as at least one person is on duty at all times to scoop out the water. I wanted to make a postcard with One- Eyed smoking a corncob pipe standing in front of his pier and house with the caption, "Wish you were here" or "Business for Sale".

One-eyed towed our boat out to the area he claims is legendary for catching huge crabs in large quantities. When we were ready to come back in, we were to hold up an oar so Connelly could see it. He would drop everything he was doing and come get us.

We caught a few crabs. This outing was productive considering that Buddy Sam, Ace of Hearts couldn't find the lines to throw out, and we rowed to different spots at least four times. Fran had to go in and wait for us because he got seasick. We used any old weight for sinkers. Like 3" washers or steel bolts or anything else that was the right weight and past it's normal utility. Fish parts and chicken parts tied to the line was the bait.

"Bill, you start holding up the oar. We're going in," requested Pop.

"I'll take a turn holding up the oar in a few minutes," agreed Pop.

"Sam, oh just forget it. Bill, try again," asked Pop after he had the job for about twenty minutes.

It took ole One-eyed at least an hour to even *see* the oar, which is why we held up the oar as soon as we caught a few. He arrived and towed us to his pier. All of us had a wonderful day with Pop, my and Pop's friends. Pop stayed awake; the friends started to drift off to sleep when One-eyed towed us out and they drifted all the way when we returned to the pier. The friends drank a couple beers each time they woke up for a few minutes. Pop had maybe two beers; the boys had none and we put a case of twenty-four empty bottles were in the trunk when we left. That didn't count the Tiger Rose and Thunderbird wines and the "soda" that kids were forbidden to drink.

I'd love to see Pop paint a portrait of Old One-eye. I wonder where One-eyed went to school or if he fought in the war like Pop did. Old One-eyed smiled when we gave him the hoagies that the seagulls turned down.

I saw One-eye's teeth when he smiled at the sight of the hoagies. He had a broad smile with no apparent missing teeth. The problem was that the teeth were green and black with no sign of whiteness. I'd bet my Mickey Mantle rokkie card that Connelly was a veteran of WWII and the war damaged his thinking and overall concern for life. Sad!

I suggested to Pop that we pay One-eyed after he tows us back, not before. Pop wanted to pay him up front. Pop couldn't wait to pay One-eye; he knew where the money was going: to some taproom nearby.

"I hope that he enjoys whatever his income is from us. "Is there a packaged goods store nearby that he could get to easily?" I thought to myself.

It's a Long Lane That Has No Turning, I hear it; it came out of nowhere. "God, forgive me for mocking Mr. One-eyed Connelly". Life is less funny since Sister Raphael talked about perfection and Sister Prophetess warned us not to give up our faith.

One-eyed saw our catch and promised it would be doubled if we came back after the spawning season in the fall. Pop gave whatever food we had left to One-eyed. He grabbed the food as if it was a life jacket and he was drowning. Feathers got up and breathed heavily the way dogs do. One-eyed and Feathers were anxious for us to leave so that they could enjoy their feast.

It's a great life for them really. Everybody is different. One-eyed hopes for at least two customers every day. I want to play for the Yankees, be an All American at Notre Dame, and become the first American pope.

32

Ace of Hearts

Lots of Schaefer's and Schmidt beers were consumed in three hours during our crabbing trip by Ace of Hearts, a man who didn't even get around to putting his line into the water. On the way home from our trip, Pop fell asleep and Fran, Vince and I braced for the joyride of our lives. Pop felt confident that Ace of Hearts was OK to drive. Ace of Hearts was driving home.

The winding roads in New Jersey looked different this time. The trees somehow merged into one very wide tree. Ace of Hearts took the car to the maximum speed it could go, not the legal limit, but the limit of the car's capability, over 100 mph. In addition, he didn't seem to be concerned about the lines in the middle of the road. Broken lines, solid lines, what did it matter? A line is a line and it's too confining for Ace of Hearts. The mile markers changed so quickly that I lost count after the first or second tenth of a mile. Things were feeling out of control when Lady Luck came our way; two New Jersey state troopers pulled us over. Our driver, the Ace (in a hole) of Hearts, had no license and very little consciousness, was taken to the local trooper station. Our trooper looked in the car as Pop was waking up.

"Ziss your car?" said one of the troopers.

"Yes, it's mine," answered my pale looking Pop.

"Your friend is at the station in bad shape. Why jah let him drive?" asked the trooper.

"I thought he'd be ok. Sorry officer," Pop followed.

"He's drunk and you have kids in the car. You can go," ended the trooper.

Pop took us to the trooper's station. Buddy Sam was silent when the troopers looked into our car.

"Mickey – Pop was called Mike or Mickey by friends and his in-laws. My Aunt Grace and Uncles Arthur and Joe called him Francis – I'm sorry about all this. Reginald was supposed to be on the road to normalcy. He's family on Cindy's side and he just got out of an institution, Byberry, where he was a model patient so they told me. He has a strange problem. He starts to act very strange; like he's not here with us. He can't think and he's smart, went to Tommy More, a Catholic school, too. He acts nutty. He starts to give orders to 'his brigade': Cindy, Angelica, and me. During these times he's convinced there are Communists in our closet. But he hasn't had beer in a while," was all that Buddy Sam could say.

Ace of Hearts couldn't answer the trooper's questions at the station.

"Do you know the speed limit around here?" asked the trooper.

"Seventy-five?" answered Ace of Hearts looking as though he's had enough of this private or corporal.

"No, thirty-five and you were doing thirty more than seventy-five," told the insubordinate trooper.

"Must be something I spotted on the horizons," said Ace, who was acting nuts.

"What's your name?" asked the trooper who just entered the room.

"Ace of Hearts, Colonel Ace of Hearts to you. Where's your commanding officer? Where's your ID?"

Don't need one on the base?" asked the very bold Colonel Ace of Hearts.

"What's your real name?" asked an impatient, yet smiling, trooper.

"Do you think I'm going to give you that information, Corporal? I'll give you my rank and serial number, that's it. Colonel 0098765004321a. Where's Mama?" Ace of Hearts asked the trooper, who couldn't control his laughter. He wanted his wife.

"She's been called. Someone else answered your phone. We're waiting for Mama to call back," answered trooper Perry.

Ace of Hearts was held overnight and wouldn't be released until he could come up with a hundred dollars bail. Pop and Sam tried to help, but the anti-Communist Colonel (soon to be General) insisted that his wife would come up with the money. She wouldn't or couldn't but didn't. I forgot what happened next. Nevertheless, I am sure that the crabs never tasted better.

It's a shame that Pop has to go back to work on Monday night. We could eat the crabs we bought on the way home for many days and Pop would like that.

It's good to be home after that nightmare with the police and the crazy driving. I thought that I'd never see Mom or Maureen, Theresa, or Vince again. Ace of Hearts is nuts. It was so crowded in the back seat with Vince and Buddy Sam. Fran is lucky this time that he gets carsick. He could sit up front, by the window. Thankfully, no one was smoking. I'm sorry that Ace of Hearts had to stay in New Jersey.

The trooper said he was drunk, somewhat nasty, and not ready to be released. No one paid Ace of Hearts' bail. He went back to headquarters - Byberry - at his request. He missed being at headquarters with his staff.

Ace of Hearts was in the war under difficult circumstances. He might have been a POW. I hope he will be happy at his headquarters with Mama visiting him as often as she could.

33

Fishman

Our Carlisle Street house had about twenty-five square feet of space suitable for growing flowers. Pop grew flowers and they were the talk of the street. He couldn't grow roses because Fran and Maureen were allergic to them. Therefore, he grew other flowers. Fran and I didn't care about the flowers, but we had to go to the fish market, a two mile walk, to ask the owner for any old fish heads and tails he had. Pop was convinced that fish heads and tails rotted in the ground and created an unusually effective fertilizer. I couldn't argue with his reasoning; the proof was in the flowers. However, I hated those trips and I think Fran hated them too. The fish market owner saw me coming and looked at me as if I was selling a used car that he knew was a lemon. He'd laugh the "gim-me a break" laugh.

The Fishman started a diatribe and stayed with it until he got it all out, "What'da heck do 'ya want kid? Your dad sent you down for some more heads? Haven't seen your brother for a long time; where's "E"? Don't 'cha think the cats need the fish heads more than your flowers? OK, I'll give you some, just wait here a minute. Some day I'm a 'gonna charge you for these things".

The Fishman's teeth and apron almost matched, both were yellowish and black in some places. The apron was more colorful than the teeth, with its red bloodstains and blue blotches. I never understood the blue blotches. The Fishman wore a white, well close to white, tee shirt under his apron. I believe that he changed his apron at the beginning of every season of the year whether it needed to be changed or not. He wiped his hands on his apron after every customer was finished. Sometimes the Fishman wore a paper hat made from folded Bulletins. He was average height, maybe five-nine, and hairy. He shaved periodically and his arms were extra hairy. He had a marking pen tied to his apron, which he used to total the customers' orders. The Fishman had a big sink where he washed the fish before he wrapped them. Gills and other fish body parts always filled the sink. The spigot dripped all the time, a slow annoying drip. Fishman wrapped the fish heads, tails, gills, etc. in newspaper then taped it together and wrote "no sale" on the tape.

"Here 'ya go kid, say hello to your brother," was his normal good bye.

Sometimes he'd say, "Tell yer Dad that I'd like some flowers for my wife; she likes any kind of flowers".

Pop would have holes dug near the roots of the flower plants, awaiting my return. He smiled and planted the heads and tails. All was ok; Pop was happy and he could take pride in his flowers and his special formula for making them grow.

Pop, you ask nothing from me, really, and you give me so much. Sorry that I give you a hard time when you asked me to get the fish heads. They're nothing compared to what I will give you in the future. I will be a source of pride to you; good grades in school, All American at Notre Dame, and the Papacy, which will get you and Mom a free trip to Rome and a place to stay. Pop, you work in a crummy job and you never miss work. You deserve beautiful flowers. Mom deserves to see beautiful flowers as well. She works at home and at some of her own crummy jobs. Mom is more beautiful than all these flowers in my eyes and Pop's eyes as well. He told me that he thought the same thing about Mom a few times.

I always have to run home from the fish shop after I reach 15th Street because that's where I saw the big red headed Tom cat, which beats up dogs if he's hungry. I don't want the fish heads to whet his appetite. The Fishman probably wakes up early to cut the heads and tails off the fish he plans to sell that day. He scrapes the gills off the fish then guts them and cleans them under the spigot. That's hard and it probably pays what the Ragman gets, which is not much. At least the Fishman and Ragman get to see what is going on outside; the Pretzel Makers never leave the cellar all day.

Some day I'm going to buy a round at Paddy's Taproom for these hard working, misunderstood men.

34

Patches

I don't know if Patches, the neighborhood Lost Soul, could draw horse heads or jump out of windows like some of our neighbors, but I do know that most hurricanes would blow him over unlike Mrs. Kleinmeister, who wouldn't budge. I'm not sure what to call him, Mr. Bradley, Mr. Gillis, Mr. X or just plain Patches. I knew him under all these names and I lucked out if I guessed right when I said hello. Mr. whatever preferred Patches, but neither of my parents would approve of me calling Mr. Unknown Patches any more than Pop would agree to refer to Mom as she, like "she" said I could. She was the cat's mother, not my mother and Pop reminded us of that all the time.

Our multi-named next-door neighbor had to have multiple names because he was a former FBI agent who could never reveal his identity. He told this to everyone he met, even the Iceman, the Milkman, Marlene, the Crazy (Crazed Husband Killer) Lady and me. J. Edgar Hoover needed Patches in Philadelphia, but he had to be anony-mous and well prepared for any "possible Red Alert coming from headquarters". His wife Gloria was really his co-worker, Anita. She was on loan from the FBI's Midwestern region until some things were under control. Patches told me all this and asked me to keep it secret or Hoover would get angry. All the neighbors knew that Gloria was really Anita. Patches told one too many people this fact and told that person to keep it secret.

Gloria was a good fake. She fooled everyone on Carlisle Street with her acting. She could fool anyone. She was a perfect agent. I'd say that Gloria was average looking and average dressed. I don't believe that she could carry a weapon on her; her clothes were too form fitting and a gun would stick out. Gloria was either snobbish, unfriendly, an introvert or an agent who had lots of critical information that she was afraid would slip out. She talked to no one and rarely left her house.

I never asked Patches what had to be under control but he revealed to me unreal details, which I had to keep secret for thirty years unless I met a man named Squirrel, who had an eye patch, who approached me. Well, that was over fifty years ago and Squirrel must have *gone nuts* or something. Patches told me that it seemed as though someone in our neighborhood was posing as a number's writer and a used watches' dealer, but he was a crook in real life. People believed that he stole millions of dollars from the local Federal Reserve Bank when the employees were on a bank holiday and nobody was at the safe to make sure the safe was safe. Apparently, the crook knew people at the Fed because he stole millions from at least two secret Fed banks in Ephrata, Pennsylvania and a secret city in central North Dakota. I really believed Patches until I observed two things.

He never went to work, ever. He sat on his front porch with his guitar and Davy Crocket hat, minus the tail, singing (I don't know what else to call it) songs about Sally Starr and Chief Halftown. The second thing was the time he went for a walk for a month or so. This might have been the Red Alert he was being ready to pounce on. Mrs. Whatever, Gloria or Anita acted as if she didn't know where he was. Great acting Gloria, you have the whole neighborhood thinking Patches is lost and not with his fellow FBI agents.

I'll keep my secrets although I wished I didn't have these secrets. Patches is a nut not an agent.

One day, while Patches was on his month long walk, I was practicing my half mooner Halfball pitches playing against a Halfball rookie from Mueller School. Patches Gillis or whatever was his current last name was in a red car with two policemen. The police car pulled up to Patches' house and both policemen got out before Patches. They opened the back door and out came the Elliot Ness of Carlisle Street; at least that's what I thought.

"Hi Mr. Gillis, it's nice to see you home again," I said to my friendly neighbor who was gone for a month.

"What did you call me?" asked that friendly neighbor with an unfamiliar voice.

I thought that Patches was in a tough position. He couldn't tell the cops his real identity due to his undercover agent position.

"Where do you live kid?" asked one of the mean looking cops, the meaner looking one.

I'm finished. I broke some code and now I'm cooked. That cop remembers me from swimming under the fireplug. None of us would tell him that Deafy turned the fireplug on. The other cop isn't smiling. Why did Patches get me into this mess? I wish we had school all year long so I could stay out of serious trouble with the law. Mom can't see this, thank God. This is the first time I am glad that Mom is at work. Grandmom will cover for me when I'm wheeled off to Riker's Island.

"Do you know this man, young man?" the meaner cop asked.

"Yes officer" I stuttered in reply.

"What's his name?" the less mean cop asked in a nice way.

"Mr. Gillis (I hope I picked the right one). He lives next door to me," I politely replied as I pictured myself in a cellblock with murders and armed robbers.

The nicer mean cop looked at me with a serious stare and said, "Thanks, now get back to the game. By the way, your halfmooner is better than your hand spraying at the fireplug. Is Deafy still around or does he stay away until the summer?"

"I don't know sir," was my weak reply.

I started to run home when Mr. Gillis asked me to show the policemen where he lived. He forgot everything in his life, even his address and FBI partner Anita.

"Mr. Gillis, you live in that house with the wooden steps and the porch with the railing with many colors," I said wondering if this was what FBI agents did.

"How do you know me?" asked Mr. Gillis with that same unfamiliar voice.

"I listened to your music and singing and you introduced yourself to me. Besides, you live next door" I told him with a bit more confidence.

Anita came out of the house and yelled, "Jim, where you've been? Are you in some kind of trouble? Why did the police bring you here? What's going on you @#%&^* @#%&^@? These words were the same words that the Ragman uses when his toss of rags to the top of the pile causes the pile to tumble down.

"Miss, are you Mrs. Hildebrand?" asked the meaner cop in a friendly voice.

"Yes officer, I am. Is there a problem here?" Mrs. Hildebrand answered and asked.

"Not really Mrs. Hildebrand. Your husband was lost and roaming the streets around the train station. If you want us to keep him until you feel comfortable, we will," volunteered the less mean cop, who had a silver badge. The mean looker had a gold badge.

"No, he's done this before, many times. He lives in a fantasy world. He thinks he's an FBI agent or informant or he thinks he's the Secretary of State or a Jesuit priest. I can take it from here," assured Mrs. Hildebrand.

Mr. Hildebrand. Where'd that come from? Now I know his name or maybe not. This could be a trick to keep the Communists away from our neighborhood. He has nine names, not nine lives.

"My names not Hildeburg like the cops said, trust me. I took the name Gillis because Reilly's friend in "The Life of Reilly" is Gillis," Patches told me. I said that I had to do homework. The cops said Hildebrand, not Hilderbrand.

"Do the nuns give you homework in the summer?" asked Patches with his normal voice.

"No, I have to shovel the ashes into the can. That's what I mean," I tried to clarify.

"Look for a big mob bust this weekend. It will be big, believe me and I will probably be on TV. I'm with the FBI. My badge number is the same as my birth date; 122522," Mr. Hildebrand gave me this insight.

Mr. and Mrs. Hilderbrand moved to points unknown in the middle of the night. Pop saw a station wagon pulling out of Carlisle Street when he came home from work. There was a mob bust on that Saturday that made the papers but didn't make TV. I watched John Facenda's news report twice, six and ten, and he didn't mention a bust.

Was he a fake or not? I'll tell anyone who wants to tell me something in secret not to talk to me. I don't want to know any more secrets. Maybe Anita-Gloria is a good actor. She seemed angry for real. Patches is different that's for sure. He belongs on Carlisle Street like the rest o us different people.

The Hilderbrands left everything as far as I could see. A small van came around to Patches and Anita's house and two or three big boxes and a heavy safe.

Make's you wonder.

35

Marlene

On the corner of Carlisle and Toronto Streets lived a strange old lady, who was never seen except when she walked to Klienies' grocery store or Cicolli's (Sig-cole-sah) candy store to get her stash of food and candy. We all knew that she brought poison from a crook hiding on 15th Street when the lady gave him the signal that she was coming. The signal was a wave of the right hand as she came out of her house. We all saw the signal. We never saw the crook but we knew he was there; Bobby and Patsy both told us. It seems as though this strange old lady got into the habit of poisoning her husbands and pushing them down the steps. She went through at least five husbands according to our calculations, though we never saw them and the police never went to her house. Marlene, that's what her next door neighbor called her, doesn't care what people think as she goes about her dreadful routine with a new partner every few years or so.

How does Marlene, who wears army boots and has a history of murder, get all the husbands? She wears very strange clothes. I never saw any woman wearing a wedding dress and shoes that looked like goulashes to walk to the store. She wears prom-type gowns with a navy watch cap. Why does she always point her head to the ground? She must know that we know what she has been doing, that's why. I wish she would look up; maybe I saw her in the movies. I think she'd make an excellent Witch or one of Cinderella's step sisters. The make-up person wouldn't have to work too hard, just a little powder here and there and put a big red pimple for the nose. She could keep her own clothes.

I heard that Marlene was once a famous movie star and that she was married to an actor who bothered her when he was practicing his lines and she wanted to practice hers. She gave him breakfast in bed, arsenic and Cheerios; that's what the big guys and Bobby said. She pushed this man down the basement steps, hoping that his neck would break. Nobody knew a famous actor who died of poison and a broken neck; I ask some of the adults I meet at the movies. Her first husband was either a bad actor or just an actor at a local theater, not a Hollywood type. I don't know where she lived when she committed her first murder, but it wasn't far from our street so I've been told.

Marlene probably buried his body in Johnson Wax's lot. She had him put under the old boxcar on the railroad spur behind Nabisco's that has just about as much track as it takes to keep the boxcar. Some hobos carried him off at night and put him under the boxcar for a swig or two of whiskey or a bottle of cheap beer or maybe ten dollars. The big guys knew this, I'm sure; they hung around Marlene's house a lot. They spied on Marlene and watched for Sonia, the beautiful Greek goddess who lived down the street.

Marlene murdered three husbands in Hollywood or on location for a movie; nobody knows for sure. She murdered her fifth husband last year in her Toronto Street, corner house with three stories. Marlene frightened her fifth husband, who probably suspected something. We knew this to be a fact because he called the cops who came and just got Marlene's autograph.

The sixth husband never left the house but you could hear him as Marlene screamed at him, especially on hot humid days, when everybody else's house had music playing. On hot days, the Dunleavys, Marlene's next-door neighbor, argued loudly when their son, Eddie Dunleavy, an older guy with a skull and crossbones tattoo on his arm, above his wrist. He got picked up by the cops. Mr. Dunleavy is a cop but the cops still picked up Eddie, who picked pockets and stole donuts from Berg's bakery. Eddie took cabs to Dawn donuts after he sold a watch or if the wallet he snatched had good money in it. The screaming was loud, but you never heard the kind of angry talk that you heard from Marlene's open windows around here.

Eddie was big but he never hit one over Good and Plenty's, it was way too high for him. Mom says that she sees Mrs. Dunleavy going to work carrying a lunch pail and a bible, Douay Reams, I bet. Most Catholics don't memorize the bible; they read Matthew, Mark, Luke and John and they use a bible with an imprimatur. The servants who filled the jugs with water at Cana

are probably going to heaven for obeying and the servant who fetched the fatted calf for the Prodigal Son's father will be there too. They have to be. Father Melley said that the Good Thief is the only person we are sure went to heaven, Jesus said so. Why not the servants at Cana and the servants of the Rich man whose prodigal son came home? They obeyed their master and did it without complaining. Aren't they a shoe-in for Heaven?

Mr. Marlene Milquetoast, the new name for Marlene's current unseen husband, was always on the receiving end of her anger. He didn't get angry it seemed, but he listened to his share of anger and more. One night after playing baseball at Johnson's Wax, I heard Marlene and Milquetoast talking. Marlene, of course, went first.

"What-cha mean Jean Harlow? she's nothing special. Jack wanted me but I wasn't in his stable at that time. MGM wouldn't let me go, you know that. Bette Davis stinks outloud. She's ugly and nasty. I'm told I'm beautiful and I know I'm not nasty. At least I read for parts. You never got to read even for a bit part; you were a mess as an actor. Maybe you should have played the Hunchback and not Laughton. You could've saved money for the producer 'cause you wouldn't need makeup and you could wear that stupid Tarzan outfit Weissmuller gave you. I didn't read for "The Grapes of Wrath" because I had the part 'til that broad what's her name started the smiling and the 'yes siring' all the big shots all over the lot. Fonda told me that he was "fonda" me. I wish I read for Gone with the Wind. That part was me," Marlene went on and on".

Milquetoast followed, "Darling Dear Honey, let's go to the Uptown. They always have the latest movies. You must take these chains off me. If I don't get exercise and fresh air, I'll die".

"You're not 'gonna' to die. You'll die when I tell you to die and not any sooner. Do you hear me?" demanded Marlene.

"Yes Sweetheart, Angel; will you forgive me? Sweetie, you were the best, I agree. Cagney and Flynn loved you, I saw that myself. You married me because you needed my money; you told me so. I'm sorry that we ran out of money, but I can make more if you'll let me," said Milquetoast in a very meek way.

"Stop all the screaming you fool, the neighbors can hear you," screamed Marlene.

"Yes Madam Delightful, I'll talk softly but you tell me I sound like a little girl when I talk softly," moaned Milquetoast.

"Just keep quiet while I think, you moron," were Marlene's last words.

Milquetoast is next and he doesn't know it. He's a week away from the poisoned tea. He can't run away because he's in chains. Mom said that Marlene is rehearsing for a new play, which she wrote and plays both parts. She was the one screaming and she was Milquetoast at the same time. I hope Mom's right. Can actresses sound like men if they're rehearsing? Milquetoast doesn't sound like a man. Can she play the roles of husband and wife? I heard number 6 talked about chains. He must be chained to the radiator or something. He can't get out. Number 6 must be told what to look forward to all the time and not to drink anything that she brings home in an unmarked bottle and definitely not to stand at the top of the upstairs steps.

36

Sir Rodney and Amigo

"Ben Franklin's bookstore was right here, on the corner of 2nd and Market. Ben started the first library, first fire department, first zoo, and Poor Richard's Almanac in one of these shops. Probably where Maria's Sunday (sic) is," cried the Town Crier, Sir Rodney. Pop and I were reminded about this once or twice by the Town Crier, who walked around the historic sections of Philadelphia as we left Maria's to go to Lenard's at 3rd Street to get soup or hot dogs and seltzer water for Pop, who gulped the water down, belched discretely and got in line. The Town Crier was the expert historian on the Revolutionary War, Sir Rodney St. Clair, of Lankershire (sic) near London where Her Highness, Queen Anne, knighted Sir Rodney in 1939. The palace where all this took place was right behind Big Ben, London's famous clock. Sometimes it was Queen Mary or Queen Anne Mary who did the crowning; Rodney couldn't keep his story straight. He couldn't keep his walk straight either. He bobbed and wove all around the street as he led a group of visitors around Market Street from 2nd to about Seventh.

"Washington crossed the Delaware across the street, where the docks are today. Jefferson wrote the Declaration of Independence where the crabs are sold down about five blocks from where we're standing".

"Washington crossed the Delaware up river, around Trenton, didn't he?" a visitor asked.

"Trenton was too far away, into another state and Washington wouldn't go out of Philadelphia just to cross a river," responded our excellent historian, "besides, he had family on 2nd Street" responded Sir Rodney, a bit perturbed by the dumb question.

"General Grant notified the troops that the Red Coats were coming and John Hancock practiced his signature as he drank ale right there on 3rd Street, down from the comic book stand". Sir Roger – sometimes Sir Rodney referred to himself as Sir Roger – looks like a skinny Billy Gilbert when Foggy the Gremlin confuses him and gets him all in a flutter. When Sir Rodney (Roger) feels challenged about his facts, he, like Gilbert, gets all in a flutter and talks fast until he dreams up a response.

Sir Rodney used to be Agent XXZ, of the Royal Canadian Mounted police on special assignment to learn how Americans live in big cities, considering crime, weather, houses and American Bandstand. Roger changed to Rodney after some visiting Canadians took offense at being labeled "a bunch of spoiled foreigners" by Sir Rodney, an American born undercover Royal Canadian Mounted police officer, who was upset when he didn't know where the capitol of Canada was when asked by a little girl. That's when he went home, spent the weekend in recovery and emerged as Sir Rodney. I knew Rodney's brother, Larry Milligan who bragged about his older brother, Kenneth, who could imitate John Wayne, Patti Page and Jimmy Stewart. Kenneth couldn't make any money doing imitations, I guess. That's when he became a Royal Mounted Policeman. In between, however, Kenneth quit school and joined the More ens (Marines) but had to leave due to conflicts with his DI and his agent over salary and position. The More ens wanted Kenneth to go to officer's school and he wanted to go to spy school.

Rodney is harmless. Visitors like him and give him big tips. He really shouldn't wear a Davy Crockett hat when he's telling visitors about The Revolution.

"Sir Rodney, I think that General Grant was in the Civil War, not the Revolutionary War," a Canadian asked.

"Not the same person, the Grant in the Civil War would be too young to fight, I would think, wouldn't you?" scolded Sir Rodney.

Yes, of course, but you did say that Franklin founded the first zoo, is that correct?"

"Yes, he started off with horses, dogs, and cats. He found snakes in the water that flooded the front of his store from the Delaware. He kept some for the zoo. Loyal patriots from here to Boston, though not New York, would bring him raccoons, deer, lizards, and lobsters. New Yorkers refused to give him animals because they didn't want him to gain more fame than he had. Franklin stopped collecting animals for his zoo when he flew his kite with a key attached. It took him a fourth night (sic) to recover".

"General Grant wasn't in the Revolutionary War. Where's Lankeshire?

"Do you mean Lancaster?"

"John Hancock didn't have to practice his signature. How do you know what he did?"

"All fair questions to an ace historian, but better kept inside than to embarrass this one. Sir Roger never charged for his tour guiding services. Pop never asked Sir Rodney about his facts, instead he marveled at his "competence". Sir Rodney was thin. He could stand behind Olive Oyl and you'd only see his head. He was tall and tended to lean forward when he walked. He looks like a scarecrow partially blown over by the wind. He looked like he is in all his glory on Market Street between 2nd and Fifth. He walks north to Arch Street – about four blocks - to Betsy Ross' house where he teaches interested visitors what they didn't know about Betsy and the first flag.

"Washington didn't want Betsy to make the flag because she was not a 'Quaker Oats' kinda person and he wasn't sure what religion she was; she drank ale on Sundays too even in 'leaped' years according to Sir Rodney," Sir Rodney told his visitors.

The visitors smiled and looked like people who couldn't find the twenty dollar bill in their wallet or pockets they knew they had that morning: puzzled and frazzled. Sir Rodney needed money for lunch or other things. Usually an astute, kindly "Grand Dame from Kent" or a friendly "Gent from Oxford" (that's what Sir Rodney called nice people) or other places read him perfectly and offered to buy his lunch or give him a buck or two to find his own restaurant. Rodney accepted "on behalf of Her Majesty, who wants to keep good friends and relatives in Philadelphia".

When Rodney wore his Confederate soldier's hat or his Revolutionary War officer's hat or his Davy Crockett hat on tours, visitors wanted to take pictures with him. Sir Rodney confuses the Civil War with the Revolutionary War at times, but few people care. I see visitors walking with Sir Rodney as he explains what they are seeing as well as the history of the churches and buildings in the Olde Town section of Philadelphia. Rodney bends down to talk to short people and little kids. He is overly courteous to make up for his lack of knowledge and to not so subtly lobby for a tip. An occasional slip of the tongue and a lapse of the English accent only make his followers follow and enjoy him more. The English accent, like Doc the Clock's imitations, is way off. Rodney didn't have to push hard for a tip. He was probably the one person that every visitor wanted to have a picture taken with. He made a bundle with tips.

Rodney once told Pop, Maria, Sunny, and me that he really wasn't English. He suspected that we would be very surprised by that revelation. He told us that he practiced his English accent from the time he was in 3rd grade in St. John's home for boys. He believed that the accent wasn't perfected until he quit high school in his sophomore year. The principal at St. Tommy More High School wanted Rodney to go to a VoTech school where he could become a mechanic or a welder. The Prefect at St. John's wanted Rodney to join the military, preferably the Navy or Air Force, not the Marines or Army. Rodney attempted to join the Marines, but he failed their physical; he was "entirely too fit for the Marines" and was told by a Marine recruiter to stay home and protect women and children.

"I got a 4F rating," bragged Rodney, "and the average is 2Fs".

He worked for a few years on South Street, comb-ing the area for any spies or "people imported from Russia or other Communist countries". Some of the South Street storeowners liked Rodney and they chipped in each week to pay Rodney for keeping the street safe. Rodney quit his job on South Street and, after having read at least ten comic books about Ben Franklin and Thomas Dewey, he started his tour guide business. He didn't want to charge for his services because he would have to pay taxes and tell the FBI the secrets he had about Stonewall Jackson and Patrick Henry. Sir Rodney's best friend in Olde Philly was a proud businessman, named Amigo. He was Jewish but he could speak Spanish.

Actually, Amigo couldn't speak Spanish. He knew "amigo" and "manana". He called every male customer Jose and every female customer Senorita. Amigo looked like the guys on South Street, but slightly taller. He was medium built with what looked like a wig, a black wig. He was always well dressed in casual clothes. He showed Pop his shoes one day. They were unusually long, narrow and red. He said they were cordovan; they were bright cordovan then. He waited outside his shop for customers. He waited many hours. Something made Amigo nervous because he never stood still even if he was talking to a customer.

Amigo paced back and forth in front of his store on 3rd Street, between Market and Chestnut, on the right side coming from Market Street. He smoked as he paced or he paced as he smoked. Amigo took a drag then took the cigarette out of his mouth to look at it for a few seconds then got back to smoking. He only went into the store when a customer went in and looked around at the unbelievable inventory of toys, trinkets, trains, dolls, pens, pencils, pots, pans, fishing gear, shaving materials, comics, cards, mops, day old newspapers, yoyo's, school companions, tricycles, and many, many other related and unrelated products. Amigo could never have a fire sale. It would take him too long to get the good stuff out before the fire started.

Amigo used the same story many times a day. "My grandfather started this place in the nineteenth century. He never envisioned we'd ever get to this point. He wanted to keep a small inventory of a few products. He'd be very proud of where it is today. My father started to expand into household essentials, as you see here. I took over after the war when I graduated from Temple. I added toys and ashtrays. The attic has the old stuff, like rolling pins, scrub boards, and authentic As uniforms. I got Pete Suter's and Ferris Fain's and I sold Joe Astroth's and Elmer Valo's".

"Do you have any Phillies uniforms?" was a standard question.

"No sir, but a couple of the Whiz Kids gave me their hats, which I gave to a couple ah cops' kids" was the standard answer.

This soliloquy was the greeting to all Amigo's new customers and it turned many of them off and around. The ones who stayed either needed an unusual doll or tool or a cheap gift or a gag gift or to use Amigo's bathroom. Amigo had a sign that said, "You can use my toilet but only in an emergency, you know what I mean".

Since there were no bathrooms nearby for visitors' use, Amigo thought this would attract customers – Lenard's Diner wouldn't let non-customers use their facilities. He was right. Customers would come into his store, listen to his story, thank him, use his rest rooms and then walk to South Street or Market Street where they made real purchases. Amigo's inventory was 90% junk. He got much of it from 5&10 Cent Stores or other legitimate stores which were about to toss the stuff out. Headless or armless dolls, chipped plates and cups, statues with chipped off ears, pants with holes in obvious places and so many other discrepancies and damages that it looked like a

Broken, Damaged Goods Store. Once I saw a chipped statue of a little girl with two sheep at her feet.

"It's yours for three dollars young man. I know your Dad; he's a good man. Isn't he the guy who walks all around the area and gets seltzer from Lenard's?" Amigo asked.

"He's the one and only" I answered.

"The chip is easy to hide; just keep the two sheep in the rear, turned to a wall. Nobody will ask you to let him or her see it".

"I can't Amigo; I have just forty-two cents".

"I'll take the forty-two cents. I'd like to see you make your parents happy".

"No thanks Amigo that is Mr. Amigo, Thanks anyway".

"Maybe someday you could own this place," Amigo suggested even though he knows that his primary source of revenue in the shop was not from selling junk to nice people.

I left and started for South Street, one of my favorite Philly sites. I remember thinking that I had to study and get a good job so I didn't have to own Amigo's shop. On South Street at the corner of 4th, was a South Street's Favorite Novelty Shop which stood out from among the two shirt stores and the ten or so clothing stores. I went in and browsed around for a while. I saw the statue of the little girl and the sheep. There was no damage and the girl had a staff, which she didn't have at Amigo's.

"Two ninety-five and we gift-wrap for the little woman," said the high school aged red headed girl.

"I'm in seventh grade," I said though I didn't think I had to.

"I know son, just kidding. Do you have a girl friend?" said this girl maybe five years older than I.

"Well, do you know Fortitude Farrell, the famous model?"

"Never hide-of-err. We'll gift wrap for your mother," answered this girl who tried to sound like she was dumb or tough. She appeared to be neither.

"I have two dollars, and I need a dime to get home on the subway".

"Give me a dollar and a half and remember me when you get rich".

"It's a deal madam," it was my turn to have fun.

The girl took a dollar and threw in two pairs of stockings to boot. Another girl wrapped the statue and I ran to the subway to give the gift to Mom. Mom was at the Z's house down the street saying goodbye and giving them her famous upside down pineapple cake. She loved the statue and put it on the mantelpiece, next to the plaster of Paris tea cups Maureen and Theresa baked at a Junior Catholic Daughters' meeting and the plant Vince got from JohnsonWax's lot. Mom put the plant, a weed if there ever was one, in a Coke bottle. The pink lamb that Fran bought for Mom with our rags and paper money was there too. Pop's pencil sketching of Mom's coffee clutch was framed and nearby.

Thank God I didn't have forty-two cents in change. I would have bought Amigo's statue. I didn't want him to see my dollar bills since I told him I had only forty-two cents on me. God has to know that I had no choice; Amigo was a hard bargainer. He dropped from three dollars to forty-two cents quickly.

I felt good that day. Everything worked out for the best. Mom was happy which made Pop happy.

I wonder why that sales girl was messing around with me. Maybe she noticed my odd shaped head or maybe she didn't know I was Irish like she is. I guess I'll never know.

37

Matthew, Mark, Luke and John

At times in the beginning of summer, when the school kids, including me, were gearing up for some serious street games, two or three men came to our street and got us off to a good start. They got us the lost pimple and pink balls that we couldn't get ourselves. I'm not sure how to describe these men, but they cleaned out our sewers and cleaned them well. One time there were four men; one each for the four sewers on our block. All four men used their sewer-cleaning poles to pull out all kinds of junk. They, all of them, put pimple balls and pinkies on the side, away from the larger pile of junk. This larger pile ended up on the garbage truck. A good scoop could render up to ten pimples and five or six pinkies. The men were interesting to say the least. They were all capable of better things, but they were victims of bad breaks or bad decisions. Sometimes they simply didn't know who they were because of negative feedback from parents, friends or coworkers. The ones I remember the most were just plain hard working, proud people who were on the job solely to raise their families.

One man in particular knew that his job was essential to a clean neighborhood. His pile of filthy, yet sought after, pimple balls was the largest among the four because his sewer was at the end of the street where the water flowed and pimple balls rolled most frequently. I knew that I could catch a few balls myself when playing Fistball or Hardball. Water ran fast down Carlisle Street while it was raining and right after a rainstorm. We never let rain stop us, so off went the balls. Sometimes, after a storm, we could remove the sewer cover and hold on to the sides of the hole and, using our feet, retrieve the balls. This was easy because the watermark was high – not high enough to lay on the ground and lean into the sewer to grab the balls, which we did on occasion. If the water level was low and out of reach, we'd hang Richie upside down into the sewer to retrieve the balls. We'd position Richie where the balls were. He didn't seem to mind but Pop went nuts when he heard about what we were doing. Richie's father would have had us picked up by his friends with the long black cars.

"But Pop, three of us were holding his ankles," I plead.

"That makes no difference; he could fracture his skull. Bill, you cannot do that anymore," Pop decided.

"OK. But Richie won't get into too many games. He's allowed to play only if we need someone or he retrieves balls".

"Bill, stop that immediately".

"It's not my rule Pop".

"Whose rule is it?"

"The big kids started it with their own small kid".

"You be a leader and change the rules. Those kids are probably in the Army by now".

We got an idea from watching Matthew, Mark, Luke and John, the sewer cleaners, not the gospel writers. We would get a broom handle, tie a tin can, like a big coffee can, to it, and use this device to scoop up the pimple balls. We would scoop pinkies if they happen to be in the sewer, but we wouldn't open the sewer just for pinkies. Richie was to be eligible to play sewer or no sewer. Pop said so and that was that. Fran would enforce Pop's decree, if necessary. It wasn't necessary and we moved ahead.

We dropped the idea when we couldn't figure out how to tie a Maxwell House coffee can to a broom handle. Richie was the most upset that we couldn't do what we planned.

Height had to be a criterion for hiring sewer cleaners; the four men on our street were of basketball player height and build, tall and lean. Matthew wore a Yankee's hat with the sewer cleaners' uniform: black pants, grey short-sleeved shirt with "Department of Sanitation of the City of Philadelphia," and waders. He could have actually written the first book of Gospels with his cunning smile that only a tax collector in Christ's time, who enjoyed the hatred he received from the taxpayers, could muster up. He had the lone tattoos among the four. One was the usual "Mom" on the arm; another had the Marine Corps emblem on his forearm. The third was a heart with "Mandy" in the middle. Matt's hair was sparse for a young man, and red as a Campbell soup label.

"How come you have tattoos? The other guys don't have them." I asked Matthew.

"Neither did I until my friend Tommy had one and I didn't. Tommy and I wished we had wires like yours for Wireball. We lived on Lehigh Avenue and played on 8th street. We shot cap guns, played cops, robbers, and cowboys and Indians. We ran everywhere and we will be friends for life and beyond. My other friend Barney Mulholland looked like you. You're gonna be six foot and your black hair will stay the same at least until you're nineteen or twenty. You'll continue to love Notre Dame, Our Lady and the school. You'll be just like Barney. I hope there's no war going on in your lifetime. He was my best friend and the Germans got him in Italy. He was a Marine. I was in the Navy, in the Philippines, on a destroyer, on duty and saying a rosary when he died. I was on the third Glorious mystery when it happened; I'll never forget," Matt got a bit nostalgic. I got emotional, like I got listening to the St. Stephen's choir.

Why does America have to give up so many lives for everybody in the world? Mom and Pop would be upset if I told them I wanted to change my name to Barney.

"How'd yah know the actual time?"

"I know because I noticed that my rosary was missing a bead in the third mystery and it was a Wednesday. I know it was not missing before. Barnreally couldn't afford anything, like a car or a house so he was saving up to get a Ford. When the Japanese hit us at Pearl Harbor Barney wasted no time in signing up to be a Marine. I thought he'd become a priest but he beat that; he became a saint.

"I'm gonna play for the Yankees because they're my favorite team".

"Why are yah crying Yankee fan?"

"Because I want you and Barney to get married to St. Ed's or St. Stephen's girls and raise kids and be friends for a long time".

"Now you got me crying too. Get on, go away so I can finish my surgery".

"See ya!"

"Not so fast Irish. What's your name?"

"Bill, but I want to be called either Barney or Irish".

"Well, Barney Irish, I should let you know that Barney, the real Barney, loved Notre Dame and their football team. He talked about Leahy, Lattner and Worden and Heap, and Guglieomo, and Leon

Hart. He mostly loved Our Blessed Mother and the Golden Dome. We watched games on Saturdays and Sunday mornings. Leahy and Bertelli went in the Army and a couple others did too. That's what I liked about the Irish, the Fightin' Irish. Barney's mother gave me his rosary and his Notre Dame Football scrapbook. I wouldn't trade either one for the Mona Lisa".

"Did you two guys play football for Catholic high?"

"I didn't make the freshman team so I decided to practice catching and tackling then try for the junior varsity. I got cut again even though the coach didn't check out my skills. I asked the coach why I didn't make the team. He said, "you wouldn't look good in purple and gold".

So I gave up trying for the varsity. Barney was more into the better things in life, like science, music, painting and the Catholic faith. He wouldn't miss the Irish games no matter what".

I'm probably gonna be an All American at Notre Dame and I will dedicate ten games to Barney.

"He'd like that Barney. Barney dreamed of being a famous artist. He painted well, really good (sic). The Sisters hung his pictures up after every time we had to draw in school. I have at least fifty of his drawings and I will never part wid'em for nut'in forever. He wanted to enlist as Rockwell for the painter and against his lousy father. I always called Barney Rockwell because he wanted me to. I miss Rockwell so much because he was my best friend all my life".

"Sir, what's your name?"

"Dennis, but Barney called me Norman".

Blessed Mother, I will do a Spiritual Bouquet for Barney and Dennis: ten thousand prayers, two hundred My Jesus Mercies, fifty rosaries and a thousand Savior of the World Save Russia. Who goes to Notre Dame anyhow? Our guys are tougher than the other neighborhoods and they get cut trying to play for the junior varsity team just like Dennis. Leahy should fix this and not let any other school know his secrets. How can God be a Ghost, even a Holy Ghost? Is fighting and killing fair to the fighters and killers? I thought they were only fighting, not killing. Let the toughest guy from the enemy play Punch As Hard As You Can with the toughest guy we have. The winner wins the war and gets some land or money from the loser.

Pop could-dah been a great painter if he had money and a Pop who told him how good he was and that he loved Pop and was proud of him. I hope Eddie Fisher isn't singing *My Buddy* on the radio when I get to 16th Street. Miss Emmie plays her radio loud and never closes her window. She never pays for her papers either.

Mark worked the southeast side of our street. He was real tall, maybe six four and he wore a handkerchief around his head.

"To keep the sweat from coming in my eyes, kid. Oh. I knew what you were thinking thass-swhy I answered you before you asked. It ain't no snot rag either. My kids sewed this in sewing and religion class at Sunday school at the Zion. It's a Jesus for All time handkerchief. This here wall is a single for me. We play Wireball on six story buildings; that's a homer," Mark told me.

"How do you get to the balls on the roof?" I was curious to know.

"Jump out a hello-copter then hold on to the bottom to get home. You know Josh and Satch?"

"Heard of 'em".

"Ever seen Baker's field?"

"No sir, just Shibe Park for baseball".

"Josh hits five balls onto the roof at Shibe. I want to be on the outfield roof to get five free baseballs. Josh and Babe Ruth would be a good battle for the best".

"Satch threw upside scrambled inside out messed up pitches and beat the man even in his fifties. He controls the batter's mind and his intersides (sic) of the gut. Daddy struck out Moses the Fleetwood Walker in a sandy lot game. Fleetwood was the first Negro to play pro ball".

"Did you play ball?"

"Of course, I had to with my Dad and uncles all players in the pros somewhere. I was the handsomest third baseman in the south of Billy Penn. Couldn't hit or catch or throw, but I caught the eyes of the best presented girls in the south of Market Street".

"See some crazy stuff in the sewers?" I asked.

"Yeah, like snakes and chairs and a lamp once. Must have tah open the lid to get the big stuff in. The pinkies are no good; should I keep them for you?"

"Yes sir, I use 'em all the time".

"For what?"

"Dodgeball or Halfball if 'there snow' pimple balls left".

"Pinkies are harder than pimples and they don't have the same feel as the pimples. Once I saw a Mummer's headdress on the southwest corner of 23rd hundred block of 15th. Was an Indian chief's costume. 'Wood-dah' kept it if it wasn't so filthy. Dennis got an autographed baseball by Jimmie Foxx once. Of course, he kept it. Baseballs cleanup easier that cloths. I'll get you some baseballs when I come back".

"Thanks Mister".

"Jonas, like the whale guy in the bible; I live a whale of a life".

"Thanks Mr. Jonas".

"Just Jonas, kid, I'll tell your Dad it's ok, don't worry about that".

"See you later Jonas. I can't wait to get the baseballs".

"They'd be water soaked and that" (as spoken).

"That's ok; we can catch the extra hard balls even if they're heavy".

"Are you married? Do you have kids?"

"No, not yet, maybe not ever".

"Did you play high school or college baseball?"

"Got cut. Hit three balls into deep center field at practice and caught everything hit to me".

"And you got cut?"

"Yeah, then I joined the Marines and went to Korea. Coach said I couldn't hit but guys who really couldn't hit made the team"

Man, I'll go nuts with more real baseballs. The guys will be my friend for as long as they last. I wonder if he meant five or ten or a hundred balls. Korea stinks like the war. People killing, not just harming, other people is not fair to our soldiers and sailors. Killing is the end. God, I hope that Pop never killed anyone or anyone shot at him. I guess we're just lucky to have him home. Maybe Sr. Prophetess was right; maybe babies will be killed before they are born. Some people don't care about killing other people. Blessed Mother, I call on you again to stop all this killing before it starts. I'll stop the abortions when I'm Bishop and for sure when I'm the Pope. Jonas is a hero to me even if he wasn't in the battles. Why did Jesus let Herod kill the Holy Innocents?

"Played a little football for the Marines right after boot camp. Make sure that you go to college after high school. If you sign up, make 'em send you through college".

"I will Jonas, thanks".

"God bless you young man".

"Same here Jonas. I'm Bill".

"Bill!"

"Tucson, Jonas, Dennis, take a break for coffee," Luke yelled into his megaphone which was made by forming a zero with is two hands.

"You the boss?" I asked with respect for his position.

"Nope, just ready for a break and I want the other guys to break with me".

"Oh, that's good. Can I take the pinkies and pimple balls?"

"Yeah, but come back for more. I saw more down there".

"My Pop has a thermos and lunch pail like yours, except that he drew a cartoon of Mom and the five of us. It's actually good and funny".

"Pop an artist? So am I".

"My Uncle Joe draws Christmas cards and they're beautiful".

"I drew Christmas cards myself. I worked for a company that made the drawings that some of the card companies used. I had a cartoon, called Wild Walter Walrus and I loved making people laugh".

"Where's it now?"

"At home with over a thousand drawings I've done".

"Do you still draw for money?"

"I draw every day, but not for money".

"Do you ever draw baseball players?"

"When I was your age I drew all my favorite players and some signed them. I like drawing cowboys and western scenes".

"So does Pop".

"I should meet your Pop; sounds like we have a lot in common".

"He's not as tall as you, but almost".

"Here's 'zah' rag, take the balls. You can take that bat too; it looks just fine. People throw away the strangest things. 'Whadid-ah' Jonas tell you about baseball?"

"That the girls loved him and that he got cut from his high school team".

"All true, all true, but he didn't tell you that he played for the Phillies farm club in Delaware somewhere during the 1950 season, you know, the Whiz Kids. He could hit a ball a mile and run like Di

Maj or Mays. He actually hit Roberts and Simmons in spring training. Doubled off Roberts and singled off Simmons.

"Why didn't he get to the majors?"

"Because his minor league coach refused to let him go to the majors until his team won their championship. Jonas 'bah-gun to wale' as he put it. Went to Korea and never played baseball again. Finest man I know. I love the guy like a brother and I'm no sissy".

"Why don't you still draw for money?"

"I got drafted right before Disney made me an offer to go to California and draw animation drawings for their movies like Snow White. Take an orange kid".

"No thanks, I'm not hungry".

Boy, just think, these guys were close to being famous and rich. The war ended their chances and they are poor so no phony politician would help them. Pop and Luke could have been a pair at Disneyland. He said he was like Raphael, Italian and Scots.

"Where's the beer little man?"

"Deafy, where you've been? Deafy, this is. Raphael. Like Raphael, the artist. I'm from an Italian/Scottish background".

"I take my artistic skills from my Dad, Dion Pietro, and my humility and relaxedness from Mom, Norma. It's good to meet you Deafy. Can you hear me?"

"I can hear you Ralph. It is with pleasant distinction that I meet you," Deafy tried to be as nice as he could.

"Good to meet you too Deafy. I hear your name everywhere I go. Where'd you get the wrench?"

"What wrench?"

"Forget it!"

"My Mom's from Scotland, Portobello, and my teacher is Sister St. Raphael".

"Hey, little man, put all those balls in that bag over there. I'll turn on the plug and you can drench them".

"Thanks Bob Deafy".

"Just Deafy so the cops don't know I can hear good".

"Deafy, this is the boss of the sewer cleaners".

"I'm Luke. Luke di Assisi and I was born in Iona, off the northern west coast of Scotland. I don't have much of a brogue because my American born family forced my brogue out of me. I'm here twenty-five years and I'm thirty-two. Call me Fitz".

"OK Fitz".

The crew all came together and seemed to relish their time-out from the crummy work of pulling scum from the sewers and sorting out sporting equipment, like balls and bats. Once I saw a Sport magazine on the pile on Toronto Street. It had the Mighty Mick's picture on the front cover. It wasn't worth cleaning up or I would have and Mom and Pop would help me if they knew I wanted it. Deafy wanted to know if I knew where Sonia was and where she lived. He got the word about her agreeing to swim at the fireplug and he'd be happy to accommodate her with the water flows necessary to enjoy a good swim.

Luke was my name for Luke; how good that is. This Luke looks like the real Luke, the doctor and athlete. Mom will like to know that her fellow Scotsman is working in our street. Every twitch of any character in a cartoon requires a separate sheet. Do all the sheets have to have all the characters involved redrawn? Or can the characters be copied? Luke won't give up his Wild Walrus cartoons. I'd like one.

John hummed and quietly sung Catholic hymns, like "On This Day Oh Beautiful Mother" or the "Tantum Ergo". He was tall, like the rest, but somehow he seemed taller than his height. He looked like seven feet to me until I stood next to him. He was taller than Pop's six feet size and shorter that the other three. He was way over six feet though. His hair was white and his beard was white as snow. These white areas contrasted to his coal black complexion, and told me he'd be the perfect Uncle Remus. I told him that and he replied with "Zip-pi-dee-do-dah".

"You must be Bill judging from the description of you that my daughter gave me".

"I am Bill and is your last name Nevada?"

"It is that and my first name is Tucson. Believe it or not my wife's first name is Uma, like Yuma".

"I know your daughter and I knew that you worked in this neighborhood. Her name is Sierra and she will go to high school next year like me".

"She's going to Goretti; how about you?"

"I'll go to North Catholic for sure. St. Stephen's always sends their boys to North. The girls go to the "Big Weed" as we say about Little Flower. Can I call Sierra? Or can she call me?

That's up to you two. We live at 15th and Berks. Come by and learn how to really play basketball and baseball. Sierra tells me that you talked about the Blessed Mother and your May procession. That's unusual from a basketball team captain".

"We didn't have captains or star players. We just tried to beat a team that was better for now. We'll catch up with them in high school. Sierra mentioned that she likes to wear different clothes and that she wants to make enough money to buy fine clothes. I told her that we have to wear white shirts and dark pants and blue ties to our May procession. That's how I started to talk to Sierra".

"See here. This is a Miraculous Medal. Pope Pius XII blessed it himself. He blessed thousands of rosaries and medals that day. He was on a balcony at St. Peter's Square and thousands of anxious people were in the square to greet him".

"Were you in the war at that time?"

"Yes, I was in the Army, stationed in France. But I had a quick job to do in Rome. I wasn't in my uniform but everybody knew I was an American soldier because people like me don't speak English and travel to Rome, Italy".

"Did you see much action in France?"

"Oh, just a little bit, nothing like some others did".

"My medal's chain turns my neck green and I'd rather have a shoe string hold my medal. But that's a venial sin, I'll bet".

"Wear the shoe string young man and wear it proudly. The rosary kept me sane when I was in prison in Germany".

"Oh man, you were a POW?"

"Sorta-ah. Good luck at North. When do you graduate from St. Stephen's?"

"In June. Do you have a bar like Paddy's Taproom where you and your friends have fun?"

"Sure, I have Sugar's and we play jazz and blues music all the time. I do the Count and my wife does Eartha Kitt".

"I hope that I can go into Sugar's and bring Doc the Clock to sing and Otto the Outrageous to entertain and Bif with one F to challenge anyone to an *Arm Wrestling* or *Punch Me As Hard As You Can* match. Renaldo the Purloiner will want a beer and he'll offer to give someone a car or anything they want to get one".

"We'd be ready for you all. What kind of music do you all like?"

"I like Mummers' music and the jazz I hear at Violet's apartment, like Dorothy Dandridge, if she's a singer. Do you have a

Ragman and an Iceman and a Lamplighter? Do the kids play street games in your neighborhood? Is there somebody who opens up the fireplug like Deafy does for us?"

"Yes, yes, yes to all your questions plus our kids play Halfball with pimple balls too. And they play on Carlisle Street, the 1300 block".

"Then I guess that our neighborhoods are all alike".

"They are that Bill".

"Say hello to Sierra. Tell her that I'm coming to her street to play Halfball and that I have a drop spin pitch that nobody on the 1300 block can touch".

"I'll bet that she'd like to see you".

I learned more that day talking to the four men than I did in all my life before that day. They were a good team and somehow they enjoyed their hard-to-enjoy jobs. They had to forego great opportunities to fight for freedom. They were humble yet proud. They talked well about each other. They weren't afraid to talk about God and the Blessed Mother

The people in my neighborhood were like them or they were like the people in my neighborhood. Pop and Mom had crummy jobs yet faith in God, thank God. The big guys went to war and to work every day. Everybody went to church every Sunday from what I could tell. Well, maybe Renaldo the Purloiner missed a few times a month. Nevertheless, everybody prayed for him so God would take care of him.

"Mom and Pop, when I'm Pope Francis Mae I, I'm gonna tell all the American Cardinals that I want all the Catholic churches to be like St. Stephen's. I will suggest to the president that all cities must be like Philadelphia. I will suggest to the mayor that all neighborhoods must be like our neighborhood," I told my parents.

"Why wait until you're the Pope Bill? Start now by telling everybody about your neighborhood and parish," Mom suggested.

Mom believes in her children. She always makes us go higher than we wanted. God will see her as an extremely good Mom, a saint.

"You don't have to be the pope for me Bill. Be a good person no matter what you do," my smiling Mom said.

"Bill, you do what's right for God and you. You don't have to be All American at Notre Dame, centerfielder for the Yankees, and the first American pope for me. Be yourself, never forget where you came from and the people you knew," *advised my Pop, my hero.*

Epilogue

I hoped that I could fit everything that I wanted to convey in this first of a trilogy, but it would be impractical. The book would be entirely too long and the reader wouldn't have another book or two to look forward to. As I wrote *It's A Long Lane That Has No Turning*, I tried hard to have the readers simply love the people I knew as a kid. I wanted the readers to want to meet these people and to want to be friends with them. I hope that I succeeded with the readers. If I didn't succeed, then I want a second chance. If I did succeed then I want to tell the readers more.

My next book will be similar to this one. However, there will be more story lines. The people of *It's* will appear in many of these stories and the reader must love these people or I didn't do my job very well. These are truly lovable people and it should be easy to see that.

The last book is more about the people you met in the first two books. I will let you know what happened to some of these people. My high school years and my wonderful experiences at IBM make up the book. I'll see you "next book".

60877100R00189

Made in the USA
Middletown, DE
16 August 2019